Gender Issues in Contemporary Society

The Claremont Symposium on
Applied Social Psychology

This series of volumes highlights important new developments on the leading edge of applied social psychology. Each volume concentrates on one area where social psychological knowledge is being applied to the resolution of social problems. Within that area, a distinguished group of authorities presents chapters summarizing recent theoretical views and empirical findings, including the results of their own research and applied activities. An introductory chapter integrates this material, pointing out common themes and varied areas of practical applications. Thus each volume brings together trenchant new social psychological ideas, research results, and fruitful applications bearing on an area of current social interest. The volumes will be of value not only to practitioners and researchers, but also to students and lay people interested in this vital and expanding area of psychology.

Books in the Series

Interpersonal Processes, *Stuart Oskamp and Shirlynn Spacapan, Editors*

The Social Psychology of Health, *Shirlynn Spacapan and Stuart Oskamp, Editors*

The Social Psychology of Aging, *Shirlynn Spacapan and Stuart Oskamp, Editors*

People's Reactions to Technology, *Stuart Oskamp and Shirlynn Spacapan, Editors*

Helping and Being Helped, *Shirlynn Spacapan and Stuart Oskamp, Editors*

Gender Issues in Contemporary Society, *Stuart Oskamp and Mark Costanzo, Editors*

Gender Issues in Contemporary Society

Stuart Oskamp
Mark Costanzo

Editors

**The Claremont Symposium on
Applied Social Psychology**

SAGE Publications
International Educational and Professional Publisher
Newbury Park   London   New Delhi

For information address:

SAGE Publications, Inc.
2455 Teller Road
Newbury Park, California 91320

SAGE Publications Ltd.
6 Bonhill Street
London EC2A 4PU
United Kingdom

SAGE Publications India Pvt. Ltd.
M-32 Market
Greater Kailash I
New Delhi 110 048 India

Printed in the United States of America

Library of Congress Cataloging-in-Publication Data

Main entry under title:

Gender Issues in Contemporary Society / Stuart Oskamp, Mark Costanzo, editors.
    p. cm. — (The Claremont Symposium on Applied Social Psychology: v.6)
  Based on papers from the 9th annual Claremont Symposium on Applied Social Psychology, 1992.
  Includes bibliographical references and index.
  ISBN 0-8039-5229-5. — ISBN 0-8039-5230-9 (pbk.)
  1. Sex role—Congresses. 2. Sex differences (Psychology)—
Congresses. 3. Socialization—Congresses. 4. Gender identity — Congresses.
I. Oskamp, Stuart. II. Costanzo, Mark. III. Claremont Symposium on
Applied Social Psychology (9th : 1992 : Claremont, Calif.) IV. Series
Claremont Symposium on Applied Social Psychology (Series)
HQ1075.G4645 1993
305.3—dc20   93-9486

93 94 95 96   10 9 8 7 6 5 4 3 2 1

Sage Production Editor: Diane S. Foster

Contents

An Introduction to Gender Issues

STUART OSKAMP
MARK COSTANZO

Gender issues are important in the everyday lives of both men and women. They affect the ways that infants are treated, the socialization norms and patterns for boys and girls, the workings of the educational system, the relationships of dating and married couples, role behaviors in families, job prescriptions and working conditions, and interactions between men and women in all areas of society.

Recent examples of the importance of gender issues are easy to find. The highly publicized rape trial of William Kennedy Smith is one instance, and the Supreme Court confirmation hearing at which Anita Hill made charges about sexual harassment is another. A recent court decision ordered that the Boy Scouts of America would have to admit girls as members in the future. Other court proceedings have dealt with the issue of whether girls would be allowed to play with boys on the same sports teams in baseball and basketball. Women reporters have been variously admitted to or barred from major league locker-room postgame interviews.

In the world of work almost as many women are now employed as men, but their average income is still dramatically lower and many fields of employment are still largely sexually segregated. Courts and regulatory agencies have dealt with many cases of alleged job discrimination against women in hiring, promotion, and working conditions. The "glass ceiling" has been recognized as a constraint limiting many women's career advancement.

In home life, too, gender issues are prominent. The expected home and family roles of women and men have changed some in recent decades, but there have been many calls for faster and more radical change. Movies and television have been quick to reflect these controversial questions. How much housework and child care should men do? How much decision-making responsibility and involvement in financial affairs should women have? If marital partners' desires and preferences differ, how should the conflict be resolved?

During the past two decades the study of how gender influences social life has moved from the outskirts to the center of psychology. There is now an extensive research literature on real and perceived differences between men and women, and the influence of feminism has been felt in virtually all of psychology's subdisciplines. Researchers interested in gender have challenged some of psychology's most cherished assumptions, and feminist scholars have proposed alternative views of human development, research methods, cognitive functioning, family life, and communication. These challenges have invigorated many areas of psychology.

All of these issues, and others related to gender, are discussed by the authors in this volume. The authors are eminent researchers on gender issues. Their approach is both empirically based and practically useful, for they bring the methods and findings of scientific psychology to the applied questions about gender that affect everyone's lives. No single volume could comprehensively summarize all the important research and theory on gender. The chapters that follow, however, place the study of gender in social and historical context, and explore how gender influences human development, child rearing, school achievement, self-concepts and identity, marital interactions, family roles, work life, and social institutions such as the legal system.

What makes this book most distinctive is its emphasis on applied issues that have practical importance in the lives of men and women. The chapters that follow present up-to-date knowledge about some key gender issues and shed light on a number of problems and controversies affecting men and women. Thus this volume illustrates that applied social psychologists have useful knowledge for citizens and practical advice for practitioners and policymakers who deal with complex personal and societal problems.

This volume is written in language intended to be accessible and interesting to students and general readers who are concerned about the many aspects of gender issues. The broad coverage of the chapters and the high level of the authors' scholarship make the volume an excellent choice as a textbook for seminars on gender. Because the chapters also report much previously unpublished research, the volume will also be valuable to scholars and researchers interested in new evolving theory and exciting new research findings on gender.

Overview of the Volume

Chapters 1 and 2 provide a context for all that follows. In Chapter 1, Janet T. Spence gives an expert overview of past research on gender and explores the relationships between societal change and social-psychological studies of gender. She likens societal upheaval to earthquakes: "tensions build up, often slowly and under the surface of public awareness, and break out suddenly when the pressure becomes too strong to constrain." The aftershocks can frequently be detected in the topics investigated by social scientists. Spence shows how powerful societal trends in education, employment, career choice, child care, and domestic life have shaped relations between the sexes and the nature of research on gender. Although the study of gender has usually reflected currently dominant ideologies, Spence argues that scholarship on gender also has the capacity to challenge prevailing views and inform public policy.

In Chapter 2, Joseph E. McGrath, Janice R. Kelly, and Jean E. Rhodes present an epistemological context for research on gender. They begin with a summary of feminist critiques of the general positivistic research paradigm both "as preached and as practiced." After laying out the core premises of strict positivism, they elaborate several meta-theoretical contrasts between feminist views and positivism. McGrath, Kelly, and Rhodes propose an alternative "dilemmatic view" of the research enterprise. This perspective focuses on how the tensions between conceptual, substantive, and methodological concerns create predictable dilemmas for researchers. Their dilemmatic view also highlights how values enter the research process at the generative, empirical, and confirmatory stages. The chapter concludes by contrasting mainstream and feminist research with respect to values, knowledge, context, and purpose.

Chapters 3, 4, and 5 discuss the processes through which gender differences and gender identity are acquired in early childhood and adolescence. In Chapter 3, Carol Nagy Jacklin and Laura A. Baker challenge a widely held belief by arguing that parents exert a much weaker influence on gender-related behavior than is generally assumed. Their review of research on gender development exposes a neglect of nonparental transmitters of attitudes and behaviors. They argue for a "comprehensive interactionist model" that takes account of the interplay between biological and social influences. After reviewing gender research conducted from both social-learning and behavior-genetic perspectives, Jacklin and Baker propose a research agenda that promises to yield a deeper understanding of gender development.

In Chapter 4, Jacquelynne S. Eccles with Janis E. Jacobs, Rena D. Harold, and Kwang Suk Yoon et al. present a theoretical framework for explaining how parental attributions and expectations influence the development of school-age boys and girls. Path-analytic models based on many years of longitudinal data demonstrate that the gender-stereotypic beliefs of parents have a significant impact on their child's performance in mathematics, language, and sports. This impact is independent of both the child's actual ability and teacher judgments of the child's ability. The authors explore how the effects of parental beliefs about gender are mediated by the child's perception of his or her competencies, task-perception, emotional reactions to activities, task interest, effort devoted to mastering a specific skill, and the opportunities provided by parents.

Joseph H. Pleck, Freya Lund Sonenstein, and Leighton C. Ku focus on the values and beliefs of adolescent males in Chapter 5. They describe a program of research that examines the effects of masculinity ideology—"the endorsement and internalization of cultural belief systems about masculinity." Their findings show links between adherence to exaggerated standards of masculinity and drug use, delinquency, school problems, and early sexual activity. The authors discuss theoretical and measurement issues, and they offer the concept of masculinity ideology as a means of explaining how young men understand the meaning of their behavior.

The final section of the book (Chapters 6, 7, 8, and 9) explores key gender issues at home and at work. In Chapter 6, Andrew Christensen and Christopher L. Heavey discuss a prevalent gender-linked pattern of conflict in marital relationships. This "demand-withdraw" interaction pattern involves a woman who demands, intrudes, and criticizes and a man who passively retreats and distances himself from the conflict. Both partners see their behavior as a justifiable response to the other's behavior. Christensen and Heavey suggest that the demand-withdraw pattern is motivated by the desire either to reform or to preserve the status quo in a relationship. Studies of dating couples, couples seeking therapy, nondistressed couples, and divorcing couples all find that presence of the pattern is strongly associated with marital dissatisfaction. Indeed, reversal of the typical female-demand, male-withdraw pattern is predictive of positive changes in the relationship.

In Chapter 7, Faye J. Crosby and Karen L. Jaskar discuss how women balance the frequently conflicting demands of work and family life. They present evidence that "many women have added the role of paid worker to their lives but have not been released from the expectations and responsibilities of being a full-time housewife." Importantly, however, although acknowledging the "gender imbalance in domestic labor," the authors challenge the popular stereotype of the overstressed, dissatisfied female role-juggler. Crosby and Jaskar explore the ideological motives underlying the widespread image of the unhappy role-juggler. In contrast, they point out the important benefits of occupying multiple roles.

Susan T. Fiske and Laura E. Stevens provide a close examination of the intricate nature of gender stereotypes in Chapter 8. Their discussion of the descriptive and prescriptive components of gender stereotypes illuminates the causes of sexual discrimination and sexual harassment. In examining the "specialness" of gender, Fiske and Stevens explore the reasons why gender stereotypes are especially complex and resistant to change. Their probing analysis reveals how the basis, goals, and norms for expression of gender stereotypes differ in significant ways from those in other forms of stereotyping.

In the closing chapter, Barbara A. Gutek provides a thorough review of research and policy on sexual harassment. She explores the history and "discovery" of sexual harassment, the prevalence of the problem, the adequacy of current legal mechanisms for compensating victims of sexual harassment, and the difficulties confronted by victims seeking legal redress. Drawing on her experience as an expert witness, Gutek describes a sexual harassment case that highlights the flagrant nature of harassment in the few cases that reach the courtroom. She also describes the tactics often used to discredit plaintiffs in such cases and assesses the prospects for changes in the implementation of laws prohibiting sexual harassment.

Thus the chapters in this volume discuss the historical changes from early psychological conceptions of gender to current research findings, and they span the age range from infancy to adulthood. They mention issues of research methodology but give more attention to key empirical findings. They discuss gender-related ideology and stereotypes in terms of their practical effects in people's lives. They focus both on marital and family relationships and on career and work issues. The questions and findings they discuss have applications to many aspects of society, from child rearing to the legal system. The volume presents topics of interest to every student of and researcher on gender issues.

Acknowledgments

The annual Claremont Symposium on Applied Social Psychology is the only setting in the United States where applied aspects of social scientific theories and research findings are regularly presented and discussed in depth. Each year's symposium focuses on a single topical theme and brings together distinguished social scientists from across North America to review current theory and research, and to present exciting new developments in the research domain chosen as the focus for that year.

We are grateful to the authors of the following chapters for their stimulating presentations at the Symposium and for expanding and amplifying their papers to give a thorough overview of past and current research on their particular topic. We are also grateful to Mary Gauvain, now of the University of California at Riverside, for serving as discussant of the presentations at the ninth annual Symposium. The Symposium is made possible through the financial support of the six Claremont Colleges—Claremont Graduate School, Claremont McKenna College, Harvey Mudd College, Pitzer College, Pomona College, and Scripps College—and through royalties from Sage Publications. We also extend our thanks to all the faculty, staff, and students who have helped to make the Symposium a great success.

PART I

THE STUDY OF GENDER
IN CONTEXT

1

Women, Men, and Society: Plus Ça Change, Plus C'est la Même Chose

JANET T. SPENCE

My charge is to provide some kind of overview, to set some kind of overall context for the chapters on specific topics that follow. As I ruminated about what I might say to fulfill this assignment, I began to recall what psychology had been like 25 years ago, a couple of years before I initiated my first study devoted to gender or, if truth must be told, had even the faintest suspicion that this was a topic that would continuously engage me and a good many other colleagues over the ensuing years. Back in 1967, a quarter of a century ago, the landscape of scientific psychology had a very different look from what it does now. Its topography, however, was undergoing major change. The influence of technological advances that led to spectacular developments in what we now know as neuroscience was beginning to be realized within psychology as well as related biological sciences. Similarly, the discipline that we now identify as cognitive science was in its early evolutionary stages, and was to have profound effects on psychology.

Trends in the Psychological Study of Gender

The mid-1960s were also watershed years with respect to the study of gender. True, in the preceding decades psychologists had not completely ignored sex differences and similar topics. For example, many omnibus personality inventories had been developed that included masculinity-femininity scales. The presumption underlying these scales, seldom made explicit, is that some fundamental psychological essence differentiates the sexes and that it can be diagnosed by assessing specific characteristics and behavioral preferences that empirically distinguish between men and women (Constantinople, 1973). The further presumption was that whereas "normal" men and women fall toward the gender-appropriate pole on the bipolar score continuum, deviations from these normative patterns are indicative of maladjustment.

Developmentalists had also been quite active for some time comparing the characteristics of boys and girls. In the 1950s and early 1960s, for example, there was a flurry of attention to gender-role development. Congruent with assumptions underlying masculinity-femininity scales, the implicit premise of these later studies and the theories that inspired them was that the acquisition of the characteristics, behaviors, and role adoptions expected by society of its adult women and men was among the major developmental tasks that children must accomplish. Achievement of this task was presumed to be essential both to the orderly functioning of society and to the well-being of its individual members.

But despite these exceptions, prior to the late 1960s gender was by and large a topic that commanded little of psychologists' attention. This disinterest turned inside out in the late 1960s, when gender skyrocketed from a minor topic to one of psychology's most popular. The ideological mainsprings driving inquiries into gender also changed radically. Whereas the legitimacy of the status quo and the psychological benefits of conformity to its dictates had been taken for granted in previous investigations, the new research set out to challenge all of the old presumptions.

As far as I know, the sharp growth of research devoted to gender beginning in the late 1960s has never been formally quantified, but it can easily be observed by looking at index volumes of *Psychological Abstracts*. From a relatively small number of studies in 1967, most of them grouped under the heading of Sex Differences, both the number of study entries and the number of headings grew rapidly and, at last look, continue to expand. Figures presented in a recent article ("In the Supreme Court of the United States," 1991) provide a basis for estimating the total number of articles that have appeared in the past 25 years: It was reported that "in the psychological literature between 1967 and 1982, there were 12,689 articles published on human sex differences, 3,621 articles on sex roles generally, and 1,765 articles on sex role attitudes specifically" (p. 1063). Based on these figures, 35,000 to 40,000 gender-related articles published in social and behavioral science journals from 1967 to the present would seem to be a reasonable guess.

Why the dramatic rise? Actually, this question can be broken down into two. First, why was there so *little* attention to gender prior to the late 1960s? Second, what forces brought about the sudden change? Unlike contemporary cognitive psychology and neuroscience, whose emergence during approximately the same time period was inspired by new scientific insights and technological innovations, the initial impetus for our preoccupation with gender lay in events occurring in American society at large. As participants in society, psychologists— especially women psychologists—responded quickly to these larger, extra-scientific influences. For those engaged in research this responsiveness took the form of empirical investigations, but these were often conducted and reported with little or no formal discussion of the larger social context that inspired them. The sources of this omission are multiple, but one of the most important is related to metatheoretical currents within psychology that also help to answer my first question: What accounts for psychologists' earlier indifference to gender?

Psychology and Its Quest for Universals

In the period following World War II, not merely experimental psychologists but research-oriented psychologists in all branches of the field increasingly turned to the search for universal principles that presumably governed the behavior of all human beings, whatever their sex or culture. In pursuit of these principles, personality and social psychologists and others in the "softer" areas of the field sought to emulate their experimentalist colleagues by turning to controlled laboratory studies and other quantitatively objective methods of inquiry. An external factor that also allowed psychologists to continue to overlook gender was the temper of the times: It was an era in which there was little public challenge to traditional gender-role ideology.

In their preoccupation with the purportedly universal, most social and personality psychologists lost touch in the years following World War II with neighboring social sciences: sociology, anthropology, political science, and history. Formal consideration of the larger social forces influencing people's characteristics and behaviors was left to these disciplines. Today many psychologists have lost faith in our ability to formulate universal laws governing complex social behaviors, particularly if the laws are derived from data obtained from laboratory studies of American introductory psychology students. Nevertheless, this ahistorical, acultural approach to socially conditioned psychological phenomena largely remains true today within the social-psychological mainstream.

The topics we choose to investigate, or neglect to investigate, are often shaped by contemporary events and societal attitudes and values. Further, our theories, if not our very methods of investigation, as is now beginning to be acknowledged, are often influenced by the prevailing ideology of the times. Like other scientists, psychologists are fallible human beings who cannot hope to be completely free from their society's biases or unaffected by its preconceptions. But when our beliefs and presumptions are left unacknowledged and unexamined they pose threats to the integrity of the scientific process. Less dramatically, ignoring the broader context in which psychosocial behaviors occur can impoverish our thinking and lessen the applicability of our data to real-world problems, even within the confines of our own society.

Many who engage in gender-related research undoubtedly are primarily motivated by real-world concerns, and surely even the youngest of our colleagues are aware that events outside of the scientific community led to the escalation of psychologists' interest in gender. However, once gender became a popular, even respectable, subject of inquiry, the area has sparked much of its own internal momentum. Two desirable outcomes are that considerable methodological sophistication has been brought to the study of gender and admirable progress has been made in integrating many gender-related phenomena into the theoretical mainstream of social, personality, and cognitive psychology. However, with some notable exceptions (a number of them represented in the research reported in later chapters of this volume), many of our inquiries are becoming self-generating, inspired only by the studies that preceded them and cut off from the broad questions and societal issues that inspired them in the first place and in which much of their ultimate significance rests.

For these reasons, I have chosen not to focus inward on psychology and attempt to summarize what we have been up to in our studies of gender over the past 25 years. (Readers can consult the admirable treatments of Ashmore, 1990, and Deaux, 1984.) Rather, I look outward and place our work in a larger, historical perspective.

The 1960s and Their Aftermath

No one, even current students who were not yet born in the 1960s, needs to be reminded that those years were turbulent times in America's history. It was a decade marked by the Civil Rights movement, the Berkeley free speech movement, the sexual revolution, hippies, and the greening of America. Quite aside from the wrenching effects of the assassination of a president, his brother, and the leader of the Civil Rights movement, and the deep divisions brought about by our involvement in Vietnam, old traditions were being overturned and despite almost inevitable periods of backlash, this country would never again be quite the same.

Feminism and a self-conscious women's movement were also coming into prominence, but in the early 1960s feminism and its causes had few supporters, even among women. Opinion polls, for example, indicated that the majority of women were content with their lot and did not perceive the treatment of women and men as being in any way inequitable. This initial resistance to overt challenges to well-established values and customary patterns of behavior is hardly surprising. What *is* in need of explanation is the rapid turnaround in societal attitudes in the space of a few years. For example, women's rejection of traditional beliefs and practices, particularly as they affected differential treatment of the sexes in education and employment, increased markedly in the ensuing years, and by the early 1970s the majority of women were admitting that discrimination not only existed but was inequitable (Spence, Deaux, & Helmreich, 1985).

What, then, drove the change? The 1950s, after all, were a period of "back to normalcy" following World War II and the Korean conflict, a period in which many young Americans were establishing their families and creating the well-known "baby boom." If one believed women's magazines and other popular media, women were reveling in domestic bliss. The immediate causes of the societal changes can be found at least as much in the successes of the Civil Rights movement as in the gathering strength of the women's movement. The struggle for civil rights was largely spearheaded by African Americans on behalf of themselves and, secondarily, on behalf of members of other ethnic minorities. Women, however, were the beneficiaries of that struggle as white Americans became sensitized to issues of equity and social justice. The cause of women was substantially advanced in a tangible way by the passage of civil rights legislation that included women among its protected classes, notably the Civil Rights Act of 1964 barring job discrimination, and the 1972 Title IX amendment of that act mandating equal opportunity in education, and later federal actions such as the institution of affirmative action guidelines by the Office of Civil Rights. The message that enforcement of these legislative actions conveyed to women was that instead of being expected to confine themselves to women's work, they were being encouraged to participate with men as equals in the educational and vocational spheres. Psychologists, especially women, were quick to respond to the implications of this message. Not only did psychologists begin to initiate gender-related research, but also research designed to challenge old conceptions and to turn the presumptions of traditional ideologies upside down.

Events of the 1960s, however, were only proximal causes, insufficient to account for the very rapid change in public concerns with the status of women and women's responses to them. Other forces were at work even though they were seldom recognized or acknowledged, forces that also gave rise to what has become a women's movement. To understand them, it is necessary to go back further in history.

The Social Context: Historical Trends

Before doing so, however, a few metahistorical remarks are in order. Social movements causing upheavals in the fabric of society are frequently like earthquakes: Tensions build up, often slowly and under the surface of public awareness, and break out suddenly when the pressure becomes too strong to contain. These tensions typically arise when changes in conditions make previously accepted arrangements between groups less functional than they once were and lead people to change their behaviors in an attempt to accommodate these new conditions. Societal attitudes about what is natural, true, or morally correct are typically resistant to change, particularly on the part of those with greater power and status but often with the passive acquiescence if not the active collusion of many of those with less power and lower status. Thus beliefs about appropriate behaviors often lag behind actual changes that are taking place. The emergence of self-conscious movements protesting against the injustice of traditional practices are often early symptoms rather than causes of change, their leaders becoming bellwethers only later. Similarly, widespread acceptance of revisions in traditional beliefs and societal values may appear to cause rapid changes in actual behaviors but the reverse is more often the case. If society is to thrive when the discrepancy between beliefs and reality becomes too great to sustain, attitudes and values must go through a period of "catch up" to allow new, more effective, social arrangements to be devised.

The 1960s and 1970s were just such a period. To understand what happened and is happening today, we must go back at least a century before the tumultuous 1960s, first tracing women's educational progress and then their place in the country's economy (Spence, Deaux, & Helmreich, 1985).

Education and Women's Attainments

In the latter part of the 19th century, the United States was in the process of becoming industrialized and urbanized. More workers and better educated workers were needed to run the factories and mills, and to keep up with expanding technology. It was also a period during which stereotypes about temperamental differences between the sexes were in full bloom, remnants of which are still with us today. However, beliefs were crumbling about women's literal incapacity for abstract thought or for anything beyond a rudimentary education. A feminist movement was in full swing, as reflected in the National Women's Suffrage Association, led by talented women whose political involvement, interestingly enough, had first arisen in conjunction with their work for the abolitionist cause prior to the Civil War (Hymowitz & Weissman, 1978).

Although many of the goals of these early feminists would not be accomplished for many decades, the rising need for an educated populace led to higher education becoming open to women. During the last 30 years of the century, a number of women's colleges were established with curricula similar to those offered to men, and a good many all-male institutions, most of them in the East, became coeducational. As new colleges and universities were established, they too tended to be coeducational. Slow progress was also being made in allowing women to enter graduate programs and professional schools.

A federal law passed in 1912 mandating compulsory education further closed the gap between the educational achievements of the sexes. Girls as well as boys had access in the public schools to both a primary and secondary education and, equally important, exposure to the same academic courses.

Although women's average educational attainments gradually caught up with men's, even surpassing them in the mid-1970s, the sexes were distinguished by the subjects that attracted them (Stockard, Schmuck, Kempner, Edson, & Smith, 1980). Few college women attempted to major in mathematics, science, or engineering, often having been actively discouraged from entering these male-dominated fields and made uncomfortable if they tried. But the chilling effects of post-1960 civil rights legislation and the growing, if initially grudging, acceptance of women in these male-dominated fields have weakened these particular exterior barriers. Nonetheless, the proportion of women electing these specialties, although increasing, remains disappointingly low (National Science Board, 1991). This outcome suggests that whatever factors lead to this avoidance, they have largely become internalized by the time girls reach college age. Similarly, in all fields combined, fewer women than men with similar credentials seek postgraduate training.

In summary, the country's requirements for a well-educated work force have steadily increased over the last century and a half as the United States passed into the industrial and postindustrial eras. Political agitation has sometimes been necessary to gain women access to the same educational opportunities as men, but at other times access has come almost automatically. The outcome is that as educated women as well as men are needed, women's level of education has risen along with men's. In actual attainments, however, discrepancies between the sexes remain. Ironically, the country will soon be in a position in which women should not merely be permitted to enter male-dominated fields but must be persuaded to do so. I will amplify this point later on, but I turn now to employment.

Changing Patterns of Employment

The Industrial Revolution and the urbanization it brought about had the effect of separating people's place of work from where they lived. This change gave rise to an idealized model of the family in which it was the husband who earned the family's income by working at a job outside the household whereas the wife remained in the home and confined her labors to domestic affairs. Nonetheless, a fairly substantial number of urban women have always had outside, income-producing employment. Up to the middle of this century, most of these women were young, single, and whatever their age and marital status, poor. The majority of these women worked for an obvious reason: They needed the money to help support themselves and their families. However, they were able to *find* work because the economy needed their contributions. With the partial exception of the two World Wars, when women were brought into the labor market to occupy jobs previously held by men who had been called up for military service, women usually held lower paying, sex-segregated jobs, jobs that were considered suitable for women's abilities and temperament and in which men had little interest. But, particularly following World War II, there was a change in employment patterns. Most notable was the expanding number of married middle-class women with minor children who entered the labor force. During the 1950s, women with children of elementary school age sought employment in increasing numbers, followed in the 1960s by women with children of preschool age. Between 1970 and 1988, the proportion of women with children under 6 years who worked rose from approximately 30% to more than 57% (U.S. Bureau of the Census, 1990). Well-educated women were also more likely to be continuously employed than those with lesser educational attainments. The public, however, was slow to perceive or to accept these changes, to recognize that the romanticized TV families of "Leave It to Beaver" and "Father

Knows Best" were no longer the norm, and that more than half of adult women had paid employment.

Public Attitudes About Women's Roles

As more and more women entered the work force, they gained economic resources that gave them more power, both domestically and in the public arena. With greater power almost inevitably came awareness that other options were possible and, consequently, discontent with inequitable treatment and traditional restrictions on women's behaviors. These dissatisfactions were signaled first by the emerging women's movement, and later, in the late 1960s and early 1970s, by discernible changes in public opinion as a whole. With affirmative action programs acting as a catalyst, the message appeared to change from active discouragement to encouragement for women to pursue advanced education and to embark on careers, especially in prestigious fields dominated by men. These views were by no means universal, of course, and what was endorsed publicly was less than fully supported privately. Particularly resistant to change have been stereotypes about sex differences in vocationally relevant abilities and personality characteristics (Ruble, 1983). Nonetheless, women have responded to these egalitarian messages in large measure over the course of the past three decades.

Psychological discussions of these changes in employment patterns have typically highlighted factors that stimulate women to enter the labor market, such as the desire for income or their wish to express their occupational interests, or changes in gender-role attitudes that permit or encourage women to pursue careers. Similarly, explanations of the resistance that women encounter from men in their occupational endeavors often emphasize men's attempts to retain power and control as well as their beliefs in their natural rights to superiority. It is crucial to recognize, however, that the presence of a majority of women in the labor force is only partially explained by the desires and motives of individual women, and that it can also be defended for reasons other than economic necessity or egalitarian beliefs. Women's actual behaviors are determined by a complex, interactive set of forces, as this brief historical overview of trends in education and employment was intended to demonstrate. Most fundamentally, the numbers of employed women and the jobs that they hold are determined by the country's economic needs, that is, the numbers and kinds of workers that are required to keep its public and private institutions and businesses functioning.

Society in Transition

Over time, the availability of jobs waxes and wanes, with women tending to be used as a kind of reserve labor force and public attitudes about what is appropriate being influenced by these conditions. Over the course of the last century or more, however, the overall trajectory of the need for women workers has moved steadily upward as the nature of our economy has changed. Particularly these days, in which there is much talk in the media about the backlash against women (Faludi, 1991) and the purported disillusionment of many working mothers with trying to "have it all," it is essential to recognize that this need will increase in the decades ahead because of shifts in the composition of the American citizenry. What demographers have known for some time is that the native-born white population is aging. This, together with the numbers of immigrants from non-European countries, will lead white citizens to be in the minority relatively early in the next century. In order to maintain our economic competitiveness, the deficiency in the number of white adult males of working age will have to be made up in the coming decades, not merely by women and ethnic minorities of both sexes, but by members of these groups who are also well educated and well trained.

The Need for Scientists and Engineers

Particularly crucial will be the need for scientists and engineers. As is well known, science and math are subjects in which American school children have for some time lagged behind the accomplishments of children from a number of other countries (Stevenson & Stigler, 1992). Also, in recent years, white males have shown diminished interest in these occupational fields. According to some reports (Atkinson, 1990), shortages in scientists and engineers may begin to occur by the year

2000. The problem is exacerbated by the fact that these are fields that tend to be avoided by women and with the exception of Asian Americans, by members of ethnic minorities. As a result, a good deal of attention has been paid by psychologists in recent years to factors within the family, the schools, and the peer culture that discourage women from electing to enter these fields and from obtaining the educational background that will allow them to do so (Chapter 4, this volume; Eccles, 1983; Wellesley Center for Research on Women, 1992).

Child Care

If we are to have even more women in the labor force, whatever their occupation, a second crucial challenge is to establish a system of effective, affordable day care to replace the inadequate patchwork system we have today. These facilities are needed not merely to supply a safe place for children to be when their parents are at work, but also to provide children with the kinds of experience that will both meet their emotional needs and stimulate their cognitive development, enabling them to become socially responsible adults and to function in a technologically oriented economy.

The United States already lags behind most industrialized nations in its provisions for child care (Kammerman, 1991). One of the factors that may be responsible for this negligence is the discrepancy between the upswing in women's participation in the work force and the publicly expressed support of equal opportunity in education and employment, on the one hand, and, on the other hand, our attitudes and practices on the domestic front. Although decision making is close to being shared equally by husbands and wives, at least in most middle-class homes, the primary responsibility for children is still assumed by women (Nyquist, Slivken, Spence, & Helmreich, 1985). Indeed, in segments of the population it is implied or stated that married women who work are selfishly neglecting their children. Women with minor children are thus made to feel even guiltier about spending time away from them or turning their care over to strangers. In an era in which both men and women are working longer and longer hours (Schor, 1992), the burden on women is particularly severe because even women who have full-time professional careers continue to carry the bulk of mundane tasks associated with running the household. (The plight of single parents is, of course, particularly acute.) In these senses, our society remains in transition, not yet fully caught up with contemporary economic and sociological realities and the concept of equitable sharing of roles within the home. A more general problem for both men and women is to find a better balance between their obligations to their work and to their families.

Women and Violence

We are also in a transitional stage with respect to our treatment of acts of violence against women. Women have increased in status to the point where society as a whole is willing to acknowledge publicly that many women are abused by their husbands or partners and that it is in the community interest to prohibit these aggressive acts and protect victims. Public recognition of the occurrence of acquaintance rape and sexual harassment is also growing but has yet to be wholehearted. Women remain reluctant to bring charges against the perpetrators out of fear that they will be disbelieved and victimized a second time by those who attempt to discredit their claim (see Chapter 9, this volume). However, recent events give some reason for optimism. For example, according to newspaper reports, in the wake of the Anita Hill-Clarence Thomas hearings, the number of sexual harassment charges filed with the federal Equal Employment Opportunity Commission has risen; in the last quarter of 1991, there was more than a 70% increase in comparison to the same period the year before. More universities and businesses are instituting training programs in preventing harassment and dealing with complaints (Paludi & Barickman, 1991), and the Civil Rights Act in the fall of 1991 expanded the right of women who bring harassment charges to sue for monetary damages.

These aggressive acts, however, continue to be a tragic feature of the contemporary scene and are likely to remain so. Their causes are multiple and in our preoccupation with the role played by gender, we should not fail to acknowledge that they are part of a wider problem— the strain of violence that runs through American society at all socio-economic levels and our reluctance to face and to try to understand the factors that contribute to it.

Plus Ça Change . . .

It also behooves us to remind ourselves that all human societies, whatever their size or stage of development, must solve certain challenges if they are to survive. Among these are the control of aggression, rules for the expression of sexual behavior, provisions for the physical care of children and for the training that will allow them to take their place in adult society, and maintenance of an economic system that will provide for people's material needs. All societies also have some degree of specialization, a system of roles that specify how tasks, responsibilities, and privileges are divided and to whom they are to be assigned.

To meet these challenges, each society must remain responsive to changes in its current circumstances, be they in the natural world or in its human institutions. Societies are caught between the need to be conservative, on the one hand, lest too rapid change lead to destabilization, and the need to change, on the other hand, lest their systems become outmoded and dysfunctional. Unfortunately, in the past decade the tide of public opinion in this country has flowed in a more regressive direction than is desirable if these goals are to be accomplished more effectively than they now are. We, and our elected representatives, also have a history of attending only to immediate problems. Our attention is too easily captured by current crises, with little long-range planning that may ameliorate or prevent future problems. But all the gender-related issues on which I have touched have crucial implications for public policy and are in urgent need of immediate attention to ensure the country's long-term well-being.

As the chapters that follow demonstrate, psychological research has contributed substantially to the understanding of these and other problems and can be expected to contribute to their solutions. I urge us all not to lose sight of the social context of our work and its societal implications. Even more broadly, social psychologists know a good deal about techniques of persuasion. We should join together to bring this knowledge to bear on policymakers so that in their deliberations they will take advantage of what psychology has to offer.

References

Ashmore, R. D. (1990). Sex, gender, and the individual. In L. A. Pervin (Ed.), *Handbook of personality: Theory and research* (pp. 486-526). New York: Guilford.

Atkinson, R. C. (1990). Supply and demand for scientists and engineers: A national crisis in the making. *Science, 248,* 425-436.

Constantinople, A. (1973). Masculinity-feminity: An exception to the famous dictum? *Psychological Bulletin, 80,* 389-405.

Deaux, K. (1984). From individual differences to social categories: Analysis of a decade's research on gender. *American Psychologist, 39,* 105-116.

Eccles, J. (1983). Expectancies, values, and social behaviors. In J. T. Spence (Ed.), *Achievement and achievement motives: Psychological and sociological approaches* (pp. 75-146). San Francisco: Freeman.

Faludi, S. (1991). *Backlash: The undeclared war against American women.* New York: Crown.

Hymowitz, C., & Weissman, M. (1978). *A history of women in America.* New York: Bantam Books.

In the Supreme Court of the United States: *Price-Waterhouse v. Ann B. Hopkins.* Amicus Curiae Brief for the American Psychological Association. (1991). *American Psychologist, 46,* 1061-1070.

Kammerman, S. B. (1991). Child care policies and programs: An international perspective. *Journal of Social Issues, 47,* 179-176.

National Science Board. (1991). *Science and engineering indicators—1991.* Washington, DC: Government Printing Office.

Nyquist, L., Slivken, K., Spence, J. T., & Helmreich, R. L. (1985). Household responsibilities in middle-class couples: The contribution of demographic and personality variables. *Sex Roles, 12,* 15-34.

Paludi, M. A., & Barickman, R. B. (1991). *Academic and workplace sexual harassment: A resource manual.* Albany: SUNY Press.

Ruble, T. L. (1983). Sex stereotypes: Issues of change in the 1970's. *Sex Roles, 9,* 397-402.

Schor, J. (1992). *The overworked American: The unexpected decline of leisure.* New York: Basic Books.

Spence, J. T., Deaux, K., & Helmreich, R. L. (1985). Sex roles in contemporary American society. In G. Lindzey & E. Aronson (Eds.), *Handbook of social psychology* (3rd ed.) (pp. 149-178). Hillsdale, NJ: Lawrence Erlbaum.

Stevenson, H. W., & Stigler, J. W. (1992). *The learning gap: Why our schools are failing and what we can learn from Japanese and Chinese education.* New York: Summit.

Stockard, J., Schmuck, P. A., Kempner, K., Edson, S. K., & Smith, M. A. (1980). *Sex equity in education.* New York: Academic Press.

U.S. Bureau of the Census. (1990). *Statistical abstract of the United States, 1990.* Washington, DC: Government Printing Office.

Wellesley Center for Research on Women. (1992). *The AAUW report: How schools shortchange girls.* Washington, DC: AAUW Educational Foundation and National Education Association.

2

A Feminist Perspective on Research Methodology: Some Metatheoretical Issues, Contrasts, and Choices

JOSEPH E. McGRATH
JANICE R. KELLY
JEAN E. RHODES

Although logical positivism is still the dominant intellectual paradigm underlying current social and behavioral science research, it has come under severe criticism from feminists and other scholars. The criticisms of positivism have been at two levels. On the one hand, some critics have attacked the underlying assumptions of logical positivism as a metatheory for acquiring and confirming knowledge. In contrast, others have attacked not the underlying premises of the metatheory, but rather the dominant preferences or practices of mainstream research in the social and behavioral sciences—practices

AUTHORS' NOTE: Some of the material in this chapter was presented as part of a symposium on Mainstream and Feminist Perspectives on Experimental Social Psychology (Faye J. Crosby, Chair) at the 25th meeting of the Society for Experimental Social Psychology, Buffalo, October 1990.

that could be modified while still working within a general positivistic paradigm.

Feminist critics of research methodology fall into both of these camps, as do those who offer methodological critiques from other perspectives. In fact, there is much overlap between the feminist and nonfeminist critiques of methodology. But there is one striking difference. In general, critiques of positivism have had only limited impact because they have not been very successful at articulating a workable substitute for current theory and practices. Feminist critics, on the other hand, seem to have paid much more attention to the question: "if not positivism, then what?" As Parlee (1979) and others have pointed out, unlike other critics, feminists have a substantive agenda to which they have committed their scholarly energies. They have some problems they want solved and some issues they want addressed as topics of scientific inquiry—and for them, positivism as preached or as practiced just won't do the job.

In this chapter, we lay out some of the criticisms at both levels—positivism in theory and positivism in practice—giving emphasis to the issues that have been raised from a feminist perspective. In order to make the methodological issues under consideration clearer and more salient, we cast our discussion in terms of a particular "dilemmatic" view of research methodology. That methodological viewpoint has been presented in detail elsewhere (cf. Brinberg & McGrath, 1985; Kelly & McGrath, 1988; McGrath, Martin, & Kulka, 1982; Runkel & McGrath, 1972). Here, we introduce only a skeleton of concepts needed to carry our discussion forward.

Positivism as a Basis for Scientific Inquiry

Positivism makes a number of crucial core assumptions—some ontological, some epistemological, some more narrowly methodological. These have been discussed from a feminist point of view by Benston (1982), Bleier (1987), Crawford and Marecek (1989), Gergen (1988), Harding (1987), Hardy and O'Barr (1987), Hare-Mustin and Marecek (1988), Peplau and Conrad (1989), and Vickers (1982), among others. They have also been discussed from a Heideggerian view by Packer (1985); from the perspective of "the new philosophy of science" by

Manicas and Secord (1983); and from other perspectives by other scholars. Here we try to condense those extensive discussions into a more or less straightforward list of key assumptions, and then present the main criticisms of those positions and the contrasting positions of a feminist perspective.

Some Core Premises of "Strict Positivism"

The classic positivist position assumes that there is a dichotomy between the object of study and the person(s) conducting the study. (Experimenter and subject are different in kind.) This in turn assumes that there is an "objective" material reality separate from and independent of the observer. It further assumes that that reality is orderly, and knowable through rational inquiry; and that knowledge thus gained is independent of characteristics of the observer.

Positivism implies that there is a clear-cut distinction between observable phenomena, on the one hand, and metaphysical entities or religious phenomena on the other, and that this distinction is obvious and not dependent on human interpretation rooted in particular interests or values.

Positivism further assumes that knowledge of the material world is gained through measurement of natural phenomena. Measurement in a scientific sense requires quantification, which in turn requires reduction of phenomena to their essential characteristics and a rendering of those characteristics in some form of mathematical or logical description. This in turn implies that the phenomena must be studied in isolation from their surroundings, and that this can be done without altering their essential character. It also implies that the essential features of phenomena are those that can be described by a (mathematical) theory, and that such theory provides some insight into the workings of physical reality.

The positivist position further assumes that when appropriate procedures are applied systematically to observable phenomena, they yield unambiguous knowledge, without need for interpretation; and that such knowledge, once articulated, is compelling by virtue of rules of logic and mathematics.

In a strict positivist view, the primary purpose of the scientific pursuit of knowledge is for the sake of knowledge, and only secondarily to solve identified problems in extant systems. At the same time, the proper relation of science to nature is one of mastery, with the fundamental criterion of scientific progress being the ability to predict and control natural phenomena.

There have been a number of thoughtful critiques of the core premises of positivism. One such critique, from a constructionist perspective, takes issue with positivism's assertions about the directness with which we can gain knowledge about the nature of reality. Constructionism holds that we do not discover reality, we invent it. Our experience does not directly reflect what is "out there"; it is an ordering and organizing of it. Our understanding of reality is a representation—a representation not a replica. Representations of reality are shared meanings, and that sharing is made possible via language, culture, and history.

Constructionism challenges positivism's premise that reality is fixed and can be observed directly, uninfluenced by the observer. It also challenges positivism's postulate that it is possible to distinguish and cleanly separate fact and values. To constructionists, values and attitudes determine what are taken to be facts. Constructionism does not argue that formal laws and theories in psychology are wrong; rather, it argues that they are explanations based on social conventions. Whereas positivism regards science as a proper use of reason, neutral in its methods and socially beneficial in its results, constructionism insists that scientific knowledge, like all knowledge, cannot be disinterested or politically neutral.

A Feminist Critique of Positivism

The positivist assumptions attacked by constructionism are also attacked from a feminist viewpoint. Among other things, they lead positivists (a) to disregard context; (b) to believe that "facts" are unproblematic; (c) to be disinterested in the unique human experience; and (d) to be intolerant of ambiguity.

A number of feminist scholars have summarized the many ways in which research done from a feminist perspective contrasts sharply with research done from a mainstream position. We borrow heavily from discussions of such contrasts by Mary Crawford and Jeanne Marecek

(1989), Mary Gergen (1988), Sandra Harding (1987), and Jill McCalla Vickers (1982).

1. Feminist research insists that scientist and subject are interdependent rather than independent, and that the scientist therefore is part of the phenomenon studied and of its interpretation.

2. Feminist research holds that scientist and facts—the observer and the observed—are interconnected, not independent of one another.

3. Feminist research insists on studying social systems embedded in their physical, biological, and situational contexts, rather than extracted from those contexts.

4. Feminists insist that neither theory nor practice can be value-free, nor is it desirable that they be so.

5. Feminist research insists that the scientist has no privileged epistemological position, as a "knower" or as an "instrument" capable of value-free objective observation. Therefore, subject and scientist ought to be placed in the same "interpretative plane," and subjects' experiences (and their reports of it) ought to be taken seriously as empirical evidence.

6. Feminist research has a strong systemic flavor and a strong preference for studying complex patterns of relationships involving situated differences in context. In contrast, traditional positivism has a strong analytic thrust, a strong preference for universal and eternal laws, and a strong preference for reducing such laws to unidirectional cause-effect relations between variables specified at the lowest system level possible.

7. Feminist research views the purpose of scientific activity as the pursuit of knowledge for *use,* and specifically for use in ways that help us understand and improve the lives of women, rather than merely the pursuit of knowledge for its own sake.

8. Feminist research views the proper relation of science and nature as one of harmony, rather than mastery.

9. Accordingly, feminist research regards the proper criterion of progress in a science as the gaining of understanding of the systems being studied, rather than the more manipulative ideas of prediction and control of natural phenomena.

These issues can be regarded as a set of metatheoretical contrasts between feminism and positivism. The first six are quite intricately related to one another and to some features of a "dilemmatic theory of method" that we will sketch next. The last three are interrelated with one another, having to do with purpose.

A *"Dilemmatic" View of*
the Research Process

The view offered thus far presents one body of assumptions called *positivism* as if it were synonymous with "the scientific method," and contrasts it with an opposing body of assumptions called *feminism,* posited as a mutually exclusive and incompatible alternative paradigm for conduct of scientific research. We do not think that is necessarily the most useful way to view these matters. Here, we propose an entirely different way to look at the overall research enterprise—a perspective that we will call a "dilemmatic" view of research (see Brinberg & McGrath, 1985; McGrath, Martin, & Kulka, 1982; Runkel & McGrath, 1972). The dilemmatic view holds that within very broad limits, the so-called scientific method is broadly permissive (ecumenical), both in general and in any given case, regarding what procedures are best for gaining or confirming knowledge, and what means are to be considered the methods of choice. To be sure, the general scientific paradigm has some prescriptions and proscriptions. It specifies some requirements, some "rules of evidence," essential to the accumulation of knowledge as defined within that system. But these requirements themselves embed *conflicting and incompatible desiderata* that cannot all be satisfied at the same time. Furthermore, *the scientific paradigm itself has no particular rules or algorithms to make choices among these incompatibles*—to tell us, for example, how much parsimony we should trade off for increased comprehensiveness, or how much generalizability we should trade off for increased precision of measurement.

Practitioners of the scientific paradigm in any given field, on the other hand, have an elaborate set of preferences that function as if they were themselves rules about epistemic values. Often it is with the assumptions underlying such mainstream preferences that feminist and other critics wish to take issue. Often it is from such "paradigms in practice," rather than from the general paradigm in principle, that feminists wish to depart.

The matter is a bit more complex, though, even apart from constructionist or feminist critiques of positivistic theory and practice. Within the general paradigm there are multiple potential paths by which research can be carried out. These paths represent choices. Sets of such choices, taken over and over again, become norms or preferences or traditions. From the point of view of the general paradigm—ecumenical through and through—all of those paths are equally valued as potential avenues to knowing. In actual mainstream practice, however, some of those paths or research traditions have been given more status than others, and some of those traditions, or parts of them, are more amenable to or more at odds with a feminist perspective. Thus, regardless of how ecumenical the underlying paradigm is in principle, a feminist perspective would likely find cause to criticize the emphases given by the systematic preferences reflected within mainstream research practice.

If we adopt such an ecumenical view, it is no longer sensible to talk about a contrast between a logical positivism (that is somehow representative of the general scientific method) versus a contrasting and incompatible (hence "unscientific") feminist perspective. Rather, we ought to delineate the requirements of a broad and encompassing general scientific paradigm and then, within that paradigm, consider and contrast the systematic sets of preferences of (many) mainstream practitioners, on the one hand, with the preferences of the feminist perspective (or any other potential paradigmatic alternative) on the other.

We take that dilemmatic and ecumenical view here. For the remainder of this chapter we will discuss issues as contrasts between mainstream and feminist perspectives, with both perspectives set *within* the general scientific paradigm. Before continuing with those comparisons we need to introduce some concepts from that underlying dilemmatic "theory of method" (Brinberg & McGrath, 1985; Kelly & McGrath, 1988; McGrath, Martin, & Kulka, 1982; Runkel & McGrath, 1972) to make that discussion clearer (see Chart 2.1).

The dilemmatic theory of method deals with three quasi-independent intellectual domains: Conceptual, Substantive, and Methodological. These domains, respectively, raise questions about epistemological issues (e.g., what can we know and who can be a knower), about ontological issues (e.g., what is the nature of "reality" and how can we separate it out from appearance), and about methodological issues (e.g., questions about the logic of inquiry and rules of evidence).

In the dilemmatic "theory of method" the research enterprise encompasses three major *stages* and involves several levels of study within each of three intellectual domains. Within each domain there are three *conflicting and incompatible desiderata,* each of which needs to be maximized but all of which cannot be maximized simultaneously. The

DOMAINS: (C)conceptual (S)substantive (M)methodological

LEVELS: Research entails seeking relations among elements
within embedding systems.

STAGES: I. Generative: built tools in each domain
II. Empirical: combine materials from C, S, & M to obtain
set of findings
III. Confirmatory: test robustness (explore scope and
boundaries) of findings

PATHS: Theoretical: Combine C & S for set of hypotheses
then test it with some M.
Experimental: Combine C & M for study design
then implement it in some S.
Empirical: Combine M & S for set of observations
then interpret it with some C.

CONFLICTING DESIDERATA:
All domains: Generality; Differentiation; System Fidelity
C: Subsumptive range; Inferential power; Particularity/fit
S: Typicality; Unambiguity; Richness of articulation
M: Generalizability; Precision/Control; Realism of context

Chart 2.1. A Dilemmatic Theory of Method: Key Concepts

three stages are generative, empirical, and confirmatory, respectively, in their functions. In the second or empirical stage, there are at least three alternative *research paths* by which material from the three domains may be brought together in the conduct of "a study," and these paths give rise to different metatheoretical issues (and by-pass other such issues). The domains, the conflicting desiderata, and the research paths are important to what will be said later, so they are sketched briefly next.

Domains and Research Paths

Research always involves combining materials from all three do-mains—Conceptual, Substantive, and Methodological—but it usually proceeds by first combining materials from two of the domains and then bringing in the third. There are three combinations of two domains, hence three research paths:

1. The theoretical path: Researchers start by combining materials from the conceptual and substantive domains, to form a set of hypotheses that are then tested by use of some methodology.
2. The experimental path: Researchers start by combining materials from conceptual and methodological domains, to construct a study design that then is implemented on some substantive system.
3. The empirical path: Researchers start by combining materials from substantive and methodological domains to generate a set of observations—or, in our jargon, a data set—that must then be interpreted in the conceptual domain.

The conduct of a research study, as we usually speak of it, *always* requires material from all three domains. When we bring in materials from the third domain, however, we encounter different sets of problems and constraints depending on which path we are pursuing. What we can do in the third domain is already highly constrained by the choices made in structuring the other two. For example: When we pursue the theoretical path, combining conceptual and substantive material first to form sets of hypotheses, the range of methods that we can then choose for testing those hypotheses is often already seriously constrained by the terms of the theory. Similarly, when we pursue the experimental path, combining conceptual with methodological material to form a study design, which substantive systems we can then use to carry out that research design are often already seriously limited (often, for example, to artificial contexts) by constraints of the study design. Likewise, when we pursue the empirical path, combining substantive and methodological material to obtain structured data sets, the assumptions and constraints embodied in that data set often severely limit the concepts we can then use to "explain" the patterns of relations obtained.

Conflicting Desiderata and Epistemic Values

Howard (1985) has distinguished between epistemic and non-epistemic values. The former are the logical or rational values that characterize the scientific paradigm—such values as parsimony, comprehensiveness, differentiation, precision, generalizability, contextual realism, ecological validity, and so on. However, these epistemic values are conflicting desiderata not all of which can be maximized at the same time, and there is no compelling "rational" algorithm within the positivistic paradigm for resolving the conflicts among them. In the end, those resolutions—those arbitrary choices—are made on the basis of criteria that are not necessarily logical or rational. Choices among conflicting criteria in the research process get resolved on the basis of such things as "my topical interests," "current thinking in the field," "a new and powerful statistical tool," and the like. They are made on the basis of what Howard (1985) calls *nonepistemic* values. (Such nonepistemic values—the sociocultural, political, economic, ethical, aesthetic, pragmatic values—are the kind that positivists worry about entering into and contaminating our scientific endeavors.)

According to our view, the epistemic values that dominate the research process can be summarized in terms of three conflicting desiderata, each of which can be expressed both at a general level and in slightly different terms within each of the three domains. Researchers always want to maximize all three of these conflicting desiderata, but they cannot. Furthermore, the things they do to try to maximize any one of them, or optimize on two, tend to minimize the other(s).

At the general level the three conflicting desiderata are *Generality, Differentiation,* and *System Fidelity.* In the Methodological domain: Generality maps to the familiar idea of generalizability, with regard to social units, situational conditions, and actions. Differentiation maps to precision in the measurement and control of variables. System fidelity maps to contextual realism.

In the Conceptual domain: Generality maps to a preference for concepts with high subsumptive range. Differentiation maps to the inferential power or leverage afforded by the concepts and relations. System fidelity maps to the particularity, or fit, of the conceptualizations to the substantive systems involved.

In the Substantive domain: Generality maps to the degree to which typical or representative system processes are being focused upon. Differentiation maps to the degree to which system processes are being clearly and unambiguously represented. System fidelity maps to the question of how richly the system processes are being articulated within the research endeavor.

In each domain, those three criteria, or sets of epistemic values, represent *mutually conflicting desiderata*—all of which the researcher must try to maximize, but all of which cannot be maximized at the same time. Hence, in each domain the researcher faces an epistemic dilemma—and *there are no epistemic rules or algorithms for resolving those dilemmas.* Nonepistemic values are used to make those choices.

Research Choices and
Nonepistemic Values

Whenever we launch a concrete study we typically borrow heavily from the extant paradigms (i.e., the elements, relations, and embedding contexts that are the generative work of stage 1) of at least one, often two, or sometimes all three of the domains. We thereby *bundle into our work the values, biases, and assumptions of the paradigms laid down by (unknown) others* (philosophers, methodologists, and system experts) who have done the stage 1 groundwork from which we borrow.

At the same time, when we make these choices we *bundle into our work a bevy of our own values/biases/assumptions.* These are two of the main windows through which values enter into the research process. Thus much of the value-laden nature of our ostensibly value-free research comes into play in stage 1, or as we go from stage 1 to stage 2—before we even start to apply our vaunted "objective" and "value-neutral" research procedures to conduct concrete studies in stage 2. The third or confirmatory stage, too, is fraught with value issues as we attempt to explore the robustness—the scope *and* boundaries—of a given set of research findings.

As choices involving value issues arise, the paradigm itself does not provide definitive rules for resolving them. These issues get resolved under the influence of current norms of our field and of the scientific and lay cultures within which it is embedded. Some feminists have argued that any science that is embedded within a patriarchal culture will inevitably reflect androcentric bias—not value-neutrality—at all levels of those guiding norms.

Feminism Versus Mainstream:
Some Contrasts

Metatheoretical Contrasts

Earlier, we listed nine major metatheoretical contrasts between the two perspectives. The first six relate, in pairs, to the three research paths described within the dilemmatic theory of method. The last three contrasts relate to each other and to the issue of purpose, hence to the entire metatheoretical space.

These metatheoretical contrasts can be boiled down to four very complex metaissues:

    I. The Value Issue: It subsumes several facets of objectivity, and haunts the theoretical path.

    II. The Knowledge Issue: It deals with the epistemological status of scientist, subject matter, and brute facts, and haunts the empirical path.

    III. The Context Issue: It subsumes issues of analytic versus systemic patterns of causation, and haunts the experimental path.

    IV. The Purpose Issue: It encompasses questions about basic versus applied work, about scholarship versus advocacy, and haunts the entire research enterprise.

The contrasting views of mainstream and feminist perspectives on those four metaissues are shown in Chart 2.2.

As a contrast between mainstream and feminist perspectives, the fourth metaissue provides an intriguing paradox. Many mainstream positivists would argue that the primary purpose of research is the pursuit of knowledge for its own sake, and perhaps secondarily to remedy some problems in extant systems. They certainly would argue that research ought to be (politically) neutral or indifferent *with respect to choice of problems.* Many feminists, on the other hand, would hold that the pursuit of knowledge cannot be politically neutral, that the positivist's putative political neutrality is simply a covert commitment to the status quo. They argue that because research cannot be politically neutral it should be explicit in its commitments, and that feminist research ought to be politically committed to the well-being of women—to gain knowledge that will help change women's lives and circumstances for the better.

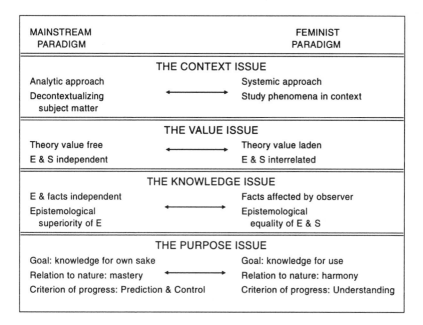

MAINSTREAM PARADIGM	FEMINIST PARADIGM
THE CONTEXT ISSUE	
Analytic approach	Systemic approach
Decontextualizing subject matter	Study phenomena in context
THE VALUE ISSUE	
Theory value free	Theory value laden
E & S independent	E & S interrelated
THE KNOWLEDGE ISSUE	
E & facts independent	Facts affected by observer
Epistemological superiority of E	Epistemological equality of E & S
THE PURPOSE ISSUE	
Goal: knowledge for own sake	Goal: knowledge for use
Relation to nature: mastery	Relation to nature: harmony
Criterion of progress: Prediction & Control	Criterion of progress: Understanding

Chart 2.2. Contrasting Paradigm Preferences at the Strategic Level

At the same time, for many positivists the criterion denoting progress in scientific inquiry is the ability to predict and control natural phenomena. This, in turn, reflects the underlying premise that the proper relation of science to nature is one of mastery. Many feminists would object to this as manipulative and androcentric, would view the proper relation of science to nature as one of harmony, and would propose that the proper criterion to denote progress in science ought to be *understanding* of the substantive systems involved, without the implication of manipulation or control.

Taken together, these seem to involve *contradictions* within both mainstream and feminist arguments, as well as opposition between them. On the mainstream side: Research for the sake of knowledge implies a politically neutral, passive stance, but research that is geared for prediction and control, in the service of mastery over nature, certainly does not. On the feminist side: Research for understanding seems politically neutral and passive, but research *for women* does not. Maybe this juxtaposition highlights still another dilemmatic choice within the research enterprise—a choice for which each of the available alternatives is ultimately unsatisfactory.

Research Choices and the
Conflicting Desiderata

Besides these broad metaissues, there are a number of less abstract issues on which mainstream and feminist perspectives can be contrasted. Some of those differences are discussed in this section in terms of the three conflicting desiderata; others are discussed in the next section in terms of each of the three research domains.

As argued above, the scientific paradigm itself carries no rules for definitive resolution of the conflicting desiderata. Thus they pose dilemmas that, strictly speaking, are unresolvable—at least in terms of *legitimate* (logical/rational) criteria, the accepted epistemic values of positivism. But they must be resolved in order to carry out any study. They get resolved, willy-nilly, by invoking nonepistemic values—that often reflect systematic preferences within the scientific practice of any one field at any one time. Feminists have been critical of the preferences regarding each of the desiderata that are reflected in mainstream work.

On the Generality criterion. Feminists have argued that mainstream researchers are too concerned with establishing wide subsumptive range for their concepts, and too often eager to claim such range (e.g., species-wide findings) even when not justified (e.g., when they have done quite narrow or biased sampling). Furthermore, feminists have argued, biased sampling of content—that is, biases in the typicality or representativeness of the system processes studied—are not random or accidental. They reflect an androcentric focus, systematically overemphasizing system processes important in the lives of men (e.g., competitive task performance), and systematically underrepresenting system processes crucial in the lives of women (e.g., child-care activities).

On the System Fidelity criterion. Feminists have argued that mainstream researchers are inclined to deal with conceptions and operations that are highly abstract (and hence are likely to fare poorly on the epistemic criterion of particularity of fit), and that their studies are likely to be done in empirical settings that have very low contextual realism. Feminists might also note that the prototypical research of mainstream practitioners is likely to focus on methodological and conceptual domains (that is, likely to follow the experimental path), thus neglecting the substantive domain. Therefore their studies are likely to involve few, abstract, and substantively impoverished system processes, reflecting emphasis on parsimony at a high cost in richness of articulation.

On the Differentiation criterion. Feminists have argued that, although mainstream researchers are properly concerned with the inferential power of their conceptualizations, they often hold too narrow a view of inference and interpretation, and too narrow a view of what constitutes evidence. They might also argue that mainstream researchers put too much reliance on manipulative and controlling strategies, and on the quantification aspects of measurement, thereby purchasing low ambiguity of concepts by vastly oversimplifying the representation of system processes—attaining clarity at a high cost in richness of articulation.

Research Choices and the Three Domains

Feminist and mainstream researchers have different preferences with respect to research paths (theoretical, experimental, and empirical). Hence, they differ in the relative emphasis they give to each of the three domains.

The Conceptual domain. Feminists have criticized mainstream practitioners for having shown a decided preference for concepts that are dichotomies, antitheses, separations rather than relations. Furthermore, our field has virtually enshrined the equilibrium idea, treating variation and change as error. We have thereby thrown in our lot with the status quo, tacitly endorsed the idea of seeking species-general laws, and focused on system stability rather than change. Moreover, we have given great weight to the criterion of parsimony, and to dealing with concepts of broad subsumptive range, at the expense of concepts that reflect the particularity of each individual social unit.

The Substantive domain. Feminists also have criticized mainstream researchers for having selected topics and systems for study with an androcentric perspective, or in ways that reflect androcentric interpretations of the world. Mainstream practitioners have given emphasis to topics that embody activities in which men dominate and predominate, and have given little attention to issues important to the lives of women. Furthermore, that androcentric bias has had a major effect on who gets defined as a potential "system expert" in various systems. Consider, for example, that it is largely male pediatricians, not midwives and not mothers, who are regarded as experts on childbearing; and it is usually educational experts (often male) rather than teachers (usually female) who are regarded as experts on the schools. This androcentric bias has also had an effect on what social units are regarded as appropriate controls or comparisons for a given set of systems under study. Such choices of comparison groups in turn affect interpretation of results.

The Methodological domain. Feminists have criticized mainstream practitioners for their heavily analytic approach, which gives high priority to precision and quantification and, generally, extracts the social unit and its behavior from the embedding context. Feminists also have decried mainstream emphasis on use of manipulative strategies, and insistence on the putative "objectivity" of measures and procedures (even though the concept of objectivity has muddled meanings and raises serious epistemological and ontological issues).

Research Choices at Design and Operational Levels

Mainstream and feminist research approaches show some contrasting preferences at study design and operational levels as well as at strategic levels. These preferences have consequences for the kinds of questions that can be asked and the kinds of answers that can be obtained.

At a study design level, mainstream research characteristically searches for *differences,* and the analytic/interpretative framework of the paradigm is designed for that purpose (e.g., hypothesis tests as attempts to reject the null hypothesis). It has been said that feminist researchers are more attuned to the study of relations, but the arguments supporting that idea are murky (see Peplau & Conrad, 1989, for a clear discussion of this).[1] It is probably more useful to talk of a feminist preference for studying multivariate and multidirectional patterns (as opposed to directional, single variable, cause-effect relations)—in effect, a preference for systemic versus analytic approaches to research.

Mainstream preferences thus tend to lead to the kinds of study designs characterized by the term "factorial" (whether or not the study actually uses ANOVA or its variants). For such designs, success hinges on the importance and power of the variables (and the levels of those variables) chosen for the study's independent variables. In contrast, feminist preferences tend to lead to study designs characterized by the term *correlational* (whether or not the study actually calculates correlation coefficients). For such designs, success hinges on identifying, articulating, and interpreting complex patterns of dependent variable results.

Unfortunately, neither mainstream nor feminist researchers can incorporate everything they want to investigate in any one study. There always is a temptation to increase the scope of a study. That temptation leads mainstream researchers to build designs that "explode," with more and more levels of more and more systematically crossed independent variables. The corresponding tendency for feminist researchers is to build designs that "implode," pursuing complex patterns of relations among more dependent variables.

There are differences in sampling pertinent to the two paradigms as well. For mainstream research, success depends on making cases "within a cell" as much alike as possible; within-cell differences are treated as "error." The assumptions underlying feminist research encourage wide and heterogeneous sampling of cases; differences among cases are treated as substantive information rather than error.

That foreshadows another sampling difference: Mainstream research favors systematic sampling of cases, with substantial numbers of cases in every cell (i.e., every combination of conditions). This gets case-costly in a hurry, as the number of systematically crossed factors increases. Furthermore, such systematically crossed designs often include combinations of crossed conditions that make little sense, and certainly have no ecological validity. Feminist research, on the other hand, favors representative sampling of cases for the sake of ecological validity. That makes interpretation of results much more problematic for interesting but low-frequency combinations of conditions.

At the operational level, mainstream practitioners and feminists also give different emphases to the importance of various data collection methods (e.g., archival, observational, self-report), and sometimes use the same methods for dramatically different functional purposes within study designs. For example: Mainstream researchers often treat participant self-reports as if they were relatively low-quality substitutes for direct observation of so-called objective behavior. Feminists, on the other hand, are likely to treat participant self-reports as valid, vital measures, yielding information about participants' perceptions and experiences.

Concluding Comments

This is not the whole iceberg by any means. There is much more to be said about positivism and feminism in regard to such issues as (a) the politics of problem selection; (b) the search for differences versus patterns, and more generally, analytic versus systemic approaches; and (c) the implications of different preferences and tendencies in study designs, such as choices of comparison groups, viewed as strategic expressions of values.

From what we have come to understand thus far, both mainstream and feminist perspectives have a lot to offer researchers in the social and behavioral sciences, but neither of them is without limitations and flaws. Each perspective contains its own paradoxes and contradictions—reflecting the dilemmatic nature of the research enterprise.

Note

1. In part, the "relations" argument here confuses an alleged feminine proclivity for effective human relationships (vs. an alleged masculine lack of such a proclivity) with a putative preference by women for the study of logical or mathematical relations (rather than differences). The confusion is made murkier when the origin of that alleged "relation" ability of women is tied to neo-Freudian object relations theory.

References

Benston, M. (1982). Feminism and the critique of scientific method. In A. R. Miles & G. Finn (Eds.), *Feminism in Canada: From pressure to politics* (pp. 47-66). Montreal: Black Rose.

Bleier, R. (Ed.). (1987). *Feminist approaches to science*. Elmsford, NY: Pergamon.

Brinberg, D., & McGrath, J. E. (1985). *Validity and the research process.* Beverly Hills, CA: Sage.

Crawford, M., & Marecek, J. (1989). Psychology reconstructs the female: 1968-1988. *Psychology of Women Quarterly, 13,* 147-166.

Gergen, M. M. (1988). Toward a feminist metatheory and methodology in the social sciences. In M. M. Gergen (Ed.), *Feminist thought and the structure of knowledge* (pp. 87-104). New York: New York University Press.

Harding, S. (Ed.) (1987). *Feminism and methodology.* Bloomington: Indiana University Press.

Harding, S., & O'Barr, J. F. (1987). *Sex and scientific inquiry.* Chicago: University of Chicago Press.

Hare-Mustin, R. T., & Marecek, J. (1988). The meaning of difference: Gender theory, postmodernism, and psychology. *American Psychologist, 43,* 455-464.

Howard, G. S. (1985). The role of values in the science of psychology. *American Psychologist, 40,* 255-265.

Kelly, J. R., & McGrath, J. E. (1988). *On time and method.* Newbury Park, CA: Sage.

Manicas, P. T., & Secord, P. F. (1983). Implications for psychology of the new philosophy of science. *American Psychologist, 38,* 399-413.

McGrath, J. E., Martin, J., & Kulka, R. C. (1982). *Judgment calls in research.* Beverly Hills, CA: Sage.

Packer, M. J. (1985). Hermeneutic inquiry in the study of human conduct. *American Psychologist, 40,* 1081-1093.

Parlee, M. B. (1979). Psychology and women. *Signs: Journal of Women in Culture & Society, 5,* 121-133.

Peplau, L. A., & Conrad, E. (1989). Beyond nonsexist research: The perils of feminist methods in psychology. *Psychology of Women Quarterly, 13*(4), 379-400.

Runkel, P. J., & McGrath, J. E. (1972). *Studying human behavior.* New York: Holt, Rinehart & Winston.

Vickers, J. M. (1982). Memoirs of an ontological exile: The methodological rebellions of feminist research. In A. R. Miles & G. Finn (Eds.), *Feminism in Canada: From pressure to politics.* Montreal: Black Rose.

PART II

SOCIALIZATION AND DEVELOPMENT

3

Early Gender Development

CAROL NAGY JACKLIN
LAURA A. BAKER

Much of the research on gender differences has focused on the early years in life, even though it is the differential expectations about adult women and men that we are ultimately interested in understanding. Perhaps this is the lingering influence of Freud's (1949) psychoanalytic theory that has led us to search for the roots of adult outcomes during childhood. Consistent with this idea, most research during the early years has examined the effects of parents, particularly mothers, on the development of an individual's gender-related behaviors.

Research in early gender development has encompassed many questions, including those concerning (a) sexual dimorphism—the physical and psychological differentiation of girls and boys; (b) sex stereotypes—differential expectations of girls and boys within a culture; (c) gender identity—one's identification with the feminine or masculine gender as part of one's self-perception; and (d) gender role—the social roles and interactions that may result from sexual dimorphisms, stereotypes, and gender identity (Wilson, 1983). Although research on stereotypes, gender identity, and gender roles certainly contributes to our understanding of the functioning of females and males in society, of central importance to the study of gender has been the extent to which there are real differences between the sexes. It is the processes by which these differences are acquired by girls and boys that we are most concerned with in this chapter.

In early childhood, two areas have been identified in which mean differences between girls and boys have been reliably found—boys are found to be more aggressive than girls, whereas girls' language development and verbal abilities exceed those of boys (Maccoby & Jacklin, 1974). However, these average differences between girls and boys are relatively minor compared to the vast individual differences within each sex. Even for characteristics showing considerable sexual dimorphism (for example, verbal skills), girls and boys typically differ by only about 0.25 of a standard deviation, suggesting considerable overlap in distributions. Much of the research on gender highlights the need to consider both within-group as well as between-sex variation in behavior to achieve a complete understanding of both females and males.

In this chapter we consider research on the development of sexually dimorphic behaviors and psychological characteristics, as well as research on sex-stereotypic behavior. We refer throughout to "gendered behaviors" and "gender outcome" as traits or behaviors either showing actual differences between girls and boys, or aspects whereby our culture expects the sexes to differ. Our focus is on influences during the early years of childhood, an area where the research emphasis has been on parents as transmitters of gendered behaviors. We describe two approaches with very different theoretical origins, social learning and behavior genetics. We argue that, despite the contrasting interpretations these two approaches provide for the observed associations between parents and children, research from both approaches yields some surprisingly similar findings. In particular, characteristics and behavior of parents provide, at best, very little prediction of young children's gender outcomes. We then consider less extensive research on other influences, including persons outside the home, peers, teachers, and other relatives, as well as characteristics of the child her- or himself.

We contend that a comprehensive interactionist model is needed for understanding gender development. This model must include both biological and social factors, as well as their interplay. Unlike previous Gesellian models of nature and nurture that focus on biological destiny and species-specific (genetic) universals (see Thelen & Adolph, 1992), we advocate an individual differences model that emphasizes genetic and cultural diversity within females and males. We also argue for the need to study factors of diversity previously not considered in gender research, including the effects of race, social class, and ethnicity.

Most importantly our conceptualization of gender and the context in which it is studied must be considered. What is needed is an understanding of the asymmetry of gender roles and the patriarchal society that the young child must come to understand.

Parents as Transmitters of Gendered Behaviors

Parents traditionally have been assumed to have profound effects on the developmental outcomes of their children, including gendered behaviors. Two different theoretical approaches to the study of parental influences, however, propose quite different mechanisms for the transmission of values, characteristics, and behaviors from parents to children. Social learning theory proposes that associations found between parental behaviors and child outcomes are primarily due to parents' socialization of the child through a system of rewards and punishments (Mischel, 1966). Imitation, or role-model effects, are additional mechanisms whereby the child is presumed to learn from parental behavior (Bandura, 1969).

Behavior geneticists, on the other hand, although not excluding the effects of socialization, recognize that parents transmit biological effects directly to their children. Thus parent-child behavior associations may reflect both genetic and cultural inheritance. For our purposes the most important implication of this interpretation is that one may not assume that changing the parent's behavior will necessarily or directly change the child's outcome (Baker & Clark, 1990; Rowe, 1990).

After a brief review of gender research stemming from both social learning and behavior genetic perspectives, we will consider their communalities in findings.

Social Learning Perspective

In the 1960s social learning theory was used to describe the learning of gender-related behavior (Mischel, 1966). In its simplest form, social learning theory hypothesizes that gender roles are learned because they are taught by social agents. Parents and other caretakers are believed to treat girls and boys differently from the very beginning of life. This process has been called *differential socialization.* Girls are thought to be rewarded for certain behaviors, and punished for other behaviors. And these are not the same sets of behaviors for which boys are thought to be rewarded or punished.

Two large-scale reviews of gender socialization by parents have found little evidence of differential socialization (Lytton & Romney, 1991; Maccoby & Jacklin, 1974). The most recent review (Lytton & Romney, 1991) is a meta-analysis of 172 studies. The authors conclude that there is only one area in which there is evidence of parents' differential socialization, and that is in the direct encouragement of gender-typed activities (see also studies by Huston, 1983, 1985). In studies of Western countries outside of North America, they found some evidence that physical punishment is used more often with boys than with girls. In 18 other areas of differential socialization (e.g., achievement encouragement, verbal interaction, restrictiveness, encouragement of dependency), Lytton and Romney found no evidence of differential socialization.

Why have empirical studies failed to confirm that differential socialization occurs, in spite of the continuing popular belief that it does? Several reasons have been suggested (Jacklin & Reynolds, in press). Psychologists may have looked too exclusively at parents as using gender stereotypes. In general, we stereotype individuals we do not know well. Yet parents know their children very well. The effects of peers, teachers, and other adults, including other family members outside the home (e.g., aunts, uncles, grandparents), may be more relevant cultural transmitters of stereotypes. What makes work on nonparental adults difficult for psychologists to study is that different children are likely to have different adults who have brought the gendered culture to them. Different relatives (or nonrelatives) will be important to different children. It is precisely these nonnormative agents that most need to be studied (Bandura, 1982). We will return to this issue below.

Behavior Genetics Perspective

Observed associations between parent and child behavior found in studies from the social learning perspective may be interpreted somewhat differently from a behavior genetics perspective. The major difference from a behavior genetic perspective is that inherited biological factors could mediate, at least in part but possibly entirely, any observed parent-child relationships.

The effects of shared environment and shared genes are estimated indirectly in behavior genetic studies through the comparison of various pairings of relatives who vary in the extent to which genes and environment are shared. For example, associations between adoptive parents and their (genetically unrelated) children are presumed to be a function of shared family environment, which may include the effects of parenting styles and socialization. On the other hand, observed similarities between biological parents and their adopted-away children would stem from genetic influences on traits (provided that the adoption agency did not seek adoptive parents who were similar to the biological parent with respect to the traits or behaviors being studied, a phenomenon known as "selective placement").

Adoption studies provide an excellent opportunity for understanding the nature of parent-child associations. During infancy and early childhood, correlations between adoptive parents and children are consistently low or negligible for personality and temperament (Plomin, 1986; Plomin & DeFries, 1985). Adopted children are generally more similar to their biological parents, even when controlling for the effects of selective placement, suggesting the important role of genetic effects in parent-child resemblance in personality (Plomin, 1990). Environmental influences on personality are primarily not shared by parents and children. Rather, environmental factors are specific to each person, and they operate to make individuals in the same family different from one another.

In adoption studies of cognitive abilities, genetic factors have also been shown to be important during infancy and childhood (Plomin, 1986; Plomin & DeFries, 1985). In contrast to results for personality, however, some effects of shared environment on cognitive abilities appear during the school years, although these effects diminish during later development. By and large, the nonshared environment is the most important class of influences on early cognitive abilities.

Studies of twins can also be used to shed light on the nature of parent-child similarities. Genetic influences are suggested by the greater resemblance of monozygotic (MZ—genetically identical) twins, compared to dizygotic (DZ) twins, who share only half their genetic material on average. Such interpretations do, of course, rest on the assumption that the effects of shared environment are equivalent for both MZ and DZ twin pairs, an assumption that has received some empirical support (Baker & Daniels, 1990; Loehlin & Nichols, 1976; Scarr, 1992). In twin studies of intellectual performance, genetically related variance has been found for most specific cognitive abilities (including those that show mean differences between girls and boys) during preschool (Wilson, 1975), and early school years (Segal, 1986), as well as adulthood (Tambs, Sundet, & Magnus, 1984). Twin studies of temperament and personality also demonstrate significant heritable influences from infancy through adulthood (Buss & Plomin, 1984). As in adoption studies, the nonshared environment is routinely found to be a major source of individual differences, in addition to genetics, in both cognition and personality in early development.

To date, few behavior genetic studies have been designed specifically to examine gender differences in behavior and their origins. Nor has there been extensive study of genetic and environmental variations in sexually dimorphic behaviors in early childhood. Most behavior genetic research focuses on within-sex variation, rather than between-sex differences.

One study of aggression in 4- to 6-year-old twins found some evidence for heritable influences (Ghodsian-Carpey & Baker, 1987), although other studies have not supported this (see Plomin, 1988). Studies of adults do suggest heritable influences in aggressiveness (Rushton, Fulker, Neale, Nias, & Eysenck, 1986) and antisocial behavior (see Raine & Dunkin, 1990). By and large, however, these results are based on variations within groups of females and males.

A few studies of twins have examined the roles of heredity and environment in gender-related personality attributes (i.e., masculinity and femininity). During preadolescence, both femininity (expressivity) and masculinity (instrumentality) have shown significant genetic variance (Mitchell, Baker, & Jacklin, 1989). The effects of environmental factors common to family members are negligible or nonexistent. The modest associations found between parental behavior and child gender outcome in the social learning studies, then, may be mediated in part by shared heredity between parents and children. Most importantly, however, the effects of experiences and other environmental factors unique to each individual appear to explain more variation in gender attributes than either genetic or common environmental influences.

Communalities in Findings

A comparison of research findings from both social learning and behavior genetics perspectives leads to a common finding: parents may not be powerful agents in the development of gender attributes. The lack of evidence for any strong relationships between parental behavior and children's gender outcomes is consistent with the repeated finding in behavior genetic research (across a wide range of psychological domains) that environmental influences are primarily not shared by family members. General parenting styles, traditionally thought to be important to child outcomes by developmental psychologists, have been found instead to play little or no role in the child's social development (Rowe, 1990).

There are also greater individual differences in child behavior within sex compared to average differences between girls and boys, even for characteristics that show the greatest sexual dimorphism (Maccoby & Jacklin, 1974). Behavior genetic research on personality in early childhood (Plomin, 1986) and gender attributes in preadolescence (Mitchell, Baker, & Jacklin, 1989) and young adulthood (Rowe, 1982) emphasizes that genetic variations within sex are important in producing these individual differences. Most important, however, is the finding that environmental influences not shared by family members are routinely the largest source of individual differences.

Moreover, although mothers and fathers may be consistent across time in their behavior toward a single child in the family, parents apparently behave differently toward their different children (Dunn, 1992; Plomin & Daniels, 1987). It may be that parents react to natural differences between their children, or that parents are different at different times of their lives, leading to the formation of multiple "micro-environments" within the same family (Scarr, 1992).

Other Transmitters of Gendered Behaviors

The Child Per Se

There are several ways in which the child her- or himself can be the transmitter of gendered behaviors. One obvious way is that genetic factors can account for the unfolding of gendered behaviors. There may be innate, biological factors, some of which may be linked to sex chromosomes, that produce both within-sex and between-sex variations.

A second, somewhat less obvious way is that the genetically based characteristics of girls and boys could elicit different responses from parents and other socializing agents. These adults may not be responding to the category of gender, but to different stimuli displayed by female and male children. The difficulty with this hypothesis is that it would entail differential treatment of girls and boys and we have seen very little evidence of differential treatment in the summaries of research above.

There is a third, more compelling way that children can be seen as responsible for their own gendered behaviors. The child may be responsible through the cognitive processing the child is known to do concerning gender. In the mid-1960s Kohlberg (1966) developed a cognitive-developmental theory of how a child might learn to understand gender through interpretation of her or his environment. He believed that sex-typed behavior is not made up of a set of independent elements acquired by imitating actions the child has seen same-sex individuals perform. Instead it develops from organized rules the child induces from what has been observed. Kohlberg's theory was patterned after the Piagetian stage theory of general cognitive development. He saw Piaget's concept of physical constancy as analogous to children's understanding of gender constancy. That is, Kohlberg believed that children could not understand concepts such as their own sex until they had reached a cognitive state that allowed them to understand that gender was a lasting or constant construct. Nevertheless, children do seem to learn gender roles very early and they seem to learn these gender roles much earlier than they develop gender-constancy. This Kohlbergian notion of the child as a cognitive processor with regard to gender has evolved into gender-schema theory.

Gender schema are networks or patterns of associations related to gender. The concept of schema has its roots in memory theory. Gender schema are sets of ideas that organize the concept of gender for individuals. These schema change and evolve with additional information. Often the schema are based on incorrect associations. A particularly compelling example is shown by a 4-year-old boy, Jeremy, who decided to wear barrettes to school one day. This was very upsetting to another boy in the preschool who kept urging Jeremy to remove the barrettes, because "only girls wear barrettes." Jeremy replied that he was a boy because he had a penis and testicles, and that the barrettes themselves did not make him a girl. After further repeated attempts by the other boy to get Jeremy to remove his barrettes, Jeremy became so upset he pulled down his pants to make his point. In response his companion remained unconvinced, saying, "Everybody has a penis, only girls wear barrettes!" (Bem, 1983, p. 612). This child's gender schema was wrong, but strongly held nonetheless.

There is ample evidence for gender schematic thinking by children (e.g., Bem, 1985). Children are themselves active in the process of understanding what gender means in each culture and applying the cultural understanding to their own behaviors.

Other Socializing Agents

As we indicated in the first section of this chapter, parents have been the focus of most of the work investigating the transmission of gendered behaviors. The role of nonparent adults has been little studied. Aunts, uncles, or grandparents may be important. On one level, nonparent adults appear to be much better candidates for gender role transmission. Unlike parents, they may be in a position to have optimal influence over a child and yet may not know the child very well. As mentioned earlier, people stereotype individuals they do not know very well, and parents tend to know their children. Thus parents are more likely to respond to individual characteristics rather than generalized stereotyped ones. It may not even be particular adults, but rather the available adults at particular times that become gender socializers. Chance events may be the major factor here (Bandura, 1982). For developmental psychologists interested in studying the influence of nonparent adults, the logistics would be formidable.

One type of nonparent adult for whom there is evidence of treating girls and boys differently is teachers. There is considerable evidence that teachers do differentially socialize girls and boys in and outside of the classroom (see Jacklin, 1982 and 1989, for reviews).

A separate line of research into gendered behaviors has been carried out cross-culturally. In their summary of the gendered behaviors of 16 cultures, Whiting and Edwards (1988) concluded that the situations that girls and boys find themselves put into are different and that is what is important. Different situations, different companions, elicit different behaviors. Thus if you are with individuals older than you, certain behaviors are called for. If you are with individuals younger than you, other behaviors are called for. For example, most humans have the same behaviors (and likely the same feelings) elicited from them when they hold an infant. These are different feelings and behaviors from those elicited by being with someone older than oneself. Whiting and Edwards conclude that we are the "company we keep." In their view, nurturance is elicited by caring for infants and children. Competitiveness is elicited by interaction with older and same-age peers. If this view is true, the crucial parent behavior may be giving girls and boys different situations and companions whose company then does the socializing.

Peers

Peers are potent transmitters of the culture of gender. Sometimes the influential peers are siblings, sometimes not. Peers' influence has been documented in two ways—as differential socializers of girls and boys, and as the individuals who provide much of the gendered associations that form the gender schema. This is an area that has not been as much studied by developmental psychologists as it has been by sociologists of childhood (e.g., Thorne, in press).

Limitations of Past Research

The early years may not be the best place to search for gender socialization. Most of the research in this area has yielded null results. There are not marked differences between girls and boys this early in life, nor are there significant differences in most aspects of how parents relate to girls and boys. Even in an individual differences framework, there are only modest associations between parents and children, part of which may be due to genetic transmission rather than socialization.

The effects of demographic variables, including race, social class, and ethnic group, have rarely been considered. More importantly, our understanding of how children learn the different values placed by society on female and male sets of behavior is not well understood. Until these factors are integrated into gender research, we may be seriously limited in our ability to understand gender per se.

A central problem of the childhood socialization viewpoint is the limited populations on which the research has been conducted. That is, the samples of children studied in the research are a small and selected subgroup of the universe of available children. Race, class, and ethnicity have been largely left out of our understandings of gender socialization. The majority of the studies we have cited in this chapter have samples of Euro-American middle-class children and adults. This problem is not limited to the literature on socialization of gender. It is equally true of much of the developmental literature and indeed of the psychological literature as a whole. We have evidence that these variables make a difference in the study of gender (Bardwell, Cochran, & Walker, 1986; Binion, 1990; Price-Bonham & Skeen, 1982), although the nature of these differences is not yet clear. In recent work there are clues on differences between girls in Afro-American, Latino, and Euro-American cultures (Bell, 1989; Grant, 1984; Reid, Trotter, & Tate, 1991). There are other clues that family variables are different in these three cultures and different still in Asian-American cultures (Gold & St. Ange, 1974; Harrison, Wilson, Pine, Chan, & Buriel, 1990; McGoldrick, Garcia-Preto, Hines, & Lee, 1989). Since our theoretical viewpoints have been based on limited samples, our viewpoints are inherently limited. Awareness of this fact coupled with the recognition that issues of gender are not the same in different cultures (Munroe, Shimmin, & Munroe, 1984; Whiting & Edwards, 1988) should help to broaden our thinking about the theoretical viewpoints that we do have.

Our conceptualization of gender itself must also be seriously questioned. There is considerable asymmetry in gender roles and the values society places on masculine and feminine behaviors. Furthermore, these values themselves may depend on whether the behaviors are displayed by females or males. An underlying assumption of most research on childhood gender development is that there are two sets of behaviors for children to learn. We have discussed different methods of transmission: differential reinforcements; genetics; and cognitive processing. A limitation of all of these perspectives is that there is more to learn than these two sets of behaviors. That is, what the child must learn is a complex patriarchal system in which the two sets of gendered behaviors are not equally valued. In most aspects male behaviors are more valued, although females may sometimes be punished for these.

The child must process more than appropriate behavior; he or she processes the levels of power among others, including parents, and other expectations of the patriarchal system (Bem, in press).

In the past decade, scholarship has begun to emphasize the value of female behaviors and celebrate female differences (e.g., Gilligan, 1982; Harding, 1986). Yet the young child must and does learn the asymmetry of gender in our culture. Our understanding of how these gender roles are learned has only begun to be conceptualized (Bem, in press).

Conclusions, Implications, and Applications

Based on our review of research on gender-related behaviors in early childhood, two major conclusions can be reached: (1) Within-sex variations are far greater than between-sex differences, even for behaviors and characteristics known to show the greatest differences between females and males. Therefore, an individual differences approach should be used, both with respect to parental behaviors toward girls and boys, as well as regarding behavior and psychological characteristics of the children themselves. (2) Models of gender development should include both biological and social influences. The pervasive effects of inherited variations in producing individual differences in most measurable characteristics of children are well established and should be carefully considered in models of social development.

Even though genetic variance may exist for within-sex variation in sexually dimorphic traits (e.g., spatial ability; aggression), between-sex effects *may* still be entirely due to environmental (cultural) differences between females and males. It is important to realize that answers to questions concerning individual differences within girls and boys do not necessarily have bearing on the answers to questions concerning between-sex differences. That is, heritable influences within each sex do not unequivocally imply that the mean difference is genetically based. In other words, genetic variations within gender do not necessarily imply that mean gender differences are heritable. Gender differences are likely to be a function of both genetic and environmental factors.

What are the social implications of gender differences being in part due to genetic differences between females and males? Historically, hereditarian viewpoints have been put to major misuse (see Minton &

Schneider, 1980). For example, immigration laws in America were set in place largely as a function of racist views that incorrectly stemmed from early findings of genetic variations for characteristics within races. Would finding a genetic basis for gender differences reinforce similar discrimination against women or men? There is ample evidence of the misuse of biological explanations (Sayers, 1982).

Biology is not destiny. We now understand genetic regulation and the effects of environmental changes on gene expression in molecular biology. Even if genetic differences explain in part the differential patterns of behavior that eventually emerge between girls and boys, these different behaviors can most likely be eliminated through environmental interventions. For example, we currently spend considerable national resources on boys who have speech and reading problems.

There is little chance of finding out the answer to these questions without further research. A well-designed behavior-genetic study of early gender development could prove very fruitful. Such a study might include child twins and their parents, which would allow the estimation of both genetic and cultural transmission of gender-related behaviors. Another alternative would be to study adult twins and their young children. Either study should include both opposite-sex twins, so that models of differences in genetic and environmental transmission could be evaluated. Given the appreciable effects of environmental factors not shared by relatives, one could predict a great deal of within-pair variation in gender-related behaviors for identical twins. An extensive assessment of which important experiences and influential role models differ between male-female identical twins would yield information about environmental factors independent of genetic variations.

A complete understanding of both the social and biological transmission of gendered behaviors in childhood has a clear implication. It could ultimately allow change of the gendered aspects of individuals and thus change the gendered aspects of the population. Childhood is not the only point in the life span at which individuals can be changed; it is simply the point we are discussing here. But if we could change the gendered aspects of individuals, in what way would we change them?

Would our goal be to make girls and boys more similar, or more different? In the 1970s the answer of feminist psychologists would have been to try to raise children without the limitations of gender roles. The goal would have been to try to raise a "gender-aschematic child in a gender-schematic society," as Bem (1983) said in her much-quoted article. Now, however, the answer is less clear. In the last decade there has been a rise in research and writing celebrating gender differences, from both a feminist point of view (e.g., Gilligan, 1982) and from a patriarchal point of view (e.g., Bly, 1990). Is the goal to emphasize differences or similarities? Feminist psychologists are now grappling with the similarities and differences viewpoints (Jacklin, 1991). The similarities tradition (e.g., Maccoby & Jacklin, 1974) uses the traditional empirical psychology methods, with all of their strengths and faults. And we conclude in the similarities tradition that there are few differences of any magnitude between females and males. The differences tradition is mainly theoretical and not empirical. Two examples are the works of Gilligan (1982) and Chodorow (1978). Chodorow hasn't gone out and counted the number of mothers who are doing X or the number of children who are doing Y. She has instead given a theoretical, psychoanalytic perspective on the socialization of gender differences.

In childhood, gender roles do limit boys but the limitations on girls are much greater (Unger & Crawford, 1992). Because of the asymmetry of power in these roles, we advocate the similarity position *between* gender groups and advocate the difference position *within* gender (and other) groupings. Knowing how gender socialization works would help parents, families, teachers, and television writers (and all socializing agents) to raise children without the limitations of these roles. And without the limitations of gender roles, there will be greater differences between individuals, and thus within groups of girls and within groups of boys.

References

Baker, L. A., & Clark, R. (1990). Genetic origins of behavior: Implications for counselors. *Journal of Counseling and Development, 68,* 597-600.

Baker, L. A., & Daniels, D. (1990). Nonshared environmental influences and personality differences in adult twins. *Journal of Personality and Social Psychology, 58,* 103-110.

Bandura, A. (1969). Social-learning theory of identificatory processes. In D. A. Goslin (Ed.), *Handbook of socialization theory and research* (pp. 213-262). Chicago: Rand McNally College Publishing.

Bandura, A. (1982). The psychology of chance encounters and life paths. *American Psychologist, 37*(7), 747-755.

Bardwell, J. R., Cochran, S. W., & Walker, S. (1986). Relationship of parental education, race and gender to sex role stereotyping in five-year-old kindergartners. *Sex Roles, 15,* 275-281.

Bell, L. A. (1989). Something's wrong here and it's not me: Challenging the dilemmas that block girls' success. *Journal for the Education of the Gifted, 12,* 118-130.

Bem, S. L. (1983). Gender schema theory and its implications for child development: Raising gender-aschematic children in a gender-schematic society. *Signs: Journal of Women in Culture and Society, 8,* 598-616.

Bem, S. L. (1985). Androgyny and gender schema theory: A conceptual and empirical integration. In T. B. Sonderegger (Ed.), *Nebraska Symposium on Motivation: Psychology of gender.* Lincoln: University of Nebraska Press.

Bem, S. L. (in press). *The lenses of gender: An essay on the social reproduction of male power.* New Haven, CT: Yale University Press.

Binion, V. J. (1990). Psychological androgyny: A black female perspective. *Sex Roles, 22*(7/8), 487-507.

Bly, R. (1990). *Iron John: A book about men.* Reading, MA: Addison-Wesley.

Buss, A. H., & Plomin, R. (1984). *Temperament: Early developing personality traits.* Hillsdale, NJ: Lawrence Erlbaum.

Chodorow, N. (1978). *The reproduction of mothering: Psychoanalysis and the sociology of gender.* Berkeley: University of California Press.

Dunn, J. (1992). Siblings and development. *Current Directions in Psychological Science, 1,* 6-9.

Freud, S. (1949). *A general introduction to psychoanalysis.* New York: Garden City Publishing.

Ghodsian-Carpey, J., & Baker, L. A. (1987). Genetic and environmental influences on aggression in 4- to 7-year-old twins. *Aggressive Behavior, 13,* 173-186.

Gilligan, C. (1982). *In a different voice: Psychological theory and women's development.* Cambridge, MA: Harvard University Press.

Gold, A. R., & St. Ange, M. C. (1974). Development of sex role stereotypes in black and white elementary school girls. *Developmental Psychology, 10,* 461.

Grant, L. (1984). Black females' "place" in desegregated classrooms. *Sociology of Education, 57,* 98-111.

Harding, S. (1986). *The science question in feminism.* Ithaca, NY: Cornell University Press.

Harrison, A. O., Wilson, M. N., Pine, C. J., Chan, S. Q., & Buriel, R. (1990). Family ecologies of ethnic minority children. *Child Development, 61,* 347-362.

Huston, A. C. (1983). Sex-typing. In P. H. Mussen (Ed.), *Handbook of child psychology* (4th ed.) (Vol. 4, pp. 387-467). New York: John Wiley.

Huston, A. C. (1985). The development of sex-typing. *Developmental Review, 5,* 1-17.

Jacklin, C. N. (1982). Boys and girls entering school. In M. Marland (Ed.), *Sex differentiation and schooling* (pp. 8-17). London: William Heinemann Educational Books.

Jacklin, C. N. (1989). Female and male: Issues of gender. *American Psychologist, 44,* 127-133.

Jacklin, C. N. (1991, March). *Research on gender similarities and differences.* Paper presented at the meeting of the Association for Women in Psychology, Hartford, CT.

Jacklin, C. N., & Reynolds, C. A. (in press). *Gender and childhood socialization.* In A. E. Beall & R. J. Sternberg (Eds.), *Perspectives on the psychology of gender.* New York: Guilford Press.

Kohlberg, L. (1966). A cognitive-developmental analysis of children's sex-role concepts and attitudes. In E. E. Maccoby (Ed.), *The development of sex differences* (pp. 82-173). Stanford, CA: Stanford University Press.

Loehlin, J. C., & Nichols, R. C. (1976). *Heredity, environment, and personality: A study of 850 sets of twins.* Austin: University of Texas Press.

Lytton, H., & Romney, D. M. (1991). Parents' differential socialization of boys and girls: A meta-analysis. *Psychological Bulletin, 109*(2), 267-296.

Maccoby, E. E., & Jacklin, C. N. (1974). *The psychology of sex differences.* Stanford, CA: Stanford University Press.

McGoldrick, M., Garcia-Preto, N., Hines, P. M., & Lee, E. (1989). Ethnicity and women. In M. McGoldrick, C. M. Anderson, & F. Walsh (Eds.), *Women in families: A framework for feminist therapy* (pp. 169-199). New York: Norton.

Minton, H. L., & Schneider, F. W. (1980). *Differential psychology.* Prospect Heights, IL: Waveland Press.

Mischel, W. (1966). A social-learning view of sex differences in behavior. In E. E. Maccoby (Ed.), *The development of sex differences* (pp. 56-81). Stanford, CA: Stanford University Press.

Mitchell, J. E., Baker, L. A., & Jacklin, C. N. (1989). Masculinity and femininity in twin children: Genetic and environmental factors. *Child Development, 60,* 1475-1485.

Munroe, R. H., Shimmin, H. S., & Munroe, R. L. (1984). Gender understanding and sex role performance in four cultures. *Developmental Psychology, 20,* 673-682.

Plomin, R. (1986). *Development, genetics, and psychology.* Hillsdale, NJ: Lawrence Erlbaum.

Plomin, R. (1988). The nature and nurture of cognitive abilities. In R. J. Sternberg (Ed.), *Advances in the psychology of human intelligence.* Hillsdale, NJ: Lawrence Erlbaum.

Plomin, R. (1990). *Behavioral genetics: A primer.* New York: Freeman.

Plomin, R., & Daniels, D. (1987). Why are children in the same family so different from each other? *Behavioral and Brain Sciences, 10,* 1-59.

Plomin, R., & DeFries, J. C. (1985). *Origins of individual differences in infancy.* Orlando, FL: Academic Press.

Price-Bonham, S., & Skeen, P. (1982). Black and white fathers' attitudes towards children's sex roles. *Psychological Reports, 50,* 1187-1190.

Raine, A., & Dunkin, J. J. (1990). The genetic and psychophysiological basis of antisocial behavior: Implications for counseling and therapy. *Journal of Counseling and Development, 68,* 637-644.

Reid, P. T., Trotter, K. H., & Tate, C. S. (1991, March). *Children's self-presentations with infants: Age gender and race comparisons.* Paper presented at the conference of the Society for Research in Child Development, Seattle, WA.

Rowe, D. C. (1982). Sources of variability in sex-linked personality attributes: A twin study. *Developmental Psychology, 18,* 431-434.

Rowe, D. C. (1990). As the twig is bent? The myth of childrearing influences on personality development. *Journal of Counseling and Development, 68,* 606-611.

Rushton, J. P., Fulker, D. W., Neale, M. C., Nias, D.K.B., & Eysenck, H. J. (1986). Altruism and aggression: Individual differences are substantially heritable. *Journal of Personality and Social Psychology, 50,* 1192-1198.

Sayers, J. (1982). *Biological politics: Feminist and anti-feminist perspectives.* London: Tavistock.

Scarr, S. (1992). Developmental theories for the 1990's: Development and individual differences. *Child Development, 63,* 1-19.

Segal, N. (1986). Monozygotic and dizygotic twins: A comparative analysis of mental ability profiles. *Child Development, 56,* 1051-1058.

Tambs, K., Sundet, J. M., & Magnus, P. (1984). Heritability analysis of the WAIS subtests: A study of twins. *Intelligence, 8,* 283-293.

Thelen, E., & Adolph, K. E. (1992). Arnold L. Gesell: The paradox of nature and nurture. *Developmental Psychology, 28,* 368-380.

Thorne, B. (in press). *The girls and the boys: Children's construction of gender.* New Brunswick, NJ: Rutgers University Press.

Unger, R., & Crawford, M. (1992). *Women and gender: A feminist psychology.* New York: McGraw-Hill.

Whiting, B. B., & Edwards, C. P. (1988). *Children of different worlds: The formation of social behavior.* Cambridge, MA: Harvard University Press.

Wilson, R. S. (1975). Twins: Patterns of cognitive development as measured on the WPPSI. *Developmental Psychology, 11,* 126-139.

Wilson, R. S. (1983). The Louisville Twin Study: Developmental synchronies in behavior. *Child Development, 54,* 298-316.

4

Parents and Gender-Role Socialization During the Middle Childhood and Adolescent Years

JACQUELYNNE S. ECCLES
in collaboration with
JANIS E. JACOBS
RENA D. HAROLD
KWANG SUK YOON
AMY ARBRETON
CAROL FREEDMAN-DOAN

A small but growing literature is emerging on the effects of parental beliefs and stereotypes. Several researchers (e.g., Eccles, Jacobs, & Harold, 1990; Goodnow & Collins, 1990;

AUTHORS' NOTE: Work on this chapter was supported by grants to the first author from the National Institute of Child Health and Human Development, the National Science Foundation, and the Spencer Foundation. We would like to thank the school districts involved in these studies and the following people for their assistance at various stages in the projects outlined: Bonnie Barber, Constance Flanagan, Toby Jayaratne, Allan Wigfield, and Doris Yee. Copies can be obtained from the first author at 5271 Institute for Social Research, University of Michigan, Ann Arbor, MI 48106-1248.

Jacobs, 1987; Yee & Eccles, 1988) have suggested that such beliefs are important because of their impact on the expectations and goals parents develop for their children, on parents' perceptions of their children's interests and talents, and on the ways in which parents interact with their children. Previous studies have documented the positive impact of parents' confidence in their children's academic abilities on children's own self-perceptions and actual performance (e.g., Alexander & Entwisle, 1988; Eccles-Parsons, Adler, & Kaczala, 1982). These studies clearly indicate that parents' expectations for their children's performance in both math and English have an impact on children's subsequent performance as well as on their view of their own math and language abilities. By late elementary school this effect is stronger than the effect of the children's own current performance levels in these subject areas. But what factors are shaping parents' expectations for their children's performance potential in various activities? And exactly how are parents' beliefs actually affecting their children's self-perceptions, interests, and performance?

This chapter outlines a theoretical framework developed by Eccles and her colleagues to investigate (a) the influences on parents' beliefs regarding their children's abilities across several activity domains, and (b) the processes through which these beliefs may affect both children's performance and involvement in various activities, and perceptions of their own competence in these activity domains (see Figure 4.1). This model is based on the assumption that parents' views of their children's competencies in various activities are influenced by several social factors in addition to the children's actual performance level in each activity domain. Primary among these social factors are the status characteristics of parents and children, and parents' interpretative belief systems. With regard to gender, parents' gender-role belief systems, in interaction with their child's sex, should affect the inferences parents draw from their children's behavior about their children's competence in various gender-role-stereotyped activity domains. These inferences, in turn, should affect parents' expectations for their children's future performance in these activities, and should affect the opportunities these parents give their children to develop skills in these activity domains. Over the past 15 years, Eccles and her colleagues have gathered extensive longitudinal information from children and their families in two different studies directly relevant to these hypotheses. This chapter summarizes the major relevant results from these two studies. The results presented represent three activity domains: math, reading/English, and sports.

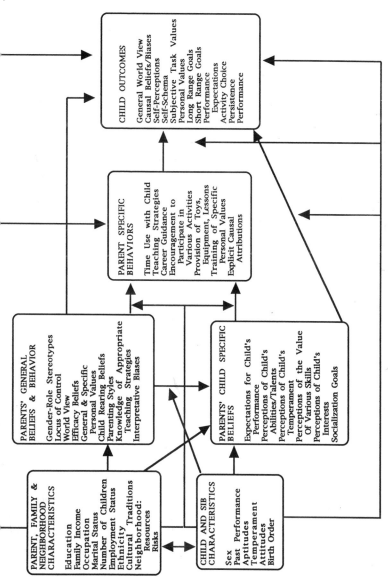

Figure 4.1. General Model of Family Socialization Influences

The boxes in the figure contain the following text:

PARENT, FAMILY & NEIGHBORHOOD CHARACTERISTICS

Education
Family Income
Occupation
Marital Status
Number of Children
Employment Status
Ethnicity
Cultural Traditions
Neighborhood:
    Resources
    Risks

CHILD AND SIB CHARACTERISTICS

Sex
Past Performance
Aptitudes
Temperament
Attitudes
Birth Order

PARENTS' GENERAL BELIEFS & BEHAVIOR

Gender-Role Stereotypes
Locus of Control
World View
Efficacy Beliefs
General & Specific
    Personal Values
Child Rearing Beliefs
Parenting Styles
Knowledge of Appropriate
    Teaching Strategies
Interpretative Biases

PARENTS' CHILD SPECIFIC BELIEFS

Expectations for Child's
    Performance
Perceptions of Child's
    Abilities/Talents
Perceptions of Child's
    Temperament
Perceptions of the Value
    Of Various Skills
Perceptions of Child's
    Interests
Socialization Goals

PARENT SPECIFIC BEHAVIORS

Time Use with Child
Teaching Strategies
Career Guidance
Encouragement to
    Participate in
    Various Activities
Provision of Toys,
    Equipment, Lessons
Training of Specific
    Personal Values
Explicit Causal
    Attributions

CHILD OUTCOMES

General World View
Causal Beliefs/Biases
Self-Perceptions
Self-Schema
Subjective Task Values
Personal Values
Long Range Goals
Short Range Goals
Performance
    Expectations
Activity Choice
Persistence
Performance

61

Background Findings and New Data Sources

In Eccles's earlier work, she documented the fact that parents' perceptions of their children's math ability have a significant effect on the children's view of their own math ability—an effect that is independent of the impact of the child's actual performance on both the parents' and children's perceptions of the children's math ability (Eccles-Parsons, Adler, & Kaczala, 1982). We have replicated and extended this work in two new studies—henceforth referred to as Study 1 and Study 2.

Study 1 (The Michigan Study of Adolescent Life Transitions—MSALT) is a 7-year longitudinal study of adolescent development in the context of the family and the school. In 1983 approximately 2,000 sixth grade, early adolescents were recruited into this study. About 1,000 of their families agreed to participate as well. These families have been participating in the study since that time. They represent a wide range of socioeconomic backgrounds. Parents were asked a series of questions regarding their perceptions of their child's competency and talent, their expectations for their child's future performance, and the importance they attach to competence in each of three domains (math, reading/English, and sports) using 7-point Likert-type response scales. Similar to Eccles's previous work, these items have good psychometric properties and factor into highly reliable scales (see Eccles-Parsons et al., 1982, and Eccles et al., 1991, for details). Due to limited space only the data from the mothers are summarized in this chapter. The fathers' data, however, yield a very similar story. In addition, only data collected in the fall and spring of the adolescents' sixth grade school year (1983-1984) are summarized herein.

The first question asked of these data was whether parents' beliefs had any influence on their children's self-perceptions, as was found by Eccles-Parsons et al. (1982). Some of the results relevant to this question are shown in Figure 4.2. Although these results are for daughters only, a similar pattern emerged for sons. As can be seen, mothers' ratings of their children's abilities in math and English are related to the teacher's ratings of the children's math ability (we had the teachers rate only the math ability due to limitations in the amount of time that teachers would spend filling out individual student ratings). But, more importantly, these results replicate Eccles's previous findings: Parents' view of their children's ability in both math and English have an

Mother's Rating of Daughter's: Daughter's Self Rating of:

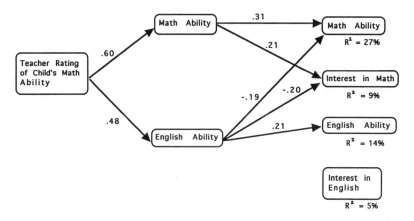

Figure 4.2. Mother's Influence on Daughter's Self-Perceptions

NOTE: All paths significant at $p < .01$ or better. Path coefficients are standardized.

important impact on the children's own self-perceptions. Furthermore, we have now analyzed this relationship using cross-lagged, longitudinal structural equation modeling procedures. Such procedures allow one to compare the relative across-time impact of parents' beliefs on changes in children's self-perceptions versus the across-time impact of children's self-perceptions on changes in parents' beliefs. The results are consistent with the hypothesized causal direction. As one would expect, the parent and child perceptions are reciprocally related at synchronous time points. Over time, however, mother's perceptions of their children's ability are more strongly related to change in the children's self-perceptions than vice versa, even when an independent indicator of the children's competence is included as a control. The goodness of fit index for this cross-lagged structural model was .98, indicating a very good fit of the model to the data.

Figure 4.2 illustrates two other important findings. First, mothers' perceptions of their daughters' English ability are negatively related to their daughters' perceptions of their own math ability. Apparently, there are two consequences of having your mother think you are very good in English: (a) you also think you are good in English and (b) you think you are less good in mathematics than your math teacher thinks you are. These results suggest that having a mother think you are very good in

English undermines your estimates of your own math ability and interest. Second, Figure 4.2 illustrates the fact that mothers' perceptions of their children's math and English abilities also mediate the impact of performance (as rated by a teacher) on the children's interest in doing mathematics and English respectively. Thus, your mother's perception of your abilities affects your interest in particular subjects as well as your estimate of your own ability in these subjects.

Based on these findings and on work by Alexander and Entwisle (1988), we have been studying the influences on parents' perceptions of their children's abilities. Clearly parents' perceptions in the academic domains are related to objective information provided by the school about how well their child is doing. But we are interested in identifying the other more subjective influences on parents' perceptions of their children's abilities. Gender is a very important organizing construct for addressing this question. We know in the academic domain, for example, that sex differences in performance in mathematics are small, don't emerge with great regularity prior to secondary school, and are not evident at any age in school grades (Eccles, 1984, 1989; Hyde, Fennema, & Lamon, 1990). Nonetheless, our previous research has shown that parents believe that gender differences in math talent exist (Yee & Eccles, 1988). We have replicated this effect in Study 1. The results are summarized in the top half of Table 4.1. In addition, there are gender-role stereotypic differences in these parents' perceptions of their children's ability in English and sports (see Table 4.1).

We have also replicated the results with a much younger sample, henceforth referred to as *Study 2* (The Michigan Study of Middle Childhood). This is a 4-year longitudinal study of the development of elementary-school-aged children in the context of the family and the school. In 1986, approximately 600 children and their families were recruited into this study and have been studied annually since then. The children were in either kindergarten, first grade, or third grade. Similar scales and items as used in Study 1 were used in Study 2. The data summarized in this chapter were collected in the spring and summer of the first year of the study (1987). The gender-of-child effects are summarized in the bottom half of Table 4.1. Gender-role stereotypic differences emerged for both English and sports. Parents of daughters rated their child as more competent in English than parents of sons and vice versa for sports. However, there was no sex-of-child effect for the parents' perceptions of these younger children's mathematical competence. Apparently this effect depends on the age of the child: Evidence

Table 4.1
Sex-of-Child Effects on Parents' Perceptions

| | DOMAINS | | | | | | | | |
| VARIABLES | Math | | | English/Reading | | | Sports | | |
	Girls' Mean	Boys' Mean	F	Girls' Mean	Boys' Mean	F	Girls' Mean	Boys' Mean	F
Adolescent Transition Study[1]									
Parent perception of current competence	5.45	5.40	<1.00	5.65	4.99	101.71***	4.84	5.22	25.75***
Parent perception of task difficulty	4.10	3.80	12.10***	3.73	4.24	39.20***	3.77	3.47	13.21***
Parent perception of natural talent	4.76	5.01	9.85*	5.03	4.51	46.76***	4.22	4.87	59.76***
Parent perception of future performance	5.36	5.34	<1.00	5.59	5.02	74.99***			
Parent perception of performance in career	5.17	5.42	11.17***	5.41	4.87	54.91***			
Parent perception of importance	6.38	6.50	9.21**	6.34	6.34	<1.00	3.80	4.10	12.90***
Middle Childhood Study[2]									
Parent perception of current competence	5.38	5.34	<1.00	5.67	5.27	10.28***	4.50	4.98	16.41***
Parent perception of task difficulty	2.08	2.02	<1.00	1.64	2.01	8.33**	2.57	2.15	11.77***
Parent perception of natural talent	5.01	5.15	1.45	5.41	5.11	7.00**	4.31	4.74	12.35***
Parent perception of future performance	5.99	5.91	<1.00	6.36	5.95	19.13***	5.02	5.52	19.91***
Parent perception of importance	6.26	6.46	8.12**	6.65	6.63	<1.00	4.20	4.72	20.00***

NOTES: 1. Mothers of 6th graders, approximate $N = 900$. 2. Parents of kindergartners, 1st, and 3rd graders, approximate $N = 500$.
$* p < .05; ** p < .01; *** p < .001$

from our previous studies and from Study 1 indicates that the gender-of-child effect in the math domain is found consistently among parents of children in Grades 6 or 7. These effects are even stronger by the time the children are in senior high school.

Questions for Analysis

The first question is: Why do parents hold these gender-differentiated perceptions of their children's competencies? The second issue of concern is the impact of parents' gender-differentiated perceptions on their children's behaviors and activity preferences. We know, for example, that males are more likely to enroll in advanced math courses and to major in math-related fields whereas females are more likely to major in languages and literature in college (see Eccles, 1984, 1987, 1989). There are also quite large gender differences in children's and adolescents' participation in various sport activities, especially competitive team sports (Eccles & Harold, 1990). Thus, the second question is: Do these gender differences result from parents' gender-differentiated expectations for their daughters and sons?

Why Do Parents Hold
These Gender-Differentiated Beliefs?

Many explanations have been offered to account for the gender-role stereotyping of people's ratings of males' and females' competencies in various domains. The most critical issue for this chapter is the extent to which parents' stereotypical perceptions of their children are either accurate or are a reflection of processes linked to perceptual bias. This is a very difficult issue to settle unequivocally because it is impossible to reach consensus on what criteria should be used to assess the accuracy of gender-role stereotypes. There is agreement that parents' perceptions of their children's competence in academic subjects are highly correlated with teacher's ratings of the children's competence and with various indicators of the children's performance and achievement, such as school grades and standardized test scores (Alexander & Entwisle, 1988; Eccles-Parsons et al., 1982). But are their gender-role stereotyped perceptions an accurate reflection of true gender differences in either talent or competence? This question is difficult to answer because females and males are treated differently by many people from infancy on. Consequently, it is impossible to get a good indicator of natural talent that is uninfluenced by the processes associated with gender-role socialization.

For example, can it be concluded that parents' gender-role stereo-typed perceptions of their 6-year-old children's talent in sports are "accurate" if male children perform better than the female children on a standardized test of athletic skill at this age? Not really, because it is quite likely that the female and male children have already had different opportunities to develop their athletic skills. The best that can be done at this point is to use the strategy proposed by Jussim (1989). This strategy involves assessing the extent to which the perceiver's judg-ments are related to the variables of interest (in this case the child's gender) even after controlling for the possible association between the perceiver's judgment and more objective indicators of the children's actual performance level. If they are, then one can begin to try to identify the mediating cognitive processes that account for the biased portion of these perceptions (i.e., the portion not due to actual differ-ences in the performance levels of girls and boys).

Due to the extensive amount of research that has been done on gender differences in mathematics, the mathematics domain provides the most fully developed example of this logic at present. In both our own work (see Eccles-Parsons et al., 1982, and Eccles & Jacobs, 1986) and the work of Entwisle and her colleagues (see Alexander & Entwisle, 1988), it is clear that parents' perceptions of their children's competence in mathematics are influenced by the children's gender, independent of the children's actual performance in mathematics. As noted earlier, it is also clear that there are sex-of-child effects on parents' ratings of their children's competence in mathematics in populations that do not display any significant differences in the math performance of the female and male children on either grades or standardized test scores. Comparable patterns of results are now being reported in the domains of English and sports. For example, Jacobs and Eccles (1990) have found that the child's gender has an independent influence on parents' ratings of their sixth grade child's athletic talent after controlling for the teachers' ratings of the children's athletic talent.

Thus it appears that something other than overt performance is influencing the formation of parents' perceptions of their children's competence in both math and sports. What might these factors be? The following three influences seem especially important to study: (a) there may be a true sex difference in the children's aptitude; (b) aptitude differences may be minor or nonexistent but parents may attribute their children's performance to different causes, leading them to different conclusions regarding their female versus their male children's "talent"; and (c) parents may generalize their category-based, gender-role stereotypes to their target-based judgments of their own children's competence. Each of these influences is discussed below.

Real Gender Differences in Children's Aptitude

This explanation comes in two forms. First, in the domains of English and sports there are measurable gender differences in children's performance by the time they enter school. Are these differences due to real gender differences in aptitude? As noted earlier, this is difficult to assess because boys and girls are treated so differently from the time of birth. But even if there is a kernel of truth to the parents' perceptions in these domains, we present evidence later that the gender-of-child differences in parents' perceptions of their children in these domains continue to be significant even after independent indicators of the children's ability are included in the analyses as controls.

Second, in the domain of math the differences in performance are very small, do not emerge until adolescence, and depend on the particular performance measure used. Nonetheless, it is possible that there are "real" gender differences in aptitude and girls compensate by working harder than boys in order to do so well. How does one evaluate the validity of this suggestion? One way is to compare the performance of females and males on a specific task that is considered more closely related to aptitude, and less closely related to effort, than school grades. If gender differences appear on this task in a population in which there are no gender differences in math course grades, then one might conclude that there is a true aptitudinal difference that is being overcome by a gender difference in effort. Evidence reported by Benbow and Stanley (1980) is consistent with this interpretation. They found that gifted boys score higher than gifted girls on standardized test scores, and they concluded that the boys have more natural aptitude for math than the girls. Unfortunately, they did not measure either effort or prior exposure to mathematics; thus they cannot rule out the possibility that the gender differences on these "aptitude" tests are due to gender differences in either experience or test taking strategies (see Eccles & Jacobs, 1986). In addition, although there is a reliable gender difference on standardized tests of math "aptitude" among the gifted, the evidence of such differences among more normally distributed samples is much less reliable, and the differences are much smaller whenever they are obtained (Eccles, 1984; Hyde et al., 1990).

Furthermore, several findings from the Eccles-Parsons et al. (1982) study cast doubt on the notion that girls compensate for lower levels of aptitude with hard work. First and foremost, there were no gender differences on either standardized tests of math aptitude or on school math grades. Second, there was not a significant gender difference in the amount of time that boys and girls reported spending on their math homework and school work. Finally, the teachers of the boys and girls in this sample did not report any gender differences in these children's talent for mathematics (Eccles-Parsons et al., 1983). Nonetheless, there was still a significant sex-of-child effect on the parents' ratings of how difficult math was for their child. This pattern of findings makes it unlikely that the gender-of-child effects found for the parents' confidence in their children's competence in this study were due primarily to either a "real" gender difference in math talent or to "real" gender differences in the amount of work the children had invested in mastering mathematics. Although these explanations may be true in some populations, the Eccles-Parsons et al. (1982) study suggests that a child's gender can affect parents' confidence in their child's math competence even when effort and ability are controlled. Similar processes could be going on in the English and sport domains. But, because comparable studies have not been done in the domains of English and sports, the validity of the effort-compensation argument cannot be assessed at this point.

Gendered Attributional Patterns

According to attribution theory (Weiner, 1974), perceptions of another's competence depend on the causal attributions made for the person's performance. If parents of boys make different attributions for their children's math performance than do parents of girls, it would follow that these parents should develop different perceptions of their children's math competence. In a test of this hypothesis, Yee and Eccles (1988) found that parents of boys rated natural talent as a more important reason for their child's math successes than did parents of girls (boys' $\overline{X}$ = 5.00; girls' $\overline{X}$ = 5.75). In contrast, parents of girls rated effort as a more important reason for their child's math success ($\overline{X}$ = 5.75) than did parents of boys ($\overline{X}$ = 4.96). In addition, to the extent that the parents attributed their child's success in mathematics to effort, they also rated their child as less talented in mathematics. Conversely, to the extent that they attributed their child's success in mathematics to talent, they also rated their child as more talented in mathematics. Thus it appears that the gender-role stereotyped attributions parents make for their children's performance may be important mediators of the parents' gender-role stereotyped perceptions of their children's math competence.

The data from Study 1 provide a direct test of this conclusion. These mothers were asked to imagine a time when their child did very well in mathematics, reading, and sports and then to rate, on 7-point Likert scales, the importance of the following six possible causes in determining this success experience: natural talent, effort, task ease, teacher help, parent help, and current skill level. Significant sex-of-child effects were obtained on attributions of success to natural talent in each domain, and the pattern of these differences reflects the gender-role stereotyping of the domains. That is, parents were more likely to attribute their child's success to natural talent in math and sports if their child was a boy (r = .13 and r = .09, respectively, p < .05 in each case) and were more likely to attribute their child's success to natural talent in English if their child was a girl (r = −.11, p < .05).

To evaluate the mediation hypothesis we tested a series of path models using regression analyses on those mothers' perceptions. This analysis yielded a significant sex-of-child effect in each domain (see Table 4.1). According to Baron and Kenny (1986), support for a mediational hypothesis consists of demonstrating that the relationship between variables A and C is reduced or eliminated when the hypothesized mediating variable B is entered into the regression equation. The results for math are illustrated in Figure 4.3. Consistent with the mediational hypothesis, the significant relationship of child's gender to the relevant parent outcome variables (i.e., parents' perceptions of the child's current competence in math, the difficulty of math for their child, their expectations regarding the child's likely future success in both math

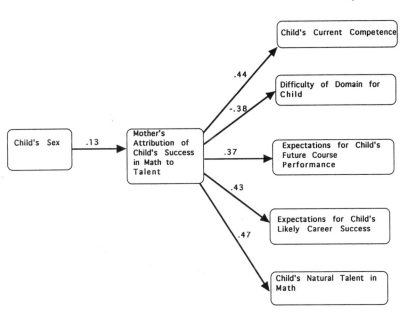

Figure 4.3. Mediating Role of Mother's Causal Attribution for Child's Success in Mathematics to Natural Talent

NOTE: All paths significant at $p < .01$ or better. Path coefficients are standardized.

courses and a math-related career, and the child's natural math talent) disappear once the relationship between the child's gender and the parents' attributions for the child's math success to talent is controlled.

Comparable results for the talent attribution emerged in both the English and sport domains (Eccles et al., 1991). In each case, as predicted, children's gender influenced their mothers' causal attributions, which, in turn, influenced the mothers' perceptions of, and expectations for, their children. But in each of these domains, the direct effect of child's gender on parents' perceptions was still significant. The size of this effect, however, was significantly reduced by including the parents' causal attribution in the path analysis, and thus the results are consistent with our mediational hypothesis. More complete details of these and other analyses summarized in this chapter have been reported elsewhere and can be obtained from the first author.

These data provide good preliminary support for the hypothesized biasing effect of causal attributions on parents' perceptions of their children's competencies. It is important to note, however, that these beliefs are all highly interrelated and the data are correlational in nature. The consistency of the findings across domains indicates that the relationships are reliable, but the actual causal direction of the relationships is still at issue. We are just beginning the longitudinal analyses necessary to pin down the predominant causal directions of influence among these various beliefs. Preliminary analyses support the causal direction illustrated in Figure 4.3. That is, causal attributions at Time 1 do appear to affect parents' perceptions of their children's ability at Time 2 (1 year later) even after controlling for the parents' Time-1 perceptions of their children's abilities.

Biasing Influence of
Gender-Role-Stereotypic Beliefs

Both Eccles and Jacobs (see Eccles, 1984; Eccles et al., 1990; Jacobs & Eccles, 1985) have hypothesized that parents' gender-role stereotypes regarding the extent to which males or females, in general, are likely to be more talented or more interested in a particular domain will affect their perceptions of their own child's ability in this domain, leading to a distortion in the parents' perceptions of their children's ability in the gender-role stereotyped direction. In other words, the impact of the child's gender on parents' perceptions of their child's ability in any particular domain will depend on the parents' gender-role stereotypes regarding ability in that domain. Furthermore, this effect should be significant even after entering an independent indicator of the children's actual level of competence in the domain as a control.

Before presenting evidence to support this hypotheses, it is important to put it in the broader context of research on the link between category-based beliefs and target-based beliefs. Although there has been very little study of this link in families, or as a developmental phenomenon, there has been quite a bit of relevant research in social psychology. Two basic views have emerged. The work in the field of stereotyping and expectancy effects has repeatedly documented the impact of the perceiver's category-based beliefs (stereotypes) on the perceiver's perceptions of specific members of the social category (e.g., Darley & Gross, 1983). In contrast, work in the area of social judgment has pointed to the power of individuating information to override the impact of stereotypical beliefs on perceptions of specific individuals (e.g., Locksley, Hepburn, & Ortiz, 1982). The latter researchers suggest that when specific individuating information about a particular person is available, such as past or present behavior, stereotypes will exert little, if any, effect on the judgments made about the person. Numerous studies have attempted to resolve the discrepancies in these two perspectives and the results are equivocal (e.g., Higgins & Bargh, 1987; Hilton & Fein, 1989). As Hilton and Fein (1989) conclude:

> Social judgment is not uniformly dominated by either categorical information or by individuating information. Perceivers do not always ignore individuating information nor do they always suspend their stereotypes when individuating information is available. Instead, the results indicate that social judgment involves a dynamic interplay between the category-based expectations of the perceiver and the information that is available from the target. (p. 208)

What do these conclusions tell us about the probability that parents' gender-role stereotypes will affect their perceptions of their own child's ability? This is a complicated question. On the one hand, parents have ample opportunity to obtain a great deal of individuating information about their child's ability in specific subject areas. And evidence suggests that when individuating information about an individual is both readily available and clearly diagnostic about the characteristic being evaluated, perceivers are likely to attend primarily to this individuating information and ignore their stereotypic beliefs (Hilton & Fein, 1989). This would suggest that parents' gender-role stereotypes will have little or no impact on their perceptions of their children's abilities.

On the other hand, the strongest support for expectancy effects typically occurs in naturalistic settings with naturally occurring beliefs and perceptions (Jussim, 1989). In addition, categorical beliefs or stereotypes may have their largest effect "when categorical information can disambiguate the diagnostic meaning of individuating information" (Hilton & Fein, 1989, p. 210). Families are clearly naturalistic settings, and both parents' gender-role beliefs and their perceptions of their children's abilities are naturally occurring social cognitions. In addition, work in attribution theory (e.g., Weiner, 1974) documents the fact that achievement-related outcomes are ambiguous as to their cause. And we have already documented the fact that parents' causal attributions for their children's competencies in gender-role-stereotyped domains are affected by their children's gender. This suggests that parents' category-based, gender-role stereotypes might affect their perceptions of their own child's competencies.

We know of no studies that have tested this hypothesis. As reported earlier, parents do hold gender-differentiated views of their children's academic and nonacademic abilities at a very early age and these beliefs are more gender-differentiated than are objective indicators of the children's actual performance in these domains (e.g., Alexander & Entwisle, 1988; Eccles et al., 1991; Eccles & Harold, 1990; Jacobs & Eccles, 1985). These studies, however, did not look at the actual relationship between parents' gender-role stereotypes and their perceptions of their own child's ability. The critical issue is not whether parents, on the average, give gender-differentiated estimates of their children's abilities. Instead, the issue is whether or not parents who endorse the culturally dominant gender-role stereotype regarding the distribution of talent and interest between males and females distort their perception of their own child's abilities in a direction that is consistent with the gender-role stereotype to a greater extent than parents who do not endorse the stereotype. Evidence from both Studies 1 and 2 supports this hypothesis.

In Study 2, mothers were asked at Time 1 who they thought was naturally better at mathematics, reading, and sports—boys, girls, or neither. They were also asked, in a separate questionnaire, to rate on a 7-point Likert scale how much natural talent their child had in each of these three domains, how difficult (or easy) each of these domains was for their child, and how important they thought it was to their child to be good in each domain. In each domain the significance of the interaction of the gender of their child with the parents' category-based gender-role stereotypes in predicting the parents' ratings of their own child's competency was tested. All nine interactions were significant (Eccles et al., 1991; Eccles, Jacobs et al., 1989), indicating that the parents who endorsed the cultural gender-role stereotype regarding which gender is "naturally" better in each domain were more likely to rate sons and daughters differently than parents who did not endorse the cultural stereotype. Furthermore, in each domain the gender-of-child effect for the parents who endorsed the cultural stereotype was in the stereotypic direction; that is, if they believed that boys in general are more talented in the domain, then the parents of sons rated their child's ability higher than the parents of daughters.

The results for mathematics were particularly interesting. As shown in Table 4.1, the gender of one's child was not significantly related as a main effect to the mothers' perceptions of either their child's math talent or the difficulty of math for their child. But the gender of their child did affect their ratings of the child's competence in math when looked at in interaction with their category-based gender-role stereotype of mathematical competence ($p < .01$). As predicted, mothers who believed that males were naturally more talented in mathematics showed a significant sex-of-child effect in ratings of their own child's math ability and the direction of this effect was consistent with their category-based stereotype. In contrast, the effect was not significant for mothers who believed that neither males nor females were naturally more talented at mathematics.

Rather similar gender-role stereotypic effects characterized the mothers' reports on their children in sports and English. For example, in comparison to parents who did not endorse this cultural stereotype, parents who endorsed the stereotype that males are generally better at sports than females were more likely to rate sons' talent higher than daughters' talent. Similarly, parents who endorsed the cultural stereotype that females are naturally better at language arts than males were more likely to rate daughters' reading talent higher than sons' than parents who did not endorse this stereotype. Although it is possible that these effects are due to the impact of target-based information on the mothers' category-based gender-role stereotypes, the extreme stability of gender-role stereotypes across time in a variety of populations makes this an unlikely alternative interpretation (Rothbart, 1989).

Jacobs and Eccles have explored these effects in the domains of math and sports more fully using data from Study 1 (Jacobs, 1987; Jacobs & Eccles, 1990). Using path-analytic techniques, they tested the impact of the interaction of the gender of one's child and one's category-based gender-role stereotypes on the mother's perceptions of their child's ability, controlling for the effect of an independent indicator of the child's actual ability level (the teacher's rating of the child's ability). The interaction term was created so that a positive coefficient indicated that the mother was distorting her impression of her child in the gender-role appropriate direction. That is, if she was talking about a boy child in a male activity domain like sports or mathematics, her perception of her child's ability was higher than what would have been predicted using only the teacher's rating; in contrast, if she was talking about a girl child, her perception was lower than what would have been predicted using only the teacher's rating.

The results for the sport domain are illustrated in Figure 4.4. Once again the findings were consistent with our hypothesis. The interaction term was significant and its coefficient was positive. Thus, to the extent that these mothers endorsed the traditional gender-role stereotypic belief that males are naturally better in sports than are girls, they distorted their perception of their child's competence in these domains in the gender-role-stereotypic direction. In addition, consistent with the findings of Eccles-Parsons et al. (1982), the mothers' perceptions of their children's competence in each domain had a significant impact on the children's own self-perceptions even after the children's actual performance in each domain was controlled. Similar findings characterized the math and reading domains (Eccles et al., 1991; Jacobs & Eccles, 1990).

These findings provide strong evidence of the processes associated with expectancy effects. But they do not indicate how well the data fit the model we are proposing. To evaluate this fit, we tested a simplified model using LISREL for each of these two domains. Because the interaction of child gender and mother's gender-role stereotype was significant, we tested a two-group hierarchical LISREL model. The specified model assumed that a mother's stereotype influenced her perception of her child's ability even after an independent indicator of the child's ability was entered as a control. It also tested whether the child's ability, as indicated by a teacher's rating of the child, influenced the mother's stereotype. The fit of the models to the data in both the math (goodness of fit index = .99) and sport domains (goodness of fit index =.97) was very good as indicated by the Joreskog's goodness-of-fit index.

In the math domain there was no significant relationship between the teacher's rating of the child's ability and the mother's stereotype for math. In contrast, there was a strong relationship (girls β = .61; boys β = .70) between the teacher's rating of the child's ability and the mother's rating of the child's ability. But most importantly for the present discussion, there was a significant positive relationship between the mother's stereotype and her perception of her son's math ability (β = .09) and a marginally significant negative relationship between the mother's stereotype and her perception of her daughter's math ability (β = −.07). Thus, as predicted, the more a mother stereotyped math as

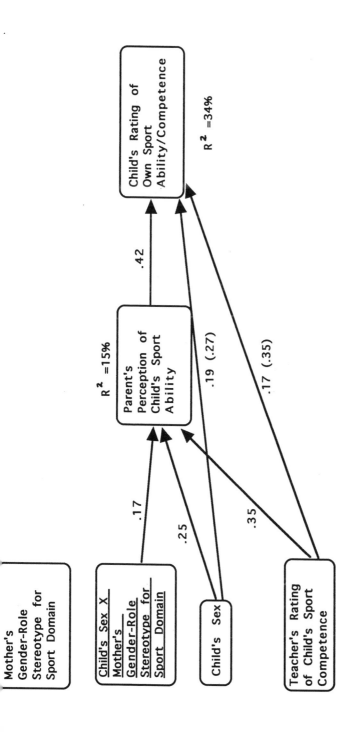

Figure 4.4. Moderating Effect of Mother's Gender-Role Stereotype for the Sport Domain on the Impact of Child's Sex and Mother's Perceptions of Child's Ability in Sports

NOTE: All paths significant at $p < .01$ or better. Path coefficients are standardized. Zero-order correlations in parentheses.

a male domain, the more she overestimated her son's math ability and underestimated her daughter's math ability relative to the level of ability indicated by the teacher's rating.

Similar results emerged in the sport domain. But in this domain, the daughter's sport ability, as rated by the teacher, was related to the mother's gender-role stereotypes ($\beta = -.20$): Mothers with more athletic daughters were less likely to stereotype sports as a male domain than other mothers. In addition, however, to the extent that the mothers stereotyped sport as a male domain, they also rated their daughters' sport ability lower than one would predict given the teacher's estimate of the girl's ability ($\beta = -.23$). This latter effect did not hold for sons. Apparently, mothers' endorsement of the cultural stereotype that males are naturally better at sports than girls only had a debilitating effect on their perceptions of daughters' sports ability. The LISREL analyses suggest that there was no enhancement effect for boys of mothers who hold the cultural stereotype in the sports domain.

These results provide support for the hypothesis that category-based beliefs do bias parents' perceptions of their own children's competencies. Given the power of individuating information and the large amount of such information that parents are exposed to as their children grow up, we did not expect the biasing effects to be large, and they are not. Nevertheless, although the effects are not large, they are both reliable and consistent across two activity domains, and they do appear to influence the development of the children's own self-perceptions in a manner consistent with the self-fulfilling prophecy hypothesis.

Behavioral Consequences of Parents' Beliefs

We have argued thus far that gender differentiation in parents' perceptions of their children's abilities in various domains results, in part, from processes associated with expectancy effects. In particular, we have presented evidence that both parents' causal attributions for their children's successes, and parents' category-based gender-role stereotypes, lead to perceptual bias in their impressions of their children's competencies in gender-role-stereotyped activity domains. Although parents' perceptions of their children's competencies in math, English, and sports are strongly related to independent indicators of their children's actual competence in these domains, the evidence clearly indicates that parents' perceptions of their children's competencies in math, English, and sports are also influenced by their children's gender and by the parents' gender-role-stereotypic beliefs about which gender is naturally more talented and interested in these domains. Furthermore, the evidence is consistent with the conclusion that these influences are independent of any actual differences that might exist in the children's competencies. Thus our findings suggest that perceptual bias is operating in the formation of parents' impressions of their children's competencies in gender-role-stereotyped activity domains.

Proponents of a self-fulfilling prophecy view of the socialization of gender differences in children's competencies would argue that differences in parents' perceptions of their children's competencies set in motion a train of events that ultimately create the very differences that the parents originally believed to exist. We have already pointed to one mechanism through which such a process might be mediated—namely, the children's self-perceptions. We have argued elsewhere that children's self- and task perceptions influence the choices children make about their involvement in various activities (see Eccles & Harold, 1990; Eccles-Parsons et al., 1983). In particular, we have documented that children spend more time engaged in activities that they think they are good at and that they value and enjoy, and that gender differences in activity choice are mediated by gender differences in self-perceptions and subjective task value. For example, in math, we have demonstrated that decisions regarding course enrollment in high school are influenced by adolescents' confidence in their math ability and by the value they attach to math (Eccles-Parsons et al., 1983). Similarly, in sports, we have demonstrated that the gender difference in the amount of free time sixth graders spend engaged in athletic activities is mediated by gender differences in both the adolescents' confidence in their athletic ability and the value they attach to athletic activities (Eccles & Harold, 1990).

Thus far in this chapter we have summarized evidence that gender differences in adolescents' self-perceptions are mediated, in part, by the gender-role-stereotyped bias in their parents' perceptions of their competencies in various activities. Together these results support the conclusion that processes associated with the self-fulfilling prophecy phenomenon contribute to the socialization of gender differences in the domains of mathematics and sports. But exactly how do parents' gender-role-stereotyped perceptions of their children's competencies influence the children's self- and task perceptions? We are just beginning to study this issue. Guided by the theoretical perspective summarized in Figure 4.1 we are testing the following sets of predictions:

1. Parents' gender-role stereotypes, in interaction with their child's gender, affect the following parent beliefs and behaviors: (a) parents' causal attributions for the child's performance, (b) the parents' emotional reaction to their child's performance in various activities, (c) the importance parents attach to their child acquiring various skills, (d) the advice parents provide their child regarding involvement in various skills, and (e) the activities and toys parents provide for their child.

2. In turn, these beliefs and behaviors influence the development of the following child outcomes across the various gender-role-stereotyped activity domains: (a) children's confidence in their ability, (b) children's interest in mastering various skills, (c) children's affective reaction to participating in various activities—and, as a consequence of these self- and task perceptions, (d) the amount of time and the type of effort that children end up devoting to mastering and demonstrating various skills.

Empirical work assessing these various causal links is now under way. Preliminary evidence looks very promising. For example, consider the link between the parents' perceptions of their children and the types of experiences they provide for their children. We tested whether parents provide different types of experiences for girls and boys in the sport domain. They clearly do: Parents reported watching sports more often with sons, playing sports more often with sons, enrolling sons more often in sports programs, and encouraging sports participation more for sons than for daughters (Eccles et al., 1991). These differences were already evident by the time the children were in kindergarten. But more importantly for the argument presented in this chapter, we used path analysis to determine whether the sex-of-child effects on the types of activities parents provide and encourage were mediated by the parents' perceptions of their children's ability and interests in each domain. Consistent with the mediational hypothesis, the sex-of-child effect on the types of experiences parents provide for their children became nonsignificant when the sex-of-child effect on parents' perceptions of their children's sport ability and interest was entered into the path analysis (Eccles et al., 1991). These results suggest the following conclusions: (a) parents form an impression of their children's ability and interest in sports at a very young age, (b) this impression depends on the gender of their child to a greater extent than justified by objective evidence of gender differences in sport performance, and (c) this impression influences the types of experiences the parents provide for their children in the sport domain. If the processes associated with expectancy effects operate, this differential provision of experience should result over time in a pattern of gender differences in actual skills that is consistent with the cultural stereotypes.

Conclusion

In conclusion, we have presented evidence of the influence of social factors on parents' perceptions of their children's abilities in various activity domains. We have focused on the child's gender as one potentially critical social factor and have presented data showing how a child's gender might influence parents' perceptions of their child's ability independent of the child's actual performance in the domain. We have also presented evidence that parents' beliefs do have an impact on children's developing self-concepts, and on the experiences parents provide for their children in various activity domains. These relationships are all likely to contribute to gender-role socialization. They also suggest possible routes to intervention. Because parents' beliefs appear to play a pivotal role in this system, interventions should be directed toward changing parents' beliefs and perceptions. We know in the math domain, for example, that teachers can convince parents that their daughters are talented in mathematics and can then enlist parents' help in encouraging young women to consider advanced math courses and occupations in math-related fields. Similar intervention efforts could be designed in other activity domains.

References

Alexander, K. L., & Entwisle, D. R. (1988). Achievement in the first two years of school: Patterns and processes. *Monograph of the Society of Research in Child Development, 53(2).*

Baron, R. M., & Kenny, D. A. (1986). The moderator-mediator variable distinction in social psychological research: Conceptual, strategic, and statistical considerations. *Journal of Personality and Social Psychology, 51,* 1173-1182.

Benbow, C. P., & Stanley, J. C. (1980). Sex differences in mathematical ability: Fact or artifact. *Science, 210,* 1262-1264.

Darley, J. M., & Gross, P. H. (1983). A hypothesis-confirming bias in labeling effects. *Journal of Personality and Social Psychology, 44,* 20-33.

Eccles, J. S. (1984). Sex differences in math participation. In M. L. Maehr & M. W. Steinkamp (Eds.), *Women in science* (pp. 93-138). Greenwich, CT: JAI Press.

Eccles, J. S. (1987). Gender roles and women's achievement-related decisions. *Psychology of Women Quarterly, 11,* 135-172.

Eccles, J. S. (1989). Bringing young women to math and science. In M. Crawford & M. Gentry (Eds.), *Gender and thought: Psychological perspectives* (pp. 36-58). New York: Springer.

Eccles, J. S., & Harold, R. (1990). Gender differences in participation in sports. *Journal of Applied Sport Psychology, 3,* 7-35.

Eccles, J. S., & Jacobs, J. E. (1986). Social forces shape math attitudes and performance. *Signs: Journal of Women in Culture and Society, 11,* 367-380.

Eccles, J. S., Jacobs, J. E., & Harold, R. (1990). Gender role stereotypes, expectancy effects, and parents' socialization of gender differences. *Journal of Social Issues, 46,* 183-201.

Eccles, J. S., Jacobs, J., Harold, R., Yoon, K. S., Arbreton, A., & Freedman-Doan, C. (1991, August). *Expectancy effects are alive and well on the home front: Influences on, and consequences of, parents' beliefs regarding their daughters' and sons' abilities and interests.* Invited address at the Annual Meeting of the American Psychological Association, San Francisco.

Eccles, J. S., Jacobs, J. E., Harold-Goldsmith, R., Jayaratne, T., & Yee, D. (1989, April). *The relations between parents' category-based and target-based beliefs: Gender roles and biological influences.* Symposium paper presented at the Annual Meeting of the Society for Research on Child Development, Kansas City, MO.

Eccles-Parsons, J., Adler, T., Futterman, R., Goff, S., Kaczala, C., Meece, J., & Midgley, C. (1983). Expectations, values and academic behaviors. In J. T. Spence (Ed.), *Achievement and achievement motivation* (pp. 75-146). New York: Freeman.

Eccles-Parsons, J., Adler, T., & Kaczala, C. (1982). Socialization of achievement attitudes and beliefs: Parental influences. *Child Development, 53,* 310-321.

Goodnow, J. J., & Collins, W. A. (1990). *Development according to parents: The nature, sources, and consequences of parents' ideas.* Hillsdale, NJ: Lawrence Erlbaum.

Higgins, E. T., & Bargh, J. A. (1987). Social cognition and social perception. *Annual Review of Psychology, 38,* 369-425.

Hilton, J. L., & Fein, S. (1989). The role of typical diagnosticity in stereotype-based judgments. *Journal of Personality and Social Psychology, 57,* 201-211.

Hyde, J. S., Fennema, E., & Lamon, S. J. (1990). Gender differences in mathematics performance: A meta-analysis. *Psychological Bulletin, 107,* 139-155.

Jacobs, J. E. (1987). *Parents' gender role stereotypes and perceptions of their child's ability: Influences on the child.* Unpublished doctoral dissertation, University of Michigan, Ann Arbor.

Jacobs, J. E., & Eccles, J. S. (1985). Gender differences in math ability: The impact of media reports on parents. *Educational Researcher, 14,* 20-25.

Jacobs, J. E., & Eccles, J. S. (1990). *The influence of parent stereotypes on parent and child ability beliefs in three domains.* Unpublished manuscript, Institute for Social Research, University of Michigan, Ann Arbor.

Jussim, L. (1989). Teacher expectations: Self-fulfilling prophecies, perceptual biases, and accuracy. *Journal of Personality and Social Psychology, 57,* 469-480.

Locksley, A., Hepburn, C., & Ortiz, V. (1982). Social stereotypes and judgments of individuals: An instance of the base-rate fallacy. *Journal of Experimental Social Psychology, 18,* 23-42.

Rothbart, M. (1989). *The stability of gender and ethnic stereotypes.* Colloquium talk given during fall semester at the University of Colorado, Boulder.

Weiner, B. (1974). *Achievement motivation and attribution theory.* Morristown, NJ: General Learning Press.

Yee, D., & Eccles, J. S. (1988). Parent perceptions and attributions for children's math achievement. *Sex Roles, 19,* 317-333.

5

Masculinity Ideology and Its Correlates

JOSEPH H. PLECK
FREYA LUND SONENSTEIN
LEIGHTON C. KU

This chapter highlights a relatively neglected research perspective on masculinity and the male gender role: the *masculinity ideology* approach. We first present the construct of masculinity ideology and relate it to other current conceptualizations used in the study of masculinity. We then present some illustrative results from our current research on adolescent males. Finally, we address some methodological and interpretive questions raised by the masculinity ideology perspective and identify future research directions.

Masculinity Ideology: Relationship to Other Constructs

Masculinity ideology refers to beliefs about the importance of men adhering to culturally defined standards for male behavior. This construct derives most directly from a line of research concerning attitudes toward masculinity (Thompson, Pleck, & Ferrera, 1993). Theoretically, it grows out of the "gender-role strain" model for masculinity (Pleck,

1981), as well as the "social constructionist" perspective on men (Brod, 1987; Kimmel, 1987; Kimmel & Messner, 1989).

How Masculinity Ideology Differs From
Masculine Gender-Related Personality Traits

Before discussing how masculinity ideology relates to these other constructs, it needs to be clearly differentiated from another concept: masculine gender-related personality traits. The latter refer to the degree to which an individual actually possesses the characteristics expected in men. It is assessed by the masculinity subscales in measures such as the Bem (1974) Sex Role Inventory (BSRI). Lenney's (1991) recent review uses *gender-role orientation* as the generic term for the construct assessed by these measures. However, Spence (1992; cf. Spence, Losoff, & Robbins, 1991) argues that a more descriptive, theoretically neutral label is preferable. Thus we use *masculine gender-related personality traits* as the master term, with *masculine personality traits* and *trait masculinity* as synonyms.

Trait masculinity and masculinity ideology are the two primary masculinity-related constructs used in research. They represent parallel but quite different conceptualizations of "masculinity." In broad terms, the former falls within the trait tradition in personality psychology, whereas the latter derives from the social-psychological and sociological conception of norms. In the former, the essence of masculinity is *being* masculine; in the latter, it is *ideologically endorsing* masculinity. Correspondingly, these two constructs are assessed differently at the individual level—the gender-role orientation conception employs trait measures (or more precisely, measures assessing traits via self-concept ratings), and the masculinity ideology conception uses attitudinal measures concerning endorsement of traditional expectations or standards for males. Thus a "traditional" male, viewed in terms of masculine personality characteristics actually *has* culturally defined masculine attributes. In contrast, from the perspective of masculinity ideology, the traditional male is one who believes that men *should* have these attributes.

Of the two constructs, trait masculinity has received far more research attention (Lenney, 1991). The nature of gender-related personality traits and how they are psychometrically organized have been interpreted in different ways, ranging from the "gender-role identity"[1] approach dominant in the 1950s and 1960s (Pleck, 1981, 1983) to the variety of perspectives represented in more recent work using the BSRI, the PAQ, and the EPAQ (Lenney, 1991). Although many interpret the M subscales of Spence and Helmreich's (1978) Personal Attributes Questionnaire (PAQ), and Spence, Helmreich, and Holahan's (1979) Extended Personal Attributes Questionnaire (EPAQ) as assessing masculine gender-role orientation, Spence's current work holds that these scale dimensions are best interpreted more narrowly as measures of what their manifest content indicates, namely gender-related instrumental and expressive traits of a desirable nature (Spence, 1992; Spence, Losoff, & Robbins, 1991). For more discussion of ways that trait masculinity measures have been interpreted, see Pleck (1981; Pleck, Sonenstein, & Ku, in press-a). The key point here, however, is that masculinity ideology differs conceptually from masculine gender-related personality traits.

Attitudes Toward Masculinity

The construct of masculinity ideology derives most directly from research on attitudes toward masculinity, as assessed by measures such as the Brannon Masculinity Scale (BMS; Brannon, 1985; Brannon & Juni, 1984) and Thompson and Pleck's (1986) Male Role Norm Scale (MRNS) (for reviews, see Beere, 1990; Thompson, Pleck, & Ferrera, 1993). Although the term *attitudes toward masculinity* is widely used as the generic category for these instruments, *masculinity ideology* is a conceptually preferable term for what they assess, for two reasons.

First, the social-psychological conception of attitude actually does not apply well to these measures. *Attitude* generally refers to a person's disposition toward an object or target, primarily on the dimension of favorability. Ordinarily, this disposition should predict some behavior toward that object. To use an example from our own research, adolescent males' attitudes toward condoms predict their use of condoms (Pleck, Sonenstein, & Ku, 1991). This usual conception of attitudes, however, does not fit the available scales for attitudes about masculinity. Masculinity, men, or the male role are not, in the customary sense, the object of the attitudinal disposition, and there is no behavior toward these objects that can be sensibly linked to it. With the exception of

Eagly and Mladinic's (1989) work, research on masculinity-related attitudes has not used the classical attitudinal approach.

Second, the more pointed term *masculinity ideology*—better than the neutral term *attitudes toward masculinity*—conveys the significance of what the available scales assess: endorsement and internalization of cultural belief systems about masculinity and male gender, rooted in the structural relationship between the two sexes. Masculinity ideology also connotes better the superordinate nature of the beliefs at issue; they are not just beliefs about a particular social object, but constitute a belief system about masculinity that entails various more specific attitudes and dispositions. Some previous research also provides a precedent for conceptualizing gender-related beliefs as ideologies (e.g., Levinson & Huffman, 1955; Lipman-Blumen, 1972; Mason & Bumpass, 1975).

Masculinity Ideology and Gender-Role Strain

Pleck (1981), synthesizing themes in the contemporary critique of masculinity, formulated a "gender-role strain" model for masculinity. Research has pursued this model in various ways (Eisler & Skidmore, 1987; Komarovsky, 1976; Mason & Bumpass, 1975; O'Neil, Helms, Gable, David, & Wrightsman, 1986). The strain model postulates that cultural standards for masculinity exist, and that socialization encourages men to attempt to live up to them. This process can have three types of negative outcomes for individual males: (a) long-term failure to fulfill male role expectations, with the continuing disjuncture between expectations and one's characteristics leading to low self-esteem and other negative psychological consequences; (b) successful fulfillment of male role expectations, but only through a traumatic socialization process with long-term negative side effects; and (c) successful fulfillment of male role expectations, but with negative consequences because the prescribed characteristics (e.g., low family participation) have inherent negative side effects. These three hypothesized negative effects correspond to three dynamics within male gender-role strain.

We formulate masculinity ideology as playing an essential part in male gender-role strain processes. For example, a male's level of endorsement of traditional masculinity ideology influences the subjective consequences of any existing discrepancies between the male's self-concept and male role standards. It should also influence the extent to which males will attempt to fulfill traditional role expectations in spite of their socialization costs or negative side effects. Pleck (1992) argues that a weakness of his 1981 formulation of male gender-role strain was its lack of attention to processes influencing how psychologically engaged or disengaged males are with traditional male role norms, as a factor influencing role strain outcomes. Thus this chapter seeks to advance the study of masculinity ideology as an essential factor in male gender-role strain. The analyses presented later do so by documenting associations between masculinity ideology and negative side effects.

Social Constructionism and Its Critique of "Sex Role"

"Social constructionism" is a dominant recent theoretical perspective in gender studies (e.g., Hunter College Women's Studies Collective, 1983), and in men's studies (Brod, 1987; Kimmel, 1987; Kimmel & Messner, 1989). As Kimmel and Messner (1989) apply the constructionist perspective to men,

> the important fact of men's lives is not that they are biological males, but that they become men. Our sex may be male, but our identity as men is developed through a complex process of interaction with the culture in which we both learn the gender scripts appropriate to our culture, and attempt to modify those scripts to make them more palatable. (p. 10)

Social constructionism and the concept of gender-role strain are theoretically compatible. Social constructionism's central concept of the learning of gender "scripts" is analogous to the gender-role strain paradigm's equally central concept of gender-role socialization. The concept of masculinity ideology can be easily integrated with social constructionism. Constructionism argues that males act in the ways they do not because of their biological characteristics, but because of the conceptions of masculinity held by their culture. Masculinity ideology is the individual-level construct that links individual males to their culture's construction of masculinity.

Social construction theorists make a pointed critique of what they describe as the "gender-role" model for understanding gender as "ahistorical, psychologically reductionist, and apolitical" (Kimmel, 1987, p. 12). Because parts of this critique potentially apply to the concept of masculinity ideology as well, they should be briefly considered here. One criticism made by Kimmel and other construction theorists is that the idea of "gender role" posits a static, historically and culturally invariant model for each sex, replicated generation after generation, which thus cannot explain how changes in women's and men's behavior occur within individuals or historically.

Actually, two quite different approaches within what Kimmel and other construction theorists label the "gender-role model" need to be distinguished: gender-role *strain* and gender-role *identity*. Construction theorists are arguing against the male gender-role *identity* model (Pleck, 1981), not the gender-role *strain* model. Gender-role identity theorists indeed made these erroneous assumptions of historical and cultural invariance and of automatic intergenerational transmission. Kimmel also links the gender-role model to functionalist sociology, which initially used the term *sex role* to refer to sex role identity (e.g., Parsons & Bales, 1955). Finally, Kimmel cites Pleck's (1981) analysis of the theory of male gender-role identity as a critique of the gender-role model.

The gender-role strain model is in fact a social constructionist model that predated the term *constructionism*. In gender-role strain theory, gender roles are explicitly *not* assumed to be invariant. In fact, strain theorists use evidence of cultural variations in each sex's behavior as evidence that gender behavior can be understood as role behavior, rather than as a result of biological gender differences. This model clearly conceptualizes gender roles as varying, and empirical research conducted within this model has made some (but not all) dimensions of variation central topics of investigation (e.g., studies of differences associated with wives' employment status).

A second, related criticism made by social construction theorists is that the gender-role model assumes a *single* standard or set of expectations for masculinity, an invalid assumption in light of the differences that exist within cultures. In social constructionism one must not speak of masculinity, but only of masculini*ties*. What role theorists represent as the male role in general is, say constructionists, really only the white heterosexual middle-class male role in the United States at this historical moment. This criticism overlooks the extent to which male gender-role theorists have explicitly argued that male role expectations include several different dimensions, the relative salience of which may vary among individuals and social groups (e.g., Brannon, 1976), and that there are multiple, competing conceptions of masculinity (Pleck, 1976).

The social constructionist criticism implies that one cannot formulate a scale assessing masculinity ideology, because there is not one ideology that is valid for all social groups. In our view, rather than glossing over group differences, measures of masculinity ideology make it possible actually to study them quantitatively, rather than simply to theorize about them. Use of a masculinity ideology scale does not necessitate a theoretical assumption that there is one universal, unvarying standard for masculinity. Rather, the argument is that a particular social construction of masculinity has been widely (though not universally) prevalent in the contemporary United States, which theorists have argued has various kinds of negative concomitants (Brannon, 1976; Doyle, 1989; Franklin, 1984; Pleck, 1976). Though the label has many pitfalls, "traditional" appears to be the best available term for this particular form of the male role (or construction of masculinity) at issue. It is possible to assess similarities and differences among different groups in the prevalence of this conception of masculinity. Researchers can also assess whether endorsing traditional masculinity has the same meaning and correlates among different groups. In these ways, research on masculinity ideology can advance our understanding of masculinity-related dynamics among different groups.

Masculinity Ideology and Adolescent Male Problem Behaviors

We will illustrate the use of the masculinity ideology approach in analyses from our work with the 1988 National Survey of Adolescent Males (Pleck, Sonenstein, & Ku, in press-a). These analyses concern the relationship between masculinity ideology and a group of behaviors known in adolescent research as "problem behaviors": sexual activity, substance use, delinquency, and school problems. One major line of current research on adolescence takes the perspective that a variety of specific deviant or unconventional behaviors are manifestations of a "problem behavior syndrome"; that is, they have common underlying causes and as a result are intercorrelated with each other (Jessor &

Jessor, 1977; Ketterlinus & Lamb, in press). In this chapter, the theoretical notion investigated is that in adolescent males one of these underlying causes is adherence to a traditional masculinity ideology. That is, the problematic behaviors shown by many adolescent males are a result of how our society defines masculinity.

This connection may seem obvious and indeed is often expressed informally. For example, in a recent article on the rising sales of malt liquors to young urban males, a youth counselor reports that "the attitude is, 'you're a man if you've got a 40 [ounce bottle] in your hand'" (Deveny, 1992). In a news report, a former male cigarette advertising model who developed lung cancer testified to a legislative committee that the underlying dynamic of the commercials in which he acted was that "we made you believe if you boys smoke, you'll be macho" (Kong, 1992).

Interestingly, the possible connection between masculinity and problem behavior has received little recent research attention. A handful of studies, many using convenience samples of male college students, identify such correlates of masculinity ideology as homophobia, Type A disposition, various behaviors relevant to close relationships, and condom use and attitudes (Bunting & Reeves, 1983; Pleck, Sonenstein, & Ku, 1990, in press-b; Snell, Hawkins, & Belk, 1988; Stark, 1991; Thompson, 1990; Thompson, Grisanti, & Pleck, 1985). However, no prior study documents the linkage of masculinity ideology specifically to adolescent male problem behaviors. Even among the large group of studies investigating correlates of the other primary masculinity-related construct, masculine personality traits, only a few have explored their association with problem behaviors (Horwitz & White, 1987; Snell, Belk, & Hawkins, 1987; Thompson, 1990; cf. Spence, Helmreich, & Holahan, 1979; Spence, Losoff, & Robbins, 1991). This relative lack of attention to masculinity in current research on problem behaviors provides an interesting contrast with earlier psychological views. In the 1950s and 1960s, under the influence of what Pleck (1981) labels the "male gender role identity paradigm," it was generally theorized that delinquency among males reflected adolescent males' conflicts or insecurity in sex role identity. However, when this and other lines of research within the male identity paradigm went into eclipse beginning in the mid-1970s, the relationship of masculinity to problem behaviors was generally no longer investigated.

Thus, in addition to arguing for the theoretical and empirical utility of the construct of masculinity ideology, the present study also intends to stimulate new interest in the link between masculinity and problem behaviors from a fresh perspective. The general hypothesis tested here is that among adolescent males, endorsement of masculinity ideology is associated with problem behaviors in four areas: school difficulties, substance use, delinquency, and sexual activity.

Method

Sample

The National Survey of Adolescent Males (NSAM) interviewed 1,880 never-married males aged 15 to 19 between April and November 1988. Its sample represented the noninstitutionalized never-married male population aged 15 to 19 in the contiguous United States. The sample was stratified to overrepresent black and Hispanic respondents, and in-person interviews averaging 75 minutes were completed with 676 young black, non-Hispanic men, 386 young Hispanic men, 755 young white, non-Hispanic men, and 63 respondents in other racial groupings. The response rate for those eligible to be interviewed was 73.9%. For other information on the sample, design, and procedures, see Sonenstein et al. (1989). Sample weights are available so that distributional results can be estimated for all noninstitutionalized never-married 15- to 19-year-old males. Analyses of distributions for problem behaviors and attitudes about masculinity use the full sample and are weighted to represent the population. Multivariate analyses use the 1,595 cases with complete data on all measures and are unweighted.

Measures

Masculinity ideology. This construct was assessed by an eight-item measure. Seven items were adapted from Thompson and Pleck's (1986) Male Role Norms Scale (MRNS), a 26-item abbreviated version of the Brannon Masculinity Scale, Short Form (Brannon, 1985). Items were chosen to represent the three factorial dimensions of the MRNS: status (3 items), toughness (2 items), and antifemininity (2 items). Items considered most relevant to an adolescent sample were selected, and wording was simplified or otherwise altered to be more appropriate for this age group. An additional item specifically about sex, a topical area absent from the MRNS, was also included (Snell et al., 1986). A guiding principle in the construction of these scales is that, as much as possible, items should refer to men in relation to male standards, rather than comparing men and women. However, one item explicitly concerns the husband-wife relationship, and another, concerning husbands' responsibility for housework, implies this relationship.

An index was derived from the eight items, with an alpha coefficient of .56. Analyses showed that all items contributed to the index, and that omission of any items would not lead to improvement in reliability. Alphas among whites, blacks, and Hispanics were .61, .47, and .54. Although this level of internal reliability is less than ideal, it was considered adequate for use in further analysis. Thompson (1990) reported a coefficient alpha of .91 in a college sample for the 26-item scale from which most of the eight items used in the present study were adapted. The lower reliability found in the present study results from the smaller number of items used.

Most measures of problem behaviors except those concerning sexual activity were composed of items from a short self-administered questionnaire (SAQ) for questions judged to be especially sensitive, which respondents completed and returned to the interviewer in a sealed envelope. For the problem behavior measures, high scores always denote being high on the construct.

School difficulties. Two items from the SAQ concerning school problems were employed. Males were asked: "Have you ever repeated a grade, or been held back a grade in school?" and "Were you ever suspended from school?"

Alcohol and drug use. The SAQ included parallel items for (a) drinking "beer, wine, hard liquor, or any other alcoholic beverage," (b) trying "cocaine or crack," and (c) trying "any other street drugs." For each, respondents were asked whether they had ever done the activity, and if so, how often they had done it during the last 12 months (never, a few times, monthly, weekly, or daily).

Delinquent activity. Males were asked in the SAQ: "Have you ever been picked up by the police for doing something wrong?" and "Have you ever done something that the police would pick you up for if they had found out?" Those answering positively were asked how often this had happened (once or twice, 3-5 times, 6-10 times, or 11 or more times).

Sexual activity. Three measures of sexual activity were selected for inclusion in this analysis. Sexual activity status was assessed by the question "Have you ever had sexual intercourse with a girl (sometimes this is called 'making love,' 'having sex,' or 'going all the way')?" Current level of sexual activity was indicated by respondents' reports of the number of different sexual partners they had in the last year; for this analysis, those not sexually active in the last year were assigned a code of zero. These two measures appeared in the interviewer-administered part of the NSAM. Finally, a measure of coercive sex was taken from the SAQ: "Have you ever tricked or forced someone else to have sex with you?"

Sociodemographic and personal background variables. Besides current age, respondents reported the level of education they thought they would ever complete (collapsed to less than high school diploma, high school diploma, some college or vocational school, 4 years of college, postgraduate). Attendance at religious services at age 14 was reported in four categories: never, less than once a month, one to three times a month, and once a week or more. Race was coded as black non-Hispanic, white non-Hispanic, Hispanic, and other race, with white non-Hispanic used as the reference category in regression analyses. Respondents estimated their family annual income in one of seven categories (in thousands: 0-10, 10-20, 20-30, 30-40, 40-50, 50-60, and 60+; coded 1-7). Region of the country was coded as the four census regions (North, Midwest, West, and South), with South as the reference category.

Results

Frequency of Problem Behaviors

Difficulties in school were relatively frequent, with 30.1% of the sample reporting repeating a grade in school, and 37.8% reporting suspension. Moreover, 21.0% reported drinking weekly or daily during the last year, and 6.6% reported using cocaine or crack in the last year. Among these, most reported cocaine use only "a few times." Use of "other street drugs" in the last year was acknowledged by 17.4%. (To a follow-up question, almost 90% reported the drug was marijuana.)

More than a quarter, 28.1%, had been "picked up" by the police. For most, this occurred only once or twice. A larger proportion, 47.6%, acknowledged ever doing something that the police would pick them up for, and 12.4% reported such activity six or more times. About 60.4% were sexually active. (Sonenstein et al., 1989, provide detailed break-downs by age and race/ethnicity.) Regarding number of different sexual partners in the last year, 45.1% had none, 27.3% had one, 15.0 % had two, 4.8% had three, and only 7.6% had four or more. For more detail, see Pleck et al. (in press-a).

Distributions of the Masculinity Ideology Items and Index. Table 5.1 provides distributional information for the items assessing traditional masculinity ideology. Item distributions may vary not only because of true differences in the rate of endorsement of one aspect of traditional male role expectations compared to another, but also because item wordings may not be precisely equivalent in intensity; because of the latter possibility, differences in means should be interpreted with caution. With this caveat, this sample reported relatively strong endorsement of traditional male role expectations concerning being respected by others, self-confidence, and avoidance of overt femininity (items 1-3, 6). By contrast, the mean levels of endorsement for the items concerning physical toughness and hypersexuality (5, 8) were close to the theoretical midpoint of 2.5. These two items also showed the largest standard deviations. Finally, respondents tended on the average to disagree with the items assessing traditional male role expectations regarding not expressing weakness and not doing housework.

Association Between Masculinity Ideology and Problem Behaviors

In these analyses, logistic regression was used to predict the problem behavior measures assessed in dichotomous form, and odds ratios are reported for predictors found to be statistically significant (Morgan & Teachman, 1988). Ordinary least squares regression was used for the problem behaviors assessed on continuous scales. In both sets of analyses, current age, expected level of education completed, frequency of religious attendance at age 14, race/ethnicity, current family income, and region of the country were included to control for sociodemographic and personal background factors.

Table 5.1
Means and Standard Deviations of Masculinity Ideology
Items and Index

Item	Mean[a]	S.D.
1. It is essential for a guy to get respect from others.	3.23	.80
2. A man always deserves the respect of his wife and children.	3.53	.71
3. I admire a guy who is totally sure of himself.	3.30	.79
4. A guy will lose respect if he talks about his problems.	1.76	.87
5. A young man should be physically tough, even if he's not big.	2.63	1.03
6. It bothers me when a guy acts like a girl.	3.33	.92
7. I don't think a husband should have to do housework.	1.72	.88
8. Men are always ready for sex.	2.13	.96
Traditional male role attitudes index	2.80	.44

NOTES: Weighted Ns for items = 1,868-1,877; weighted N for index = 1,851.
a. range: 1-4; 1 = disagree a lot, 2 = disagree a little, 3 = agree a little, 4 = agree a lot.

Results of the regression analyses of the association between masculinity ideology and problem behaviors are reported in Tables 5.2 and 5.3. Masculinity ideology showed a significant independent association with 7 of the 10 problem behaviors. Specifically, traditional masculinity expectations were associated with ever being suspended from school, drinking and use of drugs (primarily marijuana), being picked up by the police, being sexually active, number of heterosexual partners in the last year, and coercive sex. Number of partners in the last year was also predicted among the sexually active only; the coefficient for masculinity ideology remained significant (beta = .079, $p < .05$).

Based on factor analyses and reliability analyses not shown in detail here, an index combining the three substance use and the two illegal activities measures was created (alpha = .69), and results paralleled those for the individual problem behavior indicators. In addition, possible interactions between masculinity ideology and race, age, and educational expectations were examined, to detect whether the association between traditional expectations and problem behaviors might

Table 5.2
Logistic Regression Analyses of Problem Behaviors on Masculinity Ideology and Sociodemographic Factors
(N = 1,595)

Predictor	Repeated Grade		Suspended		Sexually Active		Forced Sex	
	Coeff.	Odds Ratio	Coeff.	Odds Ratio	Coeff.	Odds Ratio	Coeff.	Odds Ratio
Masculinity ideology	-.026		.398**	1.49	.698**	2.01	.657**	1.93
Age	-.022		.066		.573**	1.77	.212*	1.24
Expected education	-.511**	.57	-.435**	.64	-.126**	.88	-.063	
Religious attendance at age 14	-.130*	.88	-.142**	.87	-.215**	.81	-.327**	.72
Black[a]	.394**	1.48	.788**	2.20	1.399**	4.05	1.864**	6.45
Hispanic	.340**	1.40	.219		.218		1.491**	4.44
Other race	-.179		.133		-.017		1.981**	7.24
Family income	-.154**	.86	.017		.030		.151	
North[b]	.063		.465**	1.59	-.076		.394	
Midwest	-.620**	.54	.464**	1.59	.127		-.005	
West	-.961**	.38	.403**	1.50	-.278		-.373	
Model chi-square (11 df)	252.72		167.35		313.90		45.73	

NOTES: a. reference category for race is White.
b. reference category for region is South.
*p < .05; **p < .01

Table 5.3
Multiple Regression Analyses of Dichotomous Problem Behaviors as Predicted by Masculinity Ideology and Sociodemographic Factors (standardized regression coefficients; N = 1,595)

Predictor	Drink Alcohol	Use Cocaine	Use Other Drugs	Picked Up by Police	Police Would Pick Up	Number Partners Last Year
Masculinity ideology	.063*	.020	.064*	.090**	.026	.105**
Age	.215**	.117**	.091**	.077**	.045	.143**
Expected education	-.038	-.092**	-.100**	-.156**	.006	.066
Religious attendance at age 14	-.046	-.089**	-.083**	-.089**	-.051*	-.066**
Black[a]	-.221**	-.100*	-.154**	-.056*	-.200**	.221**
Hispanic	-.078*	.028	.037	.007	-.107**	.012
Other race	-.059	.018	.010	.010	-.044	-.013
Family income	.140**	.017	.047	.042	.121**	.081**
North[b]	.036	.039	.009	.084*	.012	.042
Midwest	.058*	-.010	.041	.145**	.011	.031
West	.002	.061*	.042	.066*	.007	-.016
Adj. R^2	.118	.044	.053	.069	.064	.097

NOTES: a. reference category for race is White.
b. reference category for region is South.
*p < .05; **p < .01

vary in different sample subgroups. In no case did inclusion of such interaction terms improve model fit. Thus there is no evidence that the association between problem behaviors and masculinity ideology differs among black, white, and Hispanic males.

In the ordinary least squares regression analyses, the size of significant associations observed between masculinity ideology and problem behaviors were modest, with betas ranging from .06 to .11. In the logistic regression analyses, an increment of one scale point (somewhat more than two standard deviations) on the masculinity ideology index was associated with about 50% greater odds of being suspended from school and about twice the odds of being sexually active and of ever forcing someone to have sex.

Implications and Issues

Our analysis indicates that adolescent males' problem behaviors are significantly associated with their endorsement of traditional masculinity ideology. The seven problem behavior indicators that demonstrated significant associations with masculinity ideology include at least one measure from each of the four broad areas of problem behaviors investigated here. These results are consistent with other research noted earlier focusing on other theoretical concomitants of masculinity attitudes, such as homophobia, Type A disposition, behaviors relevant to close relationships, and condom use and attitudes.

This analysis does have several limitations. In particular, the measures of problem behaviors utilize only self-reports, and it is not possible to specify the direction of causality: masculinity ideology may be as much a result as a cause of engaging in problem behaviors. But with these limitations acknowledged, these results have important implications from an applied perspective: adolescent males' definitions of masculinity are involved in whether or not they engage in problem behaviors.

Future research on masculinity ideology should address three interpretive or conceptual issues: (a) whether masculinity ideology is empirically distinct from masculine gender-related personality traits; (b) whether masculinity ideology is distinct from attitudes toward women; and (c) similarities and differences in the levels and concomi-tants of masculinity ideology among different groups, especially racial-ethnic groups.

Is Masculinity Ideology Independent of Masculine Gender-Related Personality Traits?

At the outset of the chapter, we argued that masculinity ideology and masculine gender-related personality traits are fundamentally distinct constructs. However, they could nonetheless be highly empirically correlated. Thus one important issue in evaluating the utility of mascu-linity ideology is whether it is really empirically different from trait masculinity. Our study did not have both kinds of measures available, so that we cannot estimate this relationship in our own data. In the studies that have both measures, however, the two constructs are gen-erally unrelated (Thompson, Pleck, & Ferrera, 1993). This is consistent with recent reviews suggesting that as a general matter, gender-related attitudes and gender-related personality traits are independent (Archer, 1989, 1990).

As noted earlier, prior research has established that trait masculinity is associated with problem behavior outcomes. Thus it appears that masculinity ideology and masculine personality traits both influence adolescent male problem behaviors (cf. Spence, 1992; Thompson, 1990). It should be noted, however, that the conceptual distance be-tween the problem outcomes considered here and masculinity ideology is greater than the distance between these outcomes and trait masculin-ity. For example, measures of trait masculinity often include males' self-ratings on aggression, toughness, and risk taking. Finding a rela-tionship between such a measure and, for example, being picked up by the police could be interpreted as simply showing that one indi-cator of toughness and aggression is correlated with another. How-ever, the association between problem behaviors and beliefs *about* masculinity—for example, between illegal acts and agreeing that males lose respect if they talk about their problems, or that men should not do housework—is far less intuitively obvious. Thus the masculinity ideol-ogy perspective hypothesizes a more theoretically ambitious relation-ship than the masculine personality traits approach.

Is Masculinity Ideology Independent of
Attitudes Toward Women?

Pleck (1981) argued that masculinity ideology and attitudes toward women are theoretically independent. For example, an individual can hold a liberal attitude toward women (e.g., believing that wives' employment is acceptable) while simultaneously holding a conservative attitude toward masculinity (e.g., viewing boys' playing with dolls as unacceptable). The two attitudes are thus conceptually independent, but what about their empirical relationship? Prior research provides two different answers.

If attitudes toward women are assessed with items concerning the desirability of women adhering to a traditional female role, without comparison to men, or describing relationships between women and men, they are relatively independent of masculinity ideology (Desnoyers, 1988; Thompson & Pleck, 1986). However, if one assesses attitudes toward women, as many scales do, with items concerning whether a behavior is relatively more desirable in women as compared to men, or with items concerning the appropriate relationship between the sexes, then the two attitudes are more related, with within-sex correlations averaging .5 (Riley, 1990; Stark, personal communication, 1991; Thompson, 1990). These latter studies used Spence and Helmreich's (1972; Spence, Helmreich, & Stapp, 1973) Attitudes Toward Women Scale (AWS), the majority of whose items compare the sexes. For example, the first item in the AWS short form is "Swearing and obscenity are more repulsive in the speech of a woman than of a man."

Thus two strategies for assessing attitudes toward women give different results concerning the degree of correlation between attitudes toward women and masculinity ideology. We can illustrate this same pattern in our own data. Table 5.4 shows the relationship between masculinity ideology and three measures of gender-related attitudes. The first two are single-item measures first used in national surveys (Mason & Bumpass, 1975). "A working mother can have just as good a relationship with her child as a mother who does not work" assesses an attitude about women fulfilling or not fulfilling a traditional role, without reference to men. The second item, "It is much better for everyone if the man earns the money and the woman takes care of the home and family," is a gender-comparative item. The third measure,

Table 5.4
Multiple Regression Analyses of Attitudes Toward Women as Predicted by Masculinity Ideology and Sociodemographic Factors ($N = 1,624$)

Predictor	Working Mother Can Have Good Relationship	Better if Man Earns the Money, Woman Takes Care of Family	Adversarial Sexual beliefs
Masculinity ideology	.041	.359***	.353***
Age	−.029	−.031	.027
Expected education	−.008	−.171**	.112*
Religious attendance at age 14	−.011	.009	−.017
Sexually active	.053*	−.059*	−.008
Black[a]	.177***	−.073**	.107***
Hispanic	.081**	.001	.064*
Other race	−.131	−.007	.010
Family income	−.026	−.099*	−.123***
North[b]	−.027	.011	−.034
Midwest	−.033	−.010	−.027
West	−.032	−.012	−.010
$F_{(12, 1611)}$	5.564***	33.656***	38.880***
Adj. R^2	.0326	.1945	.2188
Incr. to adj. R^2 due to male role attitudes index	−.0009	.1174***	.1130***

NOTES: a. reference category for race is White.
b. reference category for region is South.
*$p < .05$; **$p < .01$; ***$p < .001$

adversarial sexual beliefs, is a three-item scale drawn from Burt (1980) assessing the belief that women exploit or use men (e.g., "In a dating relationship, a girl is largely out to take advantage of a guy." This item thus concerns gender relationships. As indicated in Table 5.4, masculinity ideology is independent of the first item, but strongly related to the other items.

Our interpretation is that gender-comparative items assess what could be better labeled attitudes toward gender roles and relationships. Thus three kinds of gender-related attitudes need to be distinguished: (1) attitudes toward women (narrowly defined, not involving comparison to men), (2) attitudes toward masculinity (also narrowly defined), and (3) attitudes toward gender roles and relationships. The first two are conceptually and empirically independent, but both are conceptually part of, and are empirically correlated with, the third (Pleck et al., 1992).

In other work we have also gone further to show that attitudes toward masculinity have discriminant validity relative to both attitudes toward women and attitudes toward gender roles and relationships. That is, masculinity ideology has stronger associations with theoretically predicted concomitants than do the two other attitudes, and the associations between masculinity ideology and predicted outcomes persist when levels of the two other attitudes are controlled (Pleck et al., 1992, in press-b). Thus there is good evidence that masculinity ideology is independent of attitudes toward women. Future research should investigate how masculinity ideology, beliefs about women, and beliefs about gender roles and relationships independently and interactively shape gender-related behavior.

Masculinity Ideology and Racial-Ethnic Similarities and Differences

An especially important issue in the evaluation of masculinity ideology is its application to different populations, especially racial ethnic groups. As we argued above, use of a masculinity ideology scale does not make the theoretical assumption that there is one universal standard for masculinity. Rather, the claim is that a particular version or social construction of masculinity (not all forms of masculinity) has been widely prevalent in contemporary Western society, and this so-called traditional masculinity has various kinds of negative consequences. Masculinity ideology scales attempt to assess belief in this form of masculinity. What do our data indicate about how well this conceptualization applies to different populations?

Although various other comparisons can be made (Pleck et al., 1992, in press-b), the most important comparison is whether masculinity ideology has similar correlates among different groups. The validity concern is whether the scale and its items mean or signify the same thing to males in different groups. For example, saying that men have to get respect might be an expression of traditional masculinity ideology among whites, but not among blacks or Hispanics. There is some precedent for this concern, because 1950s masculinity-femininity scales were criticized for interpreting items like "I would like to be a singer" as revealing feminine gender-role identification among black males, unaware that in the context of black culture this interpretation may be invalid.

One way of addressing this issue is to determine whether masculinity ideology has similar correlates in different subgroups. As noted above, we tested whether the introduction of terms representing the interaction of masculinity ideology with gender led to a significant increment in explained variance in the regression models in Tables 5.2 and 5.3. Applying this formal test, there was no evidence that the association between problem behaviors and masculinity ideology differed among black, white, and Hispanic males. When the association of individual scale items to the outcomes was also examined, the items generally showed the same relationships. Although racial and ethnic differences and similarities in masculinity ideology and its correlates clearly need more research attention, the evidence to date supports the utility of the construct of masculinity ideology in different racial ethnic groups.

Conclusions

Our research supports two general conclusions. First, masculinity ideology is a distinct component of men's involvement with their gender role. It is independent of masculine gender-related personality traits and differs from men's attitudes toward women. Masculinity ideology contributes to our understanding of male behavior independently of these two other constructs. It does so because it addresses the issue of how men understand what their behavior means.

The hypothetical dynamic investigated in the present study—that problem behaviors in adolescent males are related to masculinity—is one that logically applies only to males. However, researchers should consider parallel ways in which traditional feminine ideology promotes some problem behaviors in adolescent females. A good example in the research literature is Fox's (1977) analysis of the "nice-girl dilemma" in adolescent female contraception. Fox argues that in the traditional conception of femininity, the only legitimate excuse for sex prior to marriage is being so uncontrollably in love that one is swept away by passion. Using contraception is inconsistent with this rationalization because it requires advance planning. Thus adherence to the "nice-girl" conception of femininity means not using contraception. Future research should explore the role of feminine ideology in this and other female problem behaviors.

Second, traditional masculinity ideology is associated with male behaviors that have negative consequences. Thus problem behaviors in adolescent males *are* connected to masculinity ideology. Even though masculinity-related dynamics are clearly not the only source of male problem behaviors, their role has been generally overlooked.

The results of our study might inform applied interventions. Some recent research has found cognitive approaches to be effective in youth-oriented interventions. For example, studies have documented positive effects for teen pregnancy prevention programs focusing on modifying pregnancy-related perceptions suggested by the "health beliefs model" (susceptibility to the problem, seriousness of the problem, benefits and costs of preventive action) as influencing preventive health behavior (Eisen, Zellman, & McAlister, 1990). Adolescent violence prevention efforts have employed "cognitive mediation training," attempting to alter beliefs identified as correlates of the use of aggression (Guerra & Slaby, 1990). Based on our results, one component of male youth interventions might focus on attitudes about masculinity. For example, males could discuss specific beliefs about masculinity and discuss whether masculinity is really validated by risk-taking or deviant behavior. Whatever strategy to address masculinity is employed, intervention and prevention efforts targeted to adolescent males might be more effective if they targeted these dynamics to a greater extent than they do now.

Louis Sullivan (1991), Secretary of the Department of Health and Human Services, recently urged the policy and intervention communities to address the young male "whose manhood is measured by the number of children he has fathered, and the caliber of the gun he carries." The results of our study suggest some possible avenues for doing so. Changing how manhood is measured means changing traditional masculinity ideology.

Note

1. In the literature of the 1950s and 1960s, the term was *sex role identity*. To be consistent with contemporary usage, "sex role" has been updated to "gender role" here and elsewhere.

References

Archer, J. (1989). The relationship between gender-role measures: A review. *British Journal of Social Psychology, 28,* 173-184.

Archer, J. (1990). Gender-stereotypic traits are derived from gender roles: A reply to McCreary. *British Journal of Social Psychology, 29,* 273-277.

Beere, C. A. (1990). *Gender roles: A handbook of tests and measures.* Westport, CT: Greenwood Press.

Bem, S. L. (1974). The measurement of psychological androgyny. *Journal of Personality and Social Psychology, 42,* 155-162.

Brannon, R. (1976). The male sex role: Our culture's blueprint for manhood and what it's done for us lately. In D. David & R. Brannon (Eds.), *The forty-nine percent majority: The male sex role* (pp. 1-48). Reading, MA: Addison-Wesley.

Brannon, R. (1985). A scale for measuring attitudes about masculinity. In A. G. Sargent (Ed.), *Beyond sex roles* (pp. 110-116). St. Paul, MN: West.

Brannon, R., & Juni, S. (1984). A scale for measuring attitudes about masculinity. *Psychological Documents, 14,* 6. (Ms. 2012).

Brod, H. (Ed.). (1987). *The making of masculinities: The new men's studies.* Winchester, MA: Allen & Unwin.

Bunting, A. B., & Reeves, J. B. (1983). Perceived male sex orientation and beliefs about rape. *Deviant Behavior, 4,* 281-295.

Burt, M. (1980). Cultural myths and supports for rape. *Journal of Personality and Social Psychology, 38,* 217-230.

Desnoyers, R. M. (1988). *The role of religiosity in male sex role attitudes.* Unpublished honor's thesis, Holy Cross College.

Deveny, K. (1992, March 9). Malt liquor makers find lucrative market in the urban young. *Wall Street Journal,* p. A1.

Doyle, J. A. (1989). *The male experience* (2nd ed.). Dubuque, IA: William C. Brown.

Eagly, A., & Mladinic, A. (1989). Gender stereotypes and attitudes toward women and men. *Personality and Social Psychology Bulletin, 15,* 543-558.

Eisen, M., Zellman, G., & McAlister, A. (1990). Evaluating the impact of a theory-based sexuality and contraceptive education program. *Family Planning Perspectives, 6,* 261-271.

Eisler, R., & Skidmore, J. (1987). Masculine gender role stress: Scale development and components factors in the appraisal of stressful situations. *Behavior Modification, 11,* 123-136.

Fox, G. (1977). "Nice girl": Social control of women through a value construct. *Signs: Journal of Women in Culture and Society, 2,* 805-817.

Franklin, C. W. (1984). *The changing definition of masculinity.* New York: Plenum.

Guerra, N., & Slaby, R. (1990). Cognitive mediators of aggression in adolescent offenders: 2. Intervention. *Developmental Psychology, 26,* 269-277.

Horwitz, A. V., & White, H. R. (1987). Gender role orientation and styles of pathology among adolescents. *Journal of Health and Social Behavior, 28,* 158-170.

Hunter College Women's Studies Collective. (1983). *Women's realities, women's choices.* New York: Oxford University Press.

Jessor, R., & Jessor, S. (1977). *Problem behavior and psychosocial development: A longitudinal study of youth.* New York: Academic Press.

Ketterlinus, R. D., & Lamb, M. E. (in press). *Adolescent problem behaviors.* Hillsdale, NJ: Lawrence Erlbaum.

Kimmel, M. S. (1987). Rethinking "masculinity": New directions in research. In M. S. Kimmel (Ed.), *Changing men: New directions in research on men and masculinity* (pp. 9-24). Newbury Park, CA: Sage.

Kimmel, M. S., & Messner, M. (1989). Introduction. In M. S. Kimmel & M. Messner (Eds.), *Men's lives.* New York: Macmillan.

Komarovsky, M. (1976). *Dilemmas of masculinity.* New York: Norton.

Kong, D. (1992, March 12). Same product, different message. *Boston Globe,* p. 35.

Lenney, E. (1991). Sex roles: The measurement of masculinity, femininity, and androgyny. In J. P. Robinson, P. R. Shaver, & L. S. Wrightsman (Eds.), *Measures of personality and social psychological attitudes* (pp. 573-660). New York: Academic Press.

Levinson, D. J., & Huffman, P. E. (1955). Traditional family ideology and its relations to personality. *Journal of Personality.*

Lipman-Blumen, J. (1972). How ideology shapes women's lives. *Scientific American, 226*(1), 34-62.

Mason, K. O., & Bumpass, L. L. (1975). U.S. women's sex role ideology, 1970. *American Journal of Sociology, 80,* 1212-1219.

Morgan, S. P., & Teachman, J. D. (1988). Logistic regression: Description, examples, and comparisons. *Journal of Marriage and the Family, 50,* 929-936.

O'Neil, J. M., Helms, B., Gable, R. K., David, L., & Wrightsman, L. S. (1986). Gender-role conflict scale: College men's fear of femininity. *Sex Roles, 14,* 335-350.

Parsons, T. C., & Bales, R. F. (1955). *Family socialization and interaction process.* Glencoe, IL: Free Press.

Pleck, J. H. (1976). The male sex role: Problems, definitions, and sources of change. *Journal of Social Issues, 32,* 155-164.

Pleck, J. H. (1981). *The myth of masculinity.* Cambridge: MIT Press.

Pleck, J. H. (1983). The theory of male sex role identity: Its rise and fall, 1936-present. In M. Lewin (Ed.), *In the shadow of the past: Psychology portrays the sexes* (pp. 205-225). New York: Columbia University Press.

Pleck, J. H. (1992, August). *Gender role strain, social constructionism, and masculinity.* Paper presented to the American Psychological Association, Washington.

Pleck, J. H., Sonenstein, F. L., & Ku, L. C. (1990). Contraceptive attitudes and intention to use condoms in sexually experienced and inexperienced males. *Journal of Family Issues, 11,* 294-312.

Pleck, J. H., Sonenstein, F. L., & Ku, L. C. (1991). Adolescent males' condom use: Relationships between perceived cost-benefits and consistency. *Journal of Marriage and the Family, 53,* 733-746.

Pleck, J. H., Sonenstein, F. L., & Ku, L. C. (1992). *Attitudes toward the male gender role: Levels, predictors, and discriminant validity in a national sample of adolescent males.* Manuscript under review.

Pleck, J. H., Sonenstein, F. L., & Ku, L. C. (in press-a). Problem behaviors and masculinity ideology in adolescent males. In R. D. Ketterlinus & M. E. Lamb (Eds.), *Adolescent problem behaviors.* Hillsdale, NJ: Lawrence Erlbaum.

Pleck, J. H., Sonenstein, F. L., & Ku, L. C. (in press-b). Masculinity ideology: Its impact on adolescent males' heterosexual relationships. *Journal of Social Issues.*

Riley, D. P. (1990). *Men's endorsement of male sex-role norms and time spent in psychotherapeutic treatment.* Unpublished doctoral dissertation, Boston University.

Snell, W. E., Belk, S. S., & Hawkins, R. C. (1986). The stereotypes about male sexuality scale (SAMSS): Components, correlates, antecedents, consequences, and counselor bias. *Social and Behavioral Sciences Documents, 16,* 9 (Ms. 2746).

Snell, W. E., Belk, S. S., & Hawkins, R. C. (1987). Alcohol and drug use in stressful times: The influence of the masculine role and sex-related personality attributes. *Sex Roles, 16,* 359-373.

Snell, W. E., Hawkins, R. C., & Belk, S. S. (1988). Stereotypes about male sexuality and the use of social influence strategies in intimate relationships. *Journal of Social and Clinical Psychology, 7,* 42-48.

Sonenstein, F. L., Pleck, J. H., & Ku, L. C. (1989). Sexual activity, condom use and AIDS awareness among adolescent males. *Family Planning Perspectives, 21,* 152-158.

Spence, J. T. (1992). *Gender-related traits and gender ideology: Evidence for a multifactorial theory.* Unpublished manuscript.

Spence, J. T., & Helmreich, R. L. (1972). The Attitudes Toward Women Scale: An objective instrument to measure attitudes toward the rights and roles of women in contemporary society. *JSAS Catalog of Selected Documents in Psychology, 2,* 66.

Spence, J. T., & Helmreich, R. L. (1978). *Masculinity and femininity: Their psychological dimensions, correlates, and antecedents.* Austin: University of Texas Press.

Spence, J. T., Helmreich, R. L., & Holahan, C. T. (1979). Negative and positive components of psychological masculinity and femininity and their relationships to self-reports of neurotic and acting out behaviors. *Journal of Personality and Social Psychology, 37,* 1673-1682.

Spence, J. T., Helmreich, R. L., & Stapp, J. (1973). A short version of the Attitudes toward Women Scale (AWS). *Bulletin of the Psychonomic Society, 2,* 219-220.

Spence, J. T., Losoff, M., & Robbins, A. S. (1991). Sexually aggressive tactics in dating relationships: Personality and attitudinal correlates. *Journal of Social and Clinical Psychology, 10,* 289-304.

Stark, L. P. (1991). Traditional gender role beliefs and individual outcomes: An exploratory analysis. *Sex Roles, 24,* 639-650.

Sullivan, L. (1991, May 25). US secretary urges TV to restrict "irresponsible sex and reckless violence." *Boston Globe,* p. 1.

Thompson, E. H. (1990). Courtship violence and the male role. *Men's Studies Review, 7*(3), 1, 4-13.

Thompson, E. H., Grisanti, C., & Pleck, J. H. (1985). Attitudes toward the male role and their correlates. *Sex Roles, 13,* 413-427.

Thompson, E. H., & Pleck, J. H. (1986). The structure of male role norms. *American Behavioral Scientist, 29,* 531-543.

Thompson, E. H., Pleck, J. H., & Ferrera, D. (1993). Men and masculinities: Scales *for* masculinity ideology and other masculinity-related constructs. *Sex Roles, 27,* 573-608.

PART III

HOME LIFE AND WORK LIFE

6

Gender Differences in Marital Conflict: The Demand/Withdraw Interaction Pattern

ANDREW CHRISTENSEN
CHRISTOPHER L. HEAVEY

Suppose a couple have a marital problem to which he contributes passive withdrawal while her 50% is nagging criticism. In explaining their frustrations, the husband will state that withdrawal is his only *defense against* her nagging, while she will label this explanation gross and willful distortion of what "really" happens in their marriage: namely, that she is critical of him *because* of his passivity. Stripped of all ephemeral and fortuitous elements, their fights consist in a monotonous exchange of the messages, "I will withdraw because you nag" and "I nag because you withdraw."

—Watzlawick, Beavin, and Jackson, 1967, p. 56.

This quotation describes a common interaction pattern in marriage. Other clinical theorists have described a similar interaction pattern, but used different labels for it. For example, Fogarty (1976) discussed the pursuer/distancer pattern, in which one partner advances while the other retreats. Napier (1978) described the rejection/intrusion pattern, in which one partner clasps and clings while the other pulls away. Wile (1981) described a pairing of demanding/withdrawing partners.

The quotation above not only describes an interaction pattern but makes two important assumptions about it: that its occurrence is related to marital dissatisfaction and that gender is linked to the roles in the pattern. The other clinical theorists above have made similar assumptions. This chapter describes our efforts to assess this pattern with self-report and observational measures and our empirical examination of the validity of these two important assumptions. Then we discuss our research on the antecedents of this pattern (and its gender linkage) in the personalities of the participants and in the social structure of their relationship. We conclude with some speculation about causal determinants of this pattern and the implication of our findings for future research. Throughout the chapter we use the term *demand/withdraw interaction pattern* to describe the interaction sequence.[1]

Self-Report Assessment

Our first question was whether couples could recognize the demand/withdraw pattern in their relationship and agree on its occurrence. We were interested in "what really happens" in the relationship, so we could not be satisfied with greatly divergent spouse perceptions. Only if spouses independently agreed about the occurrence of this interaction in their relationship could we be confident that it really occurred. Research indicates that couples have difficulty reaching high agreement even when reporting on specific behaviors that occur within the last 24 hours. For example, spouses achieved only an 83% level of nonchance agreement (kappa) on whether they had had sexual intercourse with each other in the previous 24 hours (Christensen & King, 1982)! Therefore, we approached the measurement of a broad interaction pattern with some trepidation.

In our first attempts at measurement, we generated vignettes of interaction patterns and asked couples to indicate whether they had interactions similar to those described in the vignettes (Christensen, Sullaway, & King, 1982; Sullaway & Christensen, 1983). Because of several difficulties in our assessments with these vignettes (see Christensen, 1987, 1988), we decided to have couples directly rate the behaviors in the demand/withdraw pattern. The clinical theory cited above suggests that there are three kinds of behaviors characteristic of this pattern. A demander is more likely to initiate problem discussions, whereas a withdrawer is more likely to avoid those discussions. A demander is more likely to nag and demand during problem discussions, while a withdrawer is more likely to be silent and withdraw from those discussions. Finally, a demander is more likely to be critical during problem discussions, while a withdrawer is more likely to be defensive. Therefore we generated items that assessed each of these pairs of behaviors. There are three items where the woman is in a demanding role and the man is in a withdrawing role and three comparable items where the roles of man and woman are reversed. Table 6.1 presents these six items.

Initially we focused on two subscales based on these items: Total Demand/Withdraw Communication, which consists of the sum total of ratings across all six items, and Demand/Withdraw Roles, which consists of the sum of the ratings on the first three items minus the sum of the ratings on the last three items. Later, we have focused separately on Woman Demand/Man Withdraw interaction (the sum of the ratings on the first three items) and Man Demand/Woman Withdraw interaction (the sum of the ratings on the last three items).

The Communication Patterns Questionnaire (CPQ, Christensen & Sullaway, 1984a) includes these six items as well as a variety of other items describing both symmetrical and complimentary interaction patterns. These items are classified under three headings: "when some problem in the relationship arises" (4 items address engagement and avoidance of discussion about the problem), "during a discussion of a relationship problem" (18 items discuss such behaviors as blaming, feeling expression, demanding, and physical violence), and "after a discussion of a relationship problem" (13 items address behaviors such as withdrawal and reactions such as guilt). Our focus will, however, be on the demand/withdraw subscale consisting of the items in Table 6.1.

In the first study with this new measure (Christensen, 1987), we examined agreement between partners in 142 married and living-together couples. Pearson correlations between partners were .57 for Total Demand/Withdraw Communication and .58 for Demand/Withdraw Roles. In this study we used the mean of each partner's responses as the unit of analysis, so the intraclass correlation coefficient was the appropriate measure of reliability for these means. These intraclass

Table 6.1
Self-Report Measure of Demand/Withdraw Interaction

Woman Demand/Man Withdraw

When some problem in the relationship arises

Discussion/Avoidance	Very Unlikely								Very Likely
Woman tries to start a discussion while Man tries to avoid a discussion.	1	2	3	4	5	6	7	8	9

During a discussion of a relationship problem

Woman nags and demands while Man withdraws, becomes silent, or refuses to discuss the matter further.	1	2	3	4	5	6	7	8	9
Woman criticizes while Man defends himself.	1	2	3	4	5	6	7	8	9

Man Demand/Woman Withdraw

When some problem in the relationship arises

Discussion/Avoidance	Very Unlikely								Very Likely
Man tries to start a discussion while Woman tries to avoid a discussion.	1	2	3	4	5	6	7	8	9

During a discussion of a relationship problem

Man nags and demands while Woman withdraws, becomes silent, or refuses to discuss the matter further.	1	2	3	4	5	6	7	8	9
Man criticizes while Woman defends herself.	1	2	3	4	5	6	7	8	9

correlations were .73 for Total Demand/Withdraw Communication and .74 for Demand/Withdraw Roles.

In more recent research we have focused on husband and wife reports of Woman Demand/Man Withdraw communication and Man Demand/ Woman Withdraw communication. We have examined interitem alphas for each of these subscales, which typically average in the low .70s. We usually treat the data from husband and wife as a separate factor in an ANOVA design, but we have never found a main effect or interaction involving this factor. The data from husband and wife have so far given us identical findings. The correlations between husbands and wives on these subscales are, however, far from perfect. Recently we examined husband and wife concordance in a study of nondistressed couples, clinic couples, and divorcing couples (Christensen & Shenk, 1991). Nondistressed couples were not in marital therapy or undergoing divorce and scored in the satisfied range on a marital adjustment measure. Clinic couples had sought out marital therapy but were assessed before therapy started. Divorcing couples had separated with their partner in the past year. Across these groups the Pearson correlation between spouses was .44 on Wife Demand/Husband Withdraw interaction and .59 on Husband Demand/Wife Withdraw interaction.

Observational Assessment

The data discussed above suggests that the Communication Patterns Questionnaire (CPQ) provided a satisfactory "insider's" perspective on the demand/withdraw interaction pattern. However, we also wanted an "outsider's" or observer's perspective on the pattern as well. The marital literature clearly indicates that insiders and outsiders have different, although often overlapping, perspectives on marital interaction. If we could develop an observational measure of the demand/withdraw interaction pattern and show similar effects with both self-report and observational measures, then our confidence in those findings would be greatly enhanced.

Observational measures of couple conflict are typically obtained by inviting couples into the laboratory, asking them to discuss a current disagreement, and videotaping the ensuing discussion. The development of an observational measure of demand/withdraw interaction based on such a scenario presented a number of challenges. First, it would not be possible to have observer items that paralleled the self-report items on the CPQ because the relevant behaviors would not occur in the typical laboratory interaction. For instance, the first demand/withdraw item from Table 6.1 describes a situation in which the woman tries to start a discussion while the man tries to avoid it. In the laboratory setting, a conflict would not begin as it usually does naturally but instead it would begin with the experimenter's instructions. If a couple has agreed to the laboratory procedure, neither member is likely to avoid discussing the topic. The second item on the demand/withdraw subscale describes the woman nagging and demanding while the man refuses to talk or withdraws. In a laboratory situation we might well see demanding and nagging, but it would be unlikely for one person to refuse to talk or to leave the situation.

Also, an observational measure must be focused around a specific topic of conflict rather than being based on the couple's general style of discussing conflict. Unlike couples, who are present at all their conflict discussions and can provide a summary report of their general patterns, observers are only present at the specific laboratory interactions that take place and can only report on these specific interactions. A third problem is that the time constraints of the observational episode (typically 5 to 15 minutes) might prevent the observer from seeing a true sequence or pattern of demand/withdraw behavior. For example, demand/withdraw interaction may occur over a longer time frame than 15 minutes, as when one partner gradually escalates demands until the other partner withdraws completely.

Because of these limitations of direct observation, our observational coding system differs from our self-report measure of demand/withdraw interaction. First, we ask observers to rate individual husband and wife behaviors rather than rating a pattern of interaction. To create a demand/withdraw subscale we sum the demand behaviors of one partner with the withdraw behaviors of the other. Second, we have observers rate behaviors that might be indicative of avoidance rather than actual avoidance, which is unlikely to occur. Table 6.2 presents the three observational items for demanding behaviors and the two observational items for withdrawing behaviors. Originally, our withdrawing scale included an item on defensiveness. We dropped this item because we wanted our measures to be consistent with Gottman and Krokoff's (1989) research and because this item lowered our interitem alpha reliability.

In four important ways the observational and self-report coding systems are similar. First, other than the exceptions noted above, the content of the items is virtually identical. Second, the items are assessed in the same way in both systems. That is, both the marital participants and the observers rate the extent to which demand and

Table 6.2
Observational Measure of Demand/Withdraw Interaction

Demands

	None							A lot	
Discussion Tries to discuss the problem (e.g., is engaged and involved in the topic at hand)	1	2	3	4	5	6	7	8	9
Blame Blames, accuses, or criticizes partner	1	2	3	4	5	6	7	8	9
Pressures for Change Requests, demands, nags, or otherwise pressures for changes in partner	1	2	3	4	5	6	7	8	9

Withdraws

	None							A lot	
Avoidance Avoids discussing the problem (e.g., hesitates, changes topics, diverts attention, or delays discussion)	1	2	3	4	5	6	7	8	9
Withdraws Withdraws, becomes silent, or refuses to discuss a particular topic	1	2	3	4	5	6	7	8	9

withdraw behaviors occur on a 9-point likelihood scale, rather than coding the presence or absence of particular behaviors. Third, both systems rely on a "cultural informant" approach (Gottman & Levenson, 1986). In this approach, members of the culture are assumed to have some ability to recognize common behaviors and interactions and thus do not need much explicit training in that process. In fact, the assumption is that too much training may alter the culturally accepted meanings of certain behaviors and interactions. In the Communication Patterns Questionnaire we provide the couple with no explicit definition of the meaning of the items. In our observational measures we provide the observers with some additional information about the meaning of these terms when applied to a brief interaction. We also provide them with several hours of training necessary to ensure adequate interobserver agreement. However, a lot of interpretation is left to the observer. Fourth, as with the self-report measure, we require at least two observers to rate all interactions. Because we require separate assessments of husband and wife behavior in our observational system, at least four observers are required for each couple, two for the husband's behavior and two for the wife's behavior. We have used Cronbach's alpha to assess consistency across observers in rating these behaviors as well as to measure consistency across items. Interobserver alphas have averaged in the .80s whereas interitem alphas have averaged in the .70s.

Relationship With Marital Satisfaction

The clinical theorists above who first described the demand/withdraw pattern of interaction suggested that it was associated with marital dissatisfaction. One of our first goals was to test this assumption empirically. Finding interactional correlates of marital satisfaction, rather than personality or demographic correlates, has been a major thrust in the clinical literature on marriage. In contrast to demographic or personality characteristics, interactional features are assumed to be more changeable, and thus they offer a more promising avenue for intervening in troubled marriages. Apart from its clinical implications, however, a correlation between an interaction pattern and marital satisfaction highlights the importance of that interaction pattern. Such data provide good grounds for further study of the causes and consequences of that interaction pattern.

Across several studies, we have consistently found a significant negative relationship between our self-report measure of demand/withdraw interaction and self-reported marital satisfaction. In a study of a diverse sample of 142 couples (Christensen, 1987) we found a Pearson correlation of −.55 between our CPQ measure of demand/withdraw interaction and the Dyadic Adjustment Scale (DAS; Spanier, 1976), a standard measure of marital satisfaction. In a recent clinical investigation, we compared demand/withdraw interaction from nondistressed couples, clinic couples prior to therapy, and divorcing couples in their last year of marriage. The clinic and divorcing couples had significantly more demand/withdraw interaction than the nondistressed couples but were not significantly different from each other (Christensen & Shenk, 1991).

Though encouraging, these findings must be interpreted with caution. We are not the first to find self-report correlates of marital satisfaction. In fact, a number of self-report measures are associated with marital satisfaction. The common method underlying these correlations (i.e., self-report) suggests that these correlations may be partly attributable to common assessment methods rather than to substantive covariation between the conceptual dimensions assessed. Couples who are unhappy with one another may reveal that dissatisfaction on virtually any measure that asks questions about their marital relationship.

Because of these concerns, we next examined the relationship between observational ratings of demand/withdraw interaction and marital satisfaction. In an initial study (Christensen & Heavey, 1990), we found a Pearson correlation of −.65 between observational ratings of total demand/withdraw interaction and average DAS scores of husband and wife. In a later study (Heavey et al., in press), observational ratings of total demand/withdraw interaction were correlated with wives' and husbands' DAS scores, $r = -.45$ and $r = -.34$, respectively.

In an important paper, Gottman and Krokoff (1989) demonstrated that longitudinal relations between marital behavior and later marital satisfaction may be different from cross-sectional relationships between marital behavior and current satisfaction. They showed, for example, that engagement in conflict, although negatively associated with current marital satisfaction, was positively associated with improvement in marital satisfaction. We also wanted to examine the longitudinal association between demand/withdraw interaction and later marital satisfaction. Recently, we examined the partial correlation between observational ratings of demand/withdraw interaction and DAS scores taken approximately one year later, controlling for DAS scores taken at the time of the interaction (Heavey et al., in press). Consistent with cross-sectional findings, wife demand/husband withdraw interaction was negatively associated with later marital satisfaction, but only for wife's marital satisfaction ($r = -.51$, $p < .05$). However, in contrast to cross-sectional findings, husband demand/wife withdraw interaction was positively associated with the wife's satisfaction one year later ($r = .92$, $p < .001$). We found no significant predictors in the demand/withdraw interaction for later husband satisfaction.

These data were obtained on only a small sample of 22 couples; clearly they need to be replicated on another sample. However, we tentatively interpret these findings as indicating that wives are satisfied in the long run when husbands show involvement in the conflicts between them by engaging in a discussion, even if it means some aversive behaviors such as criticism and demands. This interpretation is consistent with other findings and interpretations that women function more effectively than men in a negative affective climate (Gottman & Levenson, 1988) and that certain negative behaviors indicative of engagement and involvement may be associated over the long run with greater satisfaction in women (Gottman & Krokoff, 1989).

Gender Differences in Demand/Withdraw Interaction

The clinical theories of demand/withdraw interaction described above assumed a gender linkage to this pattern. One of our first goals was to test this assumption empirically: Are women more likely to be demanders and men more likely to be withdrawers? In an early study of 142 married and living-together couples (Christensen, 1987), we examined the self-report subscale of demand/withdraw roles. Across all couples, the average value on this variable was significantly different from zero in the direction of the women being more demanding and the men being more withdrawing. In later studies, we have simply compared the likelihood of man demand/woman withdraw interaction with woman demand/man withdraw interaction. We found that woman demand/man withdraw interaction was more likely than the reverse in nondistressed couples, clinic couples prior to therapy, divorcing couples, and dating couples (Christensen & Shenk, 1991; Walczynski, Schmidt, Christensen, & Sweeney, 1991).

To get a more categorical indication of how many couples fit the woman demand/man withdraw pattern and how many couples fit the man demand/woman withdraw pattern, we have classified couples simply on the basis of which of the two subscales is higher, considering both wives' and husbands' self-report. Across several investigations we find that approximately 60% of couples would be classified as woman demand/man withdraw, about 30% would be classified as man demand/woman withdraw, and about 10% are equal on these two variables. The focus of our observational research has been on the likelihood of man demand/woman withdraw interactions or the reverse in particular situations rather than in general or across the entire relationship. However, summing across the types of interactions that we have examined, we find a similar breakdown of couples as in the self-report data (Heavey et al., in press).

Supplementing our findings on a gender difference in demand/withdraw interaction is a substantial body of literature on gender differences in marital interaction. In one of the very first studies of marriage, Terman and his associates (Terman, Buttenweiser, Ferguson, Johnson, & Wilson, 1938) found differences between husbands and wives much like those we find in demand/withdraw interaction. A summary of their research (Gottman & Levenson, 1988) concluded that

> grievances of husbands centered on their wife's complaining, criticizing, and high levels of emotionality (e.g., criticizes me, too nervous or emotional, too quick tempered, feelings hurt too easily, nags me). On the other hand, wife's grievances concerned their husband's emotional withdrawal (e.g., does not talk things over, does not show affection). (p. 183)

About 50 years later Gottman and Levenson (1988) summarize gender differences in marital interaction research as follows: "The observational studies indicate that wives are more negative, more conflict engaging, more coercive, and use more emotional pressure than their husbands; husbands are more positive, reconciling, and pacifying than their wives" (p. 198).

Clearly these findings are consistent with the pattern of woman demand/man withdraw interaction. Taken together with our findings, we can safely conclude that there is a substantial gender linkage in how men and women interact during marital conflict. We now turn to an analysis of the basis of this gender linkage.

The Basis for Gender Differentiation in Demand/Withdraw Interaction

Why are women more likely to be demanders and men more likely to be withdrawers? To explore this question we need first to distinguish between the conflict of interest that a couple may have and the overt or open conflict that may result from this conflict of interest (Peterson,

1983). By *conflict of interest* we mean any difference in the needs, preferences, or desires of each member. By *open or overt conflict,* we refer to the interaction between members that attempts to resolve this difference. For example, in a particular couple, the wife, Mertle, may want a clean and tidy house and may want her husband, Homer, to participate equally in keeping the house clean and tidy. In contrast, Homer may feel quite comfortable with a messy house and have no desire to participate in the effort required to keep the house tidy. This difference between them defines a conflict of interest. Features about their individual history, their joint history, and their current circumstances may help explain the conflict of interest. For example, Mertle was raised in a very tidy home, she feels anxious when things are not in their place, and she would feel embarrassed if friends saw her in a messy environment. In contrast, Homer was raised in a fairly messy environment, he feels comfortable when things are out and about, and he would experience no embarrassment if friends visited him in a messy home. Both Homer and Mertle came to the relationship with egalitarian views about how husbands and wives should participate in household chores. Throughout their relationship they have tried to live by those views. Both Mertle and Homer are employed full time but because of Mertle's longer commute and the greater travel demands of her job, Homer actually has more time at home in which he could do household tasks. All these factors help us understand the nature of the conflict of interest between the two of them. But at its baldest level, a conflict of interest simply refers to their different preferences for household cleanliness and order.

In contrast to the conflict of interest, the overt conflict refers to the actual interaction around their different needs and preferences. In the present case, Mertle does much more housework than Homer, but often with an aloof air about her and often with some not so indirect comments about the effort she is putting out. Homer usually responds by ignoring her or lamely encouraging her not to do so much. Occasionally, Mertle blows up at Homer for his lack of equal participation in housework, to which Homer responds by attacking Mertle's "compulsiveness." Although this is their style of dealing with conflict, one can easily imagine a number of alternative ways in which Homer and Mertle could interact around this conflict of interest. For example, Mertle could nag Homer to do more housework, and he could reluctantly participate. They could attack each other for being "compulsive" and "sloppy," respectively. They could engage in detailed negotiation about who is responsible for doing what and when around the house. They could have very little verbal interaction, but instead Mertle could simply be cold to Homer after doing lots of housework whereas Homer might try to appease her subsequently by being extra nice.

With this distinction between conflict of interest and overt conflict in mind, we now consider a central conflict of interest in marriage that may lead to demand/withdraw interaction and the gender differentiation associated with it: a conflict of interest around closeness in the relationship. A number of theorists, as well as considerable empirical data, have identified closeness as an essential dimension of human relationships. Kelley and his colleagues (1983) define closeness in terms of frequent, diverse, and intense interdependence that exists over a substantial period of time. They suggest that closeness is an essential property or dimension of relationships. A number of clinical theorists have suggested that disagreements about the appropriate level of closeness in the relationship is at the heart of much marital distress (e.g., Jacobson & Margolin, 1979).

When couples enter a relationship it is unlikely that they have the same needs, desires, and preferences for closeness and independence in the relationship. Even if their desires for closeness are compatible in the early stages in their relationship, such that both partners want to spend all their free time together, these desires may diverge in later stages of their relationship. When these desires do diverge, the person wanting more closeness may desire more time together, more expression of love and affection, and more revelation of personal feelings. In contrast, the person wanting greater independence may desire more time for personal and independent activities, more privacy in what they share with each other, and more time with friends.

The participants in conflicts of interest over closeness and independence are not equal in their power to achieve what they want. Those wanting greater independence have the power to achieve that objective whether their partners cooperate or not. They may simply spend time alone or with friends, may refuse to share personal information, and may otherwise create boundaries that preserve their independence. These seekers of independence may have to suffer negative reactions from their partners but they can, nonetheless, achieve greater independence on their own. In contrast, those who seek greater closeness can only achieve their desires with the cooperation of their partners. One cannot have a close relationship alone. The partner's cooperation is essential.

Because of this difference in their goals and in their ability to achieve these goals unilaterally, those seeking independence and those seeking greater closeness will employ different interaction strategies to resolve these differences. Being dependent on the partner for goal attainment, those seeking greater closeness may be inclined toward demanding behaviors. They will try to discuss the problems with their partner, they will criticize their partner for not giving them what they want, and they will make demands for greater closeness. In fact, the very demanding behaviors they use to achieve greater closeness provide them some measure of closeness. If their partners respond in any way to their demanding attempts, they have some significant, albeit negative, interaction with their partners. In contrast, those seeking greater independence may engage in withdrawing behaviors. The withdrawal itself may provide them some measure of independence, and allows time and space to pursue private thoughts and activities. Thus the conflict of interest over independence and closeness sets the stage for an open conflict characterized by demand/withdraw interaction.

In order to examine these ideas empirically, we developed a measure to assess conflicts of interest around closeness and independence. This instrument, the Relationship Issues Questionnaire (Christensen & Sullaway, 1984b), describes a feature of this conflict of interest and then asks couples several questions about it. The one consistent item in several versions of this scale is printed below:

> Often one member (A) of a couple wants a closer relationship while the other member (B) wants more independence. For example, A may want more attention, more time together, more joint activities, more sharing of feelings, and more expressions of affection and closeness; B may want more time for independent activities, more time alone, and more personal privacy.

Following this item, couples are asked to rate the extent to which (a) this difference characterizes their relationship, (b) the man wants a closer relationship versus more independence and (c) the woman wants a closer relationship versus more independence. Items similar to the one above but that assess issues such as contact with friends and desired privacy and use the same kind of response format have also been included in our measure of conflicts of interest about closeness and independence. We generated two subscales from this measure: (a) a subscale based on the first answer to the items, which assesses the degree to which the conflict of interest is present in the relationship, and (b) a subscale based on the last two answers to the items, which assess the particular preferences that each partner has. The Relationship Issues Questionnaire also contained items assessing satisfaction with the power distribution in the relationship, but these are not relevant for our discussion here.

We wanted the Relationship Issues Questionnaire to assess actual conflicts of interest in the relationship and not merely perceptions of these conflicts. Therefore, we needed to have spouses independently agree on the conflict of interest as well as their roles in it. Across several studies, we have obtained correlations between spouses of $r = .47$ to $r = .54$ for the extent of the conflict and correlations of $r = .39$ to $r = .58$ for the different preferences. We have obtained interitem alphas of .79 to .86 for the extent of the conflict and alphas of .51 to .63 for partners' different preferences.

We have not been entirely satisfied with this measure. Married couples experience some confusion with the use of terms A and B and particularly with questions 2 and 3. For example, sometimes spouses will only mark the questions pertaining to them (e.g., husband wants) but not the questions pertaining to their partner (e.g., wife wants). Also, we were concerned that questions like the ones illustrated asked the couples to consider too much information at one time. Recently, we developed a new questionnaire, the *Closeness and Independence Questionnaire* (Heavey & Christensen, 1991), that solves some of these problems. This questionnaire breaks down several components of this conflict of interest around closeness and independence and presents these components in six easy to understand items (see Table 6.3 for several sample items).

Our initial data on this measure have been encouraging (e.g., an alpha of .79, Heavey, 1991). The data we report on below, however, is from our original Relationship Issues Questionnaire.

Across three studies we have found that a conflict of interest over closeness is associated with greater demand/withdraw interaction. In our early study with 142 couples (Christensen, 1987), we found that conflict over closeness was correlated $r = .48$ with total demand/withdraw interaction. In our study of nondistressed, clinic, and divorcing couples (Christensen & Shenk, 1991), we found correlations of $r = .45$ and $r = .36$ between conflict over closeness and woman demand/ man withdraw interaction for women's data and men's data respectively but only correlations of $r = .22$ and $r = .32$ for the comparable

Table 6.3
Closeness and Independence Questionnaire—Sample Items

Directions: Some couples want a lot of closeness and intimacy in their relationship whereas others want a lot of independence and autonomy. Often couples want both more closeness and more independence but find themselves having to choose between the two because of limited time. The following questions ask you to indicate whether, on the whole, you would like more independence *or* more closeness in your most recent or present relationship.

1. Given the limited amount of free time you have, would you prefer to spend more time with your partner or more time alone or with your friends?

More Time With Partner		No Change		More Time Alone or With Friends		
1	2	3	4	5	6	7

2. Would you like to have more sharing of feelings with your partner or more respect for privacy in your relationship?

More Sharing of Feelings		No Change		More Respect for Privacy		
1	2	3	4	5	6	7

3. On the whole, would you like more independence or more closeness in your relationship?

More Independence		No Change		More Closeness		
1	2	3	4	5	6	7

correlations for men demand/women withdraw interaction. In a recent study of dating couples (Walczynski et al., 1991), we found correlations of $r = .40$ between conflict over closeness and total demand/withdraw interaction for both men's and women's data.

In two of these investigations we also assessed (a) gender differences in desire for closeness versus independence and (b) the relationship between roles in the conflict of interest and roles in the demand/ withdraw interaction. To assess the relationship between the two roles, we examined whether the person who wanted greater closeness was also likely to be the demander and the person who wanted more independence was likely to be the withdrawer. In our early study (Christensen, 1987) we found that women were significantly more likely to want greater closeness and intimacy than men. We also found a significant correlation between roles in the conflict of interest and roles in demand/withdraw interaction of $r = .39$ in the direction predicted. However, in our dating study (Walczynski et al., 1991) we found only a marginally significant tendency for women to want greater closeness and no significant relationship between these two sets of roles. Thus across several studies we have found a consistent, positive association between a conflict of interest about closeness and demand/withdraw interaction. Furthermore, we have found evidence in a married and living-together sample, but not in a dating sample, that the person who wants greater closeness (usually the woman) will be the demander whereas the person who wants greater independence (usually the man) will be the withdrawer.

Other Conflicts of Interest

Other conflicts of interest besides the conflict over closeness and independence may generate a demand/withdraw interaction sequence. In fact, in our thinking, any conflict in which one partner's goals can only be achieved by the active cooperation of the other, whereas the other's goals can be achieved unilaterally, seems likely to lead to demand/withdraw interaction. Stated more broadly, reformers in a relationship, who are dissatisfied with the status quo and want change, would be more likely to be demanders, whereas conservatives in a relationship, who are largely satisfied with the status quo, would be more likely to be withdrawers.

Let us consider two examples: a wife who wants greater participation in housework by her husband and a husband who wants more sexual contact with his wife. These examples are admittedly stereotypical, but have some basis in empirical data in that wives want more change than husbands in housework while husbands want more change than wives in sexual activity (Margolin, Talovic, & Weinstein, 1983). In the first case, the wife who wants more participation in housework by her husband can only achieve her goals by his active participation. She is likely, therefore, to want to discuss the problem, to be critical of his past efforts at housework, and to make various demands for change. In contrast, the husband can achieve his goals of not doing more housework unilaterally (i.e., by doing nothing). He is likely not to want to discuss the problem, to be defensive about his past efforts at housework, and to want to withdraw from any discussion that gets started. A discussion will only create an argument or more housework for him. Similarly, the husband who wants more sexual activity with his wife can only achieve his goal through her active participation. He is more likely to want to talk about the problem, to criticize her past sexual behavior or lack of it, and to make various demands for change. In contrast, the wife can achieve her goal of no further sexual activity unilaterally (i.e., by doing nothing). Therefore, she is likely not to want to talk about the problem, to defend her sexual behavior, and to withdraw from discussions of the matter. A discussion will only lead to an argument or more sexual activity.

We devised a simple test of these hypotheses about conflict of interests and demand/withdraw interaction. We compared two kinds of conflicts, one in which the couple discussed an area in which the wife wanted change, and one in which the couple discussed an area in which the husband wanted change. We asked couples to fill out the Communication Patterns Questionnaire about their typical interaction around these two topics, and we had observers rate their interaction when they discussed these two particular topics in the laboratory. We expected that there would be no overall effect of gender but rather demand/withdraw interaction would shift depending upon who was invested in change. However, if there was a genuine gender linkage to demand/withdraw interaction that went beyond the particular conflicts of interest leading to the interaction, then we would find the typical women demand/men withdraw interaction consistent across the two conflicts.

Study One

This study was done in the context of a summer camp program for boys aged 7 to 12 (Christensen & Heavey, 1990). Husbands and wives in 31 couples completed a child-rearing changes questionnaire in which they indicated the types of changes they would like in the way their partner handled their son. They rated the amount of change they each wanted in five areas: being more positive with son, being more strict or consistent with son, being more involved with son, assuming more responsibility for disciplining son, and being more supportive of their own efforts with son. In each couple, a wife's issue was selected as that topic in which she wanted most change in her husband, whereas a husband's issue was selected as that topic in which he wanted most change in his wife. In counterbalanced order, husbands and wives discussed each of these issues separately for 6 minutes while being videotaped. Before each discussion, husbands and wives independently completed a short form of the Communications Patterns Questionnaire in which they rated their conversation when they discussed these two issues during their day-to-day life. Trained observers later rated demand/withdraw interaction for all videotaped discussions of husbands' and wives' issues. Thus, for each couple, we obtained self-report measures of demand/withdraw interaction during typical discussions of these two issues and observer ratings of their laboratory discussions of these two issues.

Figures 6.1 and 6.2 present the results of the data on self-report and observational measures respectively. In both cases there was a main effect of gender such that woman demand/man withdraw interaction was greater than man demand/woman withdraw interaction. This main effect was modified dramatically, however, by a powerful interaction between issue and gender. On the woman's issue, women were more likely to be demanding and men were more likely to be withdrawing; but on the man's issue, there were no differences between men and women in their demand/withdraw interaction. The nature of the discussion did dramatically alter the nature of the interaction by producing a major gender asymmetry during discussion of women's issues but no asymmetry during discussion of men's issues.

The methodology of this study may have contributed to the obtained pattern of results. Husbands and wives were only allowed to discuss changes that they wanted in each other's child-rearing practices. Since child rearing has traditionally been more a woman's than a man's responsibility, perhaps women were more invested in these discussions and this greater investment may have led to a greater gender asymmetry in men's and women's behavior. In our analysis of the results of the child-rearing changes questionnaire data, we did find that women overall wanted more change in child-rearing practices than men wanted. Furthermore, women and men tended to want different changes in each other's child-rearing behavior. For example, women wanted men to be more positive in their approach with their sons, whereas men

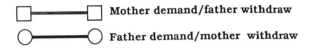

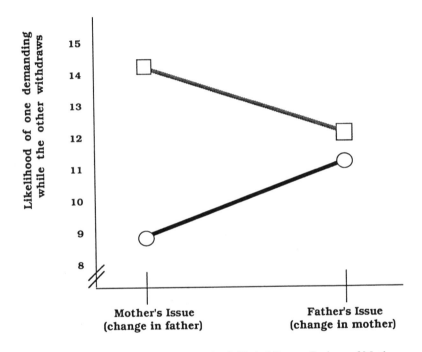

Figure 6.1. Mean of Mother's and Father's Verbal Report Ratings of Mother Demand/Father Withdraw Interaction and Father Demand/Mother Withdraw Interaction as a Function of Mother's and Father's Issues

wanted women to use stricter and more consistent discipline in their approach with their sons. Because of this pattern of results, we repeated our analysis using amount of change desired on the issue as a covariate. This new analysis did not change our overall pattern of

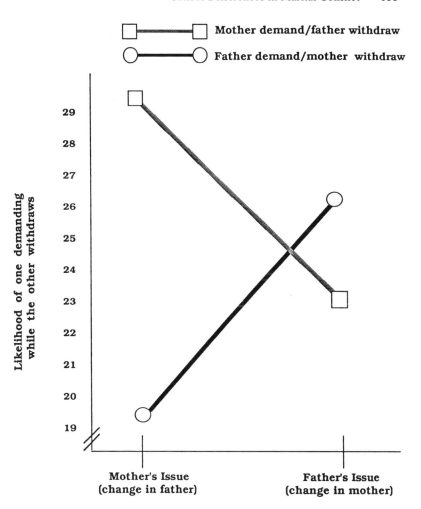

Figure 6.2. Mean Observer Ratings of Mother Demand/Father Withdraw Interaction and Father Demand/Mother Withdraw Interaction as a Function of Mother's and Father's Issue

results. Nevertheless, we could not rule out the possibility that if men and women were able to discuss any issue they wanted and if they were equally invested in those issues, the pattern of results might be quite different.

Study Two

A second study (Heavey et al., 1993) was designed to overcome the problems of the first. We had 29 couples, who each had at least one preschool child, participate in two discussions, one on a wife's issue and one on a husband's issue. Our selection of these issues, however, was quite different than in the first study. We had couples rate the amount of change they wanted on 20 common areas of change in marriage (e.g., more affection, more time together, more time spent with family). Based on these data, the experimenters selected a change that the wife wanted in her husband (wife's issue) and a change that the husband wanted in his wife (husband's issue). The selection was based on three criteria: (a) both husband and wife were willing to discuss both issues, (b) these issues were ones in which both husband and wife had high ratings of desired change or ideally their highest rating of desired change on their respective issues, and (c) both husband and wife had an equivalent rating of change on their respective issues. Because of this last restriction, sometimes we selected an issue that was not the highest one for one spouse in order to equalize it with the highest one for the partner. In most other respects the two studies were identical. Spouses completed a short form of the Communications Patterns Questionnaire about their interaction on these issues in their natural environment prior to the laboratory discussion. In counterbalanced order, they had two videotaped laboratory discussions on these two issues of 7 minutes each. In contrast to the first study, following each discussion we asked partners to fill out a questionnaire about their reactions during and immediately after the discussion.

Despite these methodological changes, the results from the second study were virtually identical to those from the first. On both self-report and observational data we found gender differences on women's issues but no gender differences on men's issues. Women were more likely to be demanding and men withdrawing when they discussed a change in men desired by women but they showed no differences in demand/withdraw interaction when they discussed a change in women desired by men. Our postdiscussion questionnaire revealed an intriguing finding that we thought might explain our pattern of results. There was evidence that both men and women were more anxious during the discussion of men's issues than they were during the discussion of women's issues. If anxiety served to moderate women's demandingness and men's withdrawingness, it could account for the lack of asymmetry in men's and women's behavior during the discussion of men's issues.

Study Three

In our third study (Heavey, 1991) we tried to replicate the findings of greater anxiety during discussion of men's issues and explore further husband's and wife's subjective experiences surrounding these discussions. We assessed their subjective reactions such as anger and anxiety prior to each of the discussions as well as after those discussions. In this study we also tried to broaden or generalize the validity of our findings. First, we conducted the study on a sample of Canadian married and living-together couples, most of whom had no children. Second, we tried to broaden the discussions beyond a narrow focus on desired changes. We asked couples to rate their dissatisfaction with a number of content areas such as finances and physical affection. There was no mention of specific changes in this list. We selected as the husband's issue the content area with which he experienced most dissatisfaction and selected as the wife's issue the content area with which she experienced most dissatisfaction. There was no attempt to balance the dissatisfaction experienced by husband and wife, but rather an attempt to discuss the area with which each experienced the most dissatisfaction (assuming of course that they were both willing to discuss these issues on videotape). Once the issues had been selected, both partners were asked on the questionnaire to answer several open-ended questions about each of the issues, such as why they thought the area was a problem and the specific changes they wanted in that area. Thus both partners wrote down the changes they might desire on each of the two issues. When the experimenter gave the instructions to begin the discussion, he or she mentioned only the content area, not the particular changes that each one might want. Third, the assessment measures did not focus on demand/withdraw interaction per se. The Communication Patterns Questionnaire was not used at all in this study. The observational coding system focused on two dimensions, engagement and constructiveness.

Despite these substantial changes in the methodology of this third study, the results were remarkably consistent with those of the previous two. When discussing the husband's issue, husband and wife were rated as equally engaged, whereas when discussing the wife's issue, the wife was much more engaged than the husband. Again, we found the striking asymmetry when discussing the wife's issue but no asymmetry when discussing the husband's issue. In contrast to our measures of engagement, the measure of constructiveness showed that the two interactions were equally constructive or destructive. Furthermore, none of the self-report measures, whether taken before or after the interaction, showed any differences in the way men and women anticipated or experienced these interactions. We did not replicate the earlier finding of greater anxiety when discussing men's issues.

Taken together, these three studies provide remarkable consistency in showing that men and women behave differently when discussing men's issues then they do when discussing women's issues. Women are more likely to be demanding and men withdrawing when they discuss women's issues, but they demonstrate no such asymmetry when discussing men's issues. We have ruled out various methodological confounds that might explain these results. Our efforts to find the causal determinant of these results in the subjective experiences of the participants, however, has not been successful. Thus our explanations for our findings at this point can only be speculative.

Conclusions

Our research has established several facts about the demand/withdraw interaction pattern. First, we have shown that we can measure the pattern reliably with both self-report and observational instruments. Second, we have shown that the pattern is strongly related to marital dissatisfaction. We have some evidence that the pattern may also be predictive of long-term dissatisfaction in marriage with the reversal of the typical pattern being predictive of positive changes in marital satisfaction. These longitudinal findings must be replicated, however, before we can feel confident about them. Third, we have shown a strong gender linkage to the pattern with women more likely to be in the demanding role and men more likely to be in the withdrawing role. Fourth, we have shown that the nature of the conflict of interest within a couple determines to some extent their gender role asymmetry. The person in the relationship who wants changes that can only be satisfied through the cooperation of the other will often take on the demanding role in discussion about those changes, whereas the partner who seeks no change or changes that can be achieved unilaterally will often take on the withdrawing role.

This information can help us explain the general finding that women are more likely to be demanding and men are more likely to be withdrawing. We know that women in general want more changes in marriage than men (Margolin et al., 1983). Three areas where women commonly want more changes are the areas of closeness, housework, and child care. Women have a greater desire for affiliation than men (Edwards, 1959) and, as reviewed above, have a stronger desire for closeness in marriage than men. Similarly, women often want more participation in housework and child care from their husbands. This desire is not surprising in that data consistently show that women take the burden of housework and child care even when both husband and wife are employed full time outside the home (Biernat & Wortman, 1991). Because the changes women want in closeness, housework, and child care (and perhaps other areas as well) can only be achieved through the cooperation of their husbands, they are likely to take on the demanding role. They are likely to want to discuss the problem, criticize their husbands' past efforts, and push for change. If men do not want greater closeness or a different allocation of housework and child-care responsibilities, they are likely to take on the withdrawing role. They are likely to avoid discussion, defend their behavior, and withdraw from discussion. Talk will only create an argument or unwanted change.

Our research can therefore explain in general why women are more demanding and men more withdrawing. However, we cannot explain the more particular finding that when we compare men's and women's issues to ensure that they both have a chance to talk about a change that can only be achieved through the other's cooperation, we find a gender asymmetry on the women's issues but no gender asymmetry on the men's issues. In exploring the gender difference that women are more likely to be demanding and men are more likely to be withdrawing, we found another, potentially more interesting, gender difference. The asymmetry between one demanding and the other withdrawing is apparent during discussions of women's issues but not men's issues. How can we explain this gender difference?

If we were inclined to blame either the men or the women, we might argue on the one hand that women are more likely to listen to men's complaints (i.e., less likely to withdraw) than men are to listen to women's complaints. On the other hand, we could argue that men present their complaints more positively (i.e., in a less demanding fashion) than women do. The evidence, however, supports neither of these explanations. There is change in both male and female behavior when moving from women's issues to men's issues. Women indeed are more engaged in and less withdrawing on men's issues than men are on women's issue, but men are indeed less demanding on their issues than women are on their issues. Thus the data are more consistent with a dyadic interpretation, that demand and withdraw feed upon each other so that when one partner is more withdrawing, the other is more demanding and when one partner is more demanding, the other is more withdrawing.

An alternate explanation might look at the history of conflict in the couple. Let us assume that couples have been more successful in resolving men's issues and accommodating to the man's needs than they have been at resolving women's issues and accommodating to the woman's needs. Three lines of evidence would support this assumption. First, men tend to have greater resources in marital relationships, and thus may be better able to get the relationship structured in the way they want. For example, husbands are typically older, more educated, and earn more money than their wives. Second, both husbands and wives may show greater deference to men's needs than to women's needs because of a shared cultural bias toward men. Third, the data indicate that women, in fact, want more changes in marriage than men (Margolin et al., 1983), perhaps resulting from their greater failure in achieving resolution of their needs in marriage. If, for these and other reasons, couples have had greater success in accommodating men's needs, we would expect the interaction around those issues to be less conflictual and less polarized. In contrast, if couples have had greater failure in resolving women's issues than in resolving men's, we would expect the interaction around women's issues to be more conflictual and polarized.

Another explanation that focuses on the history of the couple looks at the consequences of differential experience with the two issues. If women want more changes in marriage then couples are more likely to have discussions around changes that she wants than around changes that he wants. The greater frequency of discussion around these issues may, without regard to the outcome of those discussions, lead to greater polarization in the stands that men and women take. Because discussions about husbands' issues are comparatively less frequent, husbands and wives may be less polarized during their discussion of those issues.

Why would frequency by itself lead to a greater polarization? If we assume that these discussions are not easy and are often not completely successful because they revolve around genuine conflicts of interest within the couple, it seems likely that over time some rigidity in positions might develop. The one wanting change might become more and more demanding, and the one wanting the status quo might become more and more withdrawing. After many episodes of these interactions, couples may habitually take on those positions whenever the topic of the wife wanting a change comes up.

Whatever the explanations for these findings, they point to an important methodological problem. If researchers only ask couples to talk about one issue, which most observational research does, it is likely to focus on women's issues more often than on men's issues. Simply because women desire more changes in marriage than men, they are more likely to select the issue or put forward the issue for discussion. Therefore, what researchers are liable to see in that data is a discussion over a conflict of interest defined by women. They are not likely to see the very different interaction that comes about when a conflict is over an issue generated by men. We think that future research should be careful to include discussion of issues chosen by both men and women in order not to have a bias generated by who chose the issue.

A clinical example, taken from Deborah Tannen's book *That's Not What I Meant* (1986), well describes demand/withdraw interaction in the context of a conflict of interest over closeness: "Maxwell wants to be left alone and Samantha wants attention. So she gives him attention and he leaves her alone" (p. 26).

Following the golden rule, that is, doing unto others what you would have them do unto you, does not always work in marriage. Sometimes it is more desirable to follow what we will call the platinum rule: Do unto your spouse what your spouse would have done unto him or her.

Note

1. Throughout the paper we use the term *we* to refer not only to the present authors but to other current and former graduate students of Christensen, such as Christopher Layne, James Shenk, Megan Sullaway, and Pamela Walczynski. They are acknowledged through citations to specific studies.

References

Biernat, M., & Wortman, C. B. (1991). Sharing of home responsibilities between professionally employed women and their husbands. *Journal of Personality and Social
Psychology, 60,* 844-860.

Christensen, A. (1987). Detection of conflict patterns in couples. In K. Hahlweg & M. J.
Goldstein (Eds.), *Understanding major mental disorders: The contribution of family
interaction research* (pp. 250-265). New York: Family Process Press.

Christensen, A. (1988). Dysfunctional interaction patterns in couples. In P. Noller &
M. A. Fitzpatrick (Eds.), *Perspectives on marital interaction* (pp. 31-52). Philadelphia: Multilingual Matters.

Christensen, A., & Heavey, C. L. (1990). Gender and social structure in the demand/with-
draw pattern of marital interaction. *Journal of Personality and Social Psychology, 59,*
73-81.

Christensen, A., & King, C. E. (1982). Telephone survey of daily marital behavior.
Behavioral Assessment, 4, 327-338.

Christensen, A., & Shenk, J. L. (1991). Communication, conflict, and psychological
distance in nondistressed, clinic, and divorcing couples. *Journal of Consulting and
Clinical Psychology, 59,* 458-463.

Christensen, A., & Sullaway, M. (1984a). *Communication patterns questionnaire.* Unpublished questionnaire, University of California, Los Angeles.

Christensen, A., & Sullaway, M. (1984b). *Relationship issues questionnaire.* Unpublished
questionnaire, University of California, Los Angeles.

Christensen, A., Sullaway, M., & King, C. E. (1982, November). *Dysfunctional interaction patterns and marital happiness.* Los Angeles: Association for Advancement of
Behavior Therapy.

Edwards, A. L. (1959). *Edwards personal preference schedule revised manual.* New York:
Psychological Corporation.

Fogarty, T. F. (1976). Marital crisis. In P. J. Guerin (Ed.), *Family therapy: Theory and
practice.* New York: Gardner Press.

Gottman, J. M., & Krokoff, L. J. (1989). Marital interaction and satisfaction: A longitudinal view. *Journal of Consulting and Clinical Psychology, 57,* 47-52.

Gottman, J. M., & Levenson, R. W. (1986). Assessing the role of emotion in marriage.
Behavioral Assessment, 8, 31-48.

Gottman, J. M., & Levenson, R. W. (1988). The social psychophysiology of marriage. In
P. Noller & M. Fitzpatrick (Eds.), *Perspectives on marital interaction* (pp. 182-200).
Philadelphia: Multilingual Matters.

Heavey, C. L. (1991). *Causes and consequences of destructive conflicts in romantic
relationships: Cognitive, affective, and behavioral predictors of course and outcome.*
Unpublished doctoral dissertation, University of California, Los Angeles.

Heavey, C. L., & Christensen, A. (1991). *Closeness and Independence Questionnaire.*
Unpublished questionnaire, University of California, Los Angeles.

Heavey, C. L., Layne, C., & Christensen, A. (1993). Gender and conflict structure in
marital interaction: A replication and extension. *Journal of Consulting and Clinical
Psychology, 61.*

Jacobson, N. S., & Margolin, G. (1979). *Marital therapy: Strategies based on social
learning and behavior exchange principles.* New York: Brunner/Mazel.

Kelley, H. H., Berscheid, E., Christensen, A., Harvey, J. H., Huston, T. L., Levinger, G., McClintock, E., Peplau, L. A., & Peterson, D. R. (1983). *Close relationships* (pp. 20-67). New York: Freeman.

Margolin, G., Talovic, S., & Weinstein, C. D. (1983). Areas of change questionnaire: A practical approach to marital assessment. *Journal of Consulting and Clinical Psychology, 51,* 920-931.

Napier, A. Y. (1978). The rejection-intrusion pattern: A central family dynamic. *Journal of Marriage and Family Counseling, 4,* 5-12.

Peterson, D. R. (1983). Conflict. In H. H. Kelley, E. Berscheid, A. Christensen, J. H. Harvey, T. L. Huston, G. Levinger, E. McClintock, L. A. Peplau, & D. R. Peterson (Eds.), *Close relationships* (pp. 360-396). New York: Freeman.

Spanier, G. B. (1976). Measuring dyadic adjustment: New scales for assessing the quality of marriage and similar dyads. *Journal of Marriage and the Family, 38,* 15-28.

Sullaway, M., & Christensen, A. (1983). Assessment of dysfunctional interaction patterns in couples. *Journal of Marriage and the Family, 45,* 653-660.

Tannen, D. (1986). *That's not what I meant.* New York: Ballantine.

Terman, L. M., Buttenweiser, P., Ferguson, L. W., Johnson, W. B., & Wilson, D. P. (1938). *Psychological factors in marital happiness.* New York: McGraw-Hill.

Walczynski, P. T., Schmidt, G. W., Christensen, A., & Sweeney, L. (1991, August). *Demand/withdraw interaction in dating couples.* San Francisco: American Psychological Association.

Watzlawick, P., Beavin, J. H., & Jackson, D. D. (1967). *Pragmatics of human communication.* New York: Norton.

Wile, D. B. (1981). *Couples therapy: A non-traditional approach.* New York: John Wiley.

7

Women and Men at Home and at Work: Realities and Illusions

FAYE J. CROSBY
KAREN L. JASKAR

few years ago a psychologist, who was also a married working mother, attended a small intensive weekend meeting. The other participants were mostly male and none of the other females at the meeting had young children. During the period of time set aside on Saturday afternoon for exercise and relaxation, virtually everyone headed for the track, the pool, or the tennis court. The woman—feeling somewhat bedraggled—confessed that she was going to spend her free hour taking a nap. Upon hearing the confession, a friend took the woman aside and gave her a piece of career advice: "My dear, at a meeting like this, you must never admit that you need sleep. So, if anyone asks, don't say that you are going to take a nap; tell them you are going to take a power nap!"

Ever since, we have been taking power naps and feeling more powerful.

Words matter. Arranged into meaningful sequences, they become the ideas by which we interpret our own experiences. How we conceptualize social arrangements affects the ways we conduct ourselves and the ways we feel about ourselves and others. When it comes to images, the person who takes power naps is not the same as one who, old-fashioned, grabs 40 winks. And as images mold self-images, and self-images shape phenomenology, the woman with her power naps may come to experience life differently than before.

Given the importance of conceptualizations, this chapter looks equally at "the facts" about how contemporary women and men balance home and work and at the ways that researchers have interpreted the facts and even framed the search for them. We review findings of numerous studies, some of which have been reviewed before (Crosby, 1991) and some of which are new. We distinguish between conclusions that only appear to be true, given the prevalent preconceptions and assumptions about women and men, and conclusions that are actually true.

This chapter falls into three uneven segments. The first segment reviews the basics and echoes the conclusions of others (e.g., Gilbert, 1985), that women have experienced role expansion. The next section critically examines the notion that the combination of work and home roles causes problems for women. The notion appears to flow logically from what we know about role expansion; but, in fact, it is not supported by the empirical evidence. The final section discusses the possibly unsurprising conclusion that the current emphasis on the harried role-juggler is ideologically motivated, coming from the residue of misogyny in our culture and the American emphasis on individualism. The chapter ends on a note of advocacy.

Current Realities:
Reviewing the Basics

Work is not a recent invention, and women's participation in the world of work is not new either. What is new is women's participation in the paid labor market away from the family domicile. Prior to the industrial revolution in America, women contributed to the agrarian economy as did men and, to the extent they were able, children. During the industrial revolution, the home-based economy that involved all family members in a productive capacity shifted to a factory-based economy, in which productive labor was moved away from the home and became the almost exclusive domain of men. Significant changes in the status of women's roles ensued. Women's work was removed from being a direct economic contribution to the family and shifted instead to center on management of the household and child care (Fowlkes, 1987).

Women Have Entered the Paid Labor Market

The most sweeping changes made in the gender composition of the workplace occurred in the decades following World War II. The most significant of these changes has been the emergence of women into all aspects of the paid labor force. Following the end of World War II, in 1948, 38.5% of all women aged 16 to 54 participated in the work force. By 1987 this number had risen to 68.6% (Jacobs, Shipp, & Brown, 1989). These dramatic increases were true for women across racial lines. In 1954, 37% of white women and 53.4% of minority women were employed. As of 1987 these figures had swelled to 71.8% and 72.1%, respectively. This rise in the presence of women in the labor force is projected to continue into the next century. It is believed that by the year 2000, 80.8% of the women aged 25 to 54 will have entered the work force (Shank, 1988).

Many of the women in the paid labor force also fulfill family responsibilities. Crosby (1991) has termed women who carry both job and family roles "jugglers," and statistics reflect sweeping changes in the number of American women who are role-jugglers. In 1984, 68.8% of married women between 25 and 54 were in the paid labor force. Women with children were also an important part of this phenomenon. In 1967, one fourth of all mothers with children 3 years or younger worked outside the home. By 1987 this number had doubled. Also by 1987, 66.7% of all women aged 25 to 54 with a child 18 years or younger were employed (Shank, 1988). In 1920 only 9% of all households had dual-earner couples. By 1988, the figure had risen to 41% (Hayge, 1990).

The Division of Home Labor

Has women's entry into the paid labor market been matched by men's entry into domestic labor? The answer has, unfortunately, been negative: Women have moved into the work force, but their husbands have not reacted by becoming equally active in the home. Continued gender imbalances in domestic responsibilities (coupled, as we shall see, with continued difficulties at work) have left American women at a professional and personal disadvantage.

Research on the Division of Home Labor. Although the 1960s and 1970s were decades of great change for women in our culture as they entered the work force in large numbers, dramatic change was not equally evident in the sex roles practiced in the home. Such is the conclusion of a number of published reviews (e.g., Crosby, 1991; Steil, in press).

One type of study that has informed this conclusion is the time diary, which documents how North Americans spend their day. Between 1965 and 1975 husbands in this country increased their time spent on housework from an average of 81.4 minutes per day to an average of 82.5 minutes per day (Coverman & Sheley, 1986). Thus, as many women added a job outside the home to their hours spent working inside the home, their husbands reacted by increasing their time spent on housework by 1.1 minute a day. Similar findings emerged when taking the average estimates of the major time-share studies of the 1960s and 1970s. Hochschild and Machung (1989) discovered that women worked approximately 15 hours more per week than did men. Over the period of a year, these added 15 hours of work translate into an extra 3 months of 8-hours-a-day labor.

It is theoretically possible that although most American husbands have not increased their household labor over the years, husbands of employed wives have. Not so. Research specifically examining men in dual-paycheck couples found inequity in the division of home labor similar to those found in all American families. In 1976, 353 husbands were selected to keep diaries of how they spent their time. Those men married to employed women devoted 4 minutes more per day to household tasks than did men married to housewives (Berk, 1985). In the following year, these figures were validated by similar measurements recorded in the national Quality of Employment Survey (Pleck, 1985). Again in 1983, it was reported that fathers in dual-career families were likely to spend 10 minutes more per day on child care than other fathers if they were white, and 16 minutes more per day if they were black (Beckett & Smith, 1981).

The same inequality in home labor was found in dual-career couples in a reanalysis by Roubin Douhitt (1989) of a 1981 time sample of Canadian families. Among families with children 5 years or younger,

the figures indicate a consistent gender imbalance in housework participation between women and men in dual-career marriages. The employed wives in the study worked 32.6 hours a week on household tasks
and child care, whereas their husbands spent only 12.6 hours per week.

Other studies focusing on the differences in child-care practices
between men and women in dual-career families have found similar
results. One investigation found that working mothers of infants less
than 1 year old devoted a greater amount of time than fathers to almost
every child-care task except watching TV (Belsky & Volling, 1987).
This discrepancy between mothers and fathers in participation with
child care was found to be even more extreme in a survey of parents of
second graders in Texas (Nyquist, Slivken, Spence, & Helmreich,
1985). There, questionnaires distributed to parents revealed that women
performed almost all child-care chores and men almost none. A study
conducted in Ohio with professional men and women also noted a
gender imbalance in participation in child care within dual-career
families (Kilty & Richardson, 1985). Of the 457 respondents, 218 were
female, and 70% were married, with an average of 1.68 children.
Participants were asked to estimate the number of hours each week they
devoted to child care. Although the presence of a dependent child in a
household was the strongest predictor of time spent on child care by a
man or a woman, there was also a strong relationship between gender
and hours devoted to child care. Women in dual-career families spent
an average of 28 hours per week caring for children, but men in
dual-career families spent an average of 9 hours per week caring for
their children.

What accounts for the glacial rate of change in gender arrangements
at home? One reason that change has been slow is that people's behaviors are influenced by their expectations and assumptions, and most
people have assumptions about behaviors. Expectations about one's
own situation are often based on comparisons to other people of the
same gender (Crosby, 1982). Moreover, comparisons are often made to
parents. To understand her own situation, a woman may compare
herself to her mother; and to understand his own situation, a man may
compare himself to his father. The employed women studied during the
1970s and 1980s may have been using their mother's more traditional
role of housewife to evaluate their own success as a wife and mother.
So too may the men in dual-career marriages, interviewed during the
1970s and 1980s, have used their fathers as a basis for comparing their
involvement in the home, and thus they may have had just cause to

congratulate themselves on how much they were helping around the house.

The importance of people's comparisons to their families of origin has been beautifully articulated by Lisa Silberstein (1992). In the mid-1980s Silberstein conducted a qualitative study of 20 dual-career couples in the New York and New Haven area. Through in-depth interviews conducted separately with each spouse, Silberstein noted that although the couples were attempting to establish a marriage pattern significantly different from that of their parents, they continued to use their parents' traditional relationship as the basis for evaluating their own success or failure as a spouse, parent, and worker. As one man in the survey commented:

> My father had very little to do with household chores or childrearing. Jane and I aren't quite equal, but we approach it. This change has been all for the better—it's a sense of equality in home and work. It's one of the most profound changes that has occurred in my lifetime. (p. 21)

Men were not the only ones to evaluate their involvement in the home in comparison to their fathers; the women also compared their fathers' presence in the home with their husbands' participation. A woman in the survey described her feelings on the subject:

> I remember very little of my dad during my childhood. Sure, the big events—family trips, special occasions—but not the day-to-day stuff. Did he even read me a story at bedtime? I don't know. Our children will have a very different experience of Calvin being there for them, and that's really important. (p. 22)

The danger in a couple using comparisons to their parents as the method of evaluating the appropriateness of their own division of domestic labor, according to Silberstein, is that it almost inevitably reinforces patterns of inequality in the home. When people used only their parents as the yardstick against which to measure their participation in the home, it created a false sense of change as couples perceived that they were closer to achieving equality in household labor than they actually were.

As long as *either* partner in a marriage feels that the current arrangements are suitable, change is difficult. This point has been more forcefully made by sociologists (e.g., Epstein, 1987; Hochschild, 1989;

Thoits, 1987) than by psychologists. Writing of gender roles in and outside the home, Thoits (1987) has noted:

> It takes a minimum of two to make a role. Roles are relationships between people—patterned (normative) exchanges of behavior. Furthermore, for role relationships to proceed smoothly, we must . . . be able to anticipate accurately and to respond in advance to another's expectations. (p. 16)

Thoits goes on to note that societies differ in how much role innovation they encourage (or tolerate), and that societal realities both reflect and reinforce some modes of behavior in preference to others. The bargaining that takes place between wife and husband in any one household, Thoits (1987) reminds us, does not occur in isolation:

> In a static society, congruent expectations may occur because of widespread and unchanging understandings about the nature of reality. In fluid societies, shared meanings can also result from implicit or explicit negotiation between two people—that is, from interpersonal bargaining. Even in very fluid societies, however, broad structural arrangements and the degree of social consensus regarding the content or shape of particular role relationships constrain the types of bargains struck. For example, the scarcity and expense of childcare facilities is a structural arrangement limiting the kinds of role bargains that husbands and wives can strike with one another if both work. And the degree to which society confers offensive labels on husbands who clean house and care for children will also limit the kinds of bargains that husbands and wives can strike with one another. (p. 17)

Current Research

As the emergence of women into the work force has been a rapidly changing and evolving situation, it is possible that the corresponding situation regarding home labor has also changed drastically in only a few years time. Certainly there seems to have been a change in the images that are available in the media, and it would seem on all the major TV networks that husbands regularly care for children. Could it be that the conclusions based on reviews of previously published research are already obsolete?

Does the current research—that is, work published since the last reviews—show that men and women have achieved a more egalitarian relationship with respect to the division of household labor? Does it give hope of the "new male" whose participation in the home has been so eagerly awaited? To find out, we scoured the library shelves and conducted vigorous computerized searches. The results of our efforts offer slim hope for those who would like to welcome the much heralded "new husband."

In 1990 researchers surveyed 64 black families living in a small university town in Virginia (Wilson, Tolson, Hinton, & Kiernan, 1990). These families were lower middle-class, with an average of 2.4 children, and the majority of parents possessed a high school degree. Although 78% of the mothers were employed, they performed a variety of household tasks more often than any other family member 60% of the time. Mothers also performed more of the child care than any other family member, including grandmothers. Mothers, not fathers, were primarily responsible for disciplining the children.

Another recent investigation into the division of labor between men and women in the home was reported by Biernat and Wortman (1991). A longitudinal survey begun in 1986 interviewed 139 women professionals with preschool-age children and their husbands. To qualify for the study the women had to be working at least 30 hours a week and have children between the ages of 3 and 5. The women were chosen from the professional areas of academics, accounting, advertising, banking, and law. By choosing to survey couples including wives in high-status occupations, the researchers attempted to analyze how equal-status careers would affect the distribution of household tasks and child care within marriage. Results were recorded through self-report questionnaires for husbands, and interviews and questionnaires for wives. Both partners were asked to evaluate their participation in eight child care tasks and 12 household activities, as well as to rate their satisfaction with their role and their spouse's role in home labor.

Findings indicated that on every child-care task mothers were more active than fathers. There were also differences in degrees of participation among tasks. With the more enjoyable tasks, such as playing with the child, there was greater equality of involvement between men and women. The more unpleasant tasks, such as caring for a sick child or getting up in the middle of the night, remained primarily the responsibility of the mothers. The data revealed a greater degree of sharing in household chores than in child care. Although women were more likely to be primarily responsible for finances, cleaning, and cooking, husbands performed some chores dealing with laundry and household repairs. However, further questioning indicated that although couples were apparently becoming more egalitarian in the division of household tasks, the women were more likely to be responsible for seeing that all the chores were done.

In response to evaluating their own and their spouse's role in the home, Biernat and Wortman's (1991) women were more critical of their roles as spouse and parent than their husbands were of either themselves or of their wives. Perhaps the women were comparing themselves against the standard of the traditional full-time wife and mother. In their parents' generation, women could more often be available to meet every need (real and imagined) of their families; if the employed married mothers in Biernat and Wortman's study held themselves to the standards of a bygone era, it would explain why they viewed themselves more negatively.

Another study asked 490 white women who were married, working mothers of infants living in major metropolitan areas about—among other things—their husbands' practical and emotional support (Gray, Lovejoy, Piotrkowski, & Bond, 1990). Though most of the respondents were satisfied with how "understanding" their husbands were about the demands of their jobs, the traditional gender imbalance in domestic labor was evident. Identifying six traditional household tasks, the investigators found that the wives were responsible for three or more of the tasks in more than 70% of the households. In only 6.8% of the households did the husband take primary responsibility for three or more of the tasks. In nearly half of the households (45.7%) the wife was responsible for all six tasks; in none of the households was the husband responsible for all six tasks!

Role Expansion in the Absence of Role Redefinition

Because the revolution that occurred in the workplace has not yet strongly changed the roles men and women play in the home, many women have added the role of paid worker to their lives but have not been released from the expectations and responsibilities of being a full-time housewife. In recent decades, many people believed in and struggled for a new definition of gender roles in the work force and the home. Many women hoped that as they took on the demands of the workplace, their husbands would commit to increasing their participation in caring for the home and children. As research has shown, this hope has not been realized. Rather than the envisioned role redefinition for men and women, the resulting situation has created a time of *role expansion* for women as they struggle to meet obligations in many spheres.

Role expansion has left many contemporary women living what William Kessen has called "lives without margins" (Crosby, 1991). The uneven distribution of work in the home and the continuing struggle that faces many women in their offices, factories, and classrooms leaves role-jugglers feeling constantly short on time.

In every recent study in which working mothers have been interviewed, the respondents have given clear evidence that they feel extremely short of time. Arlie Hochschild and Anne Machung (1989) interviewed employed mothers about their attempts to meet their various obligations, and the women spoke of giving up their hobbies, as well as reading, television, visiting with friends, and personal time. When one woman, a bank word-processor, was asked by Hochschild about where she found leisure time, her response was "time at my terminal."

Another woman, toward the other end of the occupational continuum, commented to Lisa Silberstein (1992):

> The thing I keep coming back to is the need for more time. Not that you can generate more time, per se, but at least you can use it in more gratifying ways. . . . It gets to the point where things are so frantic you don't even know what you're doing. (p. 110)

Similar sentiments were expressed by a respondent who confided to Crosby (1991) that she felt there was not enough time to do everything well at home and at work. She went on to rephrase the shortage of time in terms of a shortage of self:

> There is not enough of me. Everybody needs so much of me. I constantly feel as if one person or one group of people has one of my arms, and another group has the other arm, and they are pulling in different directions. And then two other groups have my feet. And then the phone rings. (p. 27)

Similarly, in response to a question about balancing career and private life, a woman who graduated from a top law school reported to David Chambers (1989):

I "balance" by losing myself—my free time. I have no hobbies, little free time to assess who I am and where I want to go. I "balance" by foregoing social opportunities and chit-chat with peers. (p. 266)

It is not only qualitative in-depth investigations that have uncovered feelings of acute and chronic time starvation. Virtually every inquiry—even the most quantitative—has shown a significant proportion of working mothers as feeling in need of more minutes in the day (Crosby, 1991, pp. 23-25). In a 1989 telephone poll of more than 1,000 women and 500 men, for instance, 86% of the women in dual-worker marriages responded that they did not have enough time to themselves; only 49% of the men felt this was a problem in their lives (*The New York Times,* 1989).

A clear illustration of why role-jugglers feel short on time is presented in the breakdown of hours spent weekly on household activities by 61 working mothers employed in a university faculty (Yogev, 1981). The women on average devoted 48.5 hours per week to their careers; 35.1 hours were spent on child care, housework consumed 24.6 hours per week, and 56 hours went to sleeping. The remaining time allowed the women 3.8 hours a week to spend on everything else in their lives.

Implications

Women's rights activist and lawyer Lynn Schafran (1992) recently reminded a standing-room-only crowd of feminists that they must not confuse activity with progress. Much has happened since World War II in terms of women's participation in the paid labor force; but until these actions produce an equal reaction in the home, our discussions will need to be limited to descriptions of activity and hopes for progress. Women's roles have expanded, but men's have not expanded—or at least not expanded at the same rate. The situation today is one in which women, more than men, must work what Arlie Hochschild (1989) has vividly called "the second shift."

How long the imbalanced situation will continue depends, in part, on how we as a society understand the dynamics of gender, work, and family. Because societal understandings are often influenced by scholars, it behooves us to examine with care the evidence on role expansion and role strain among women and men. Like many observers outside the ivory tower, some scholars have made an illogical leap from the observation that role-jugglers feel a time crunch to the conclusion that juggling causes stress. The next section indicates that if we make that conceptual leap, we shall fall, empirically and conceptually, on our face.

Appearances and Realities: Illusory Conclusions

Realizing the hectic pace of life in what we have come to call "the fast food lane," a number of researchers and social commentators have wondered if the women who seek to combine careers and domestic life have been working themselves into an early grave. Given the prevalence of time crunches and other common emergencies in the lives of busy role-jugglers it may seem unexceptional to expect that women who work outside as well as within the home will feel more stress and experience more illness than other women in America today.

This section reviews evidence on that point. It shows, first, that the connection between role juggling and physical ill-health, although plausible, is unsupported by empirical evidence. Indeed, women who combine work and home life may be physically healthier than other women. It then shows that there is no empirical support for the notion that role combination is associated with psychological distress. Again, the evidence actually shows a positive association between the number of life roles, on the one hand, and good health, on the other. The third part of this section notes that the plausible connection between role juggling and stress remains plausible if—and only if—one turns a blind eye to some important evidence, such as the fact that women role-jugglers derive much pleasure from combining roles.

Does Juggling Result in Ill Health?

The documented shortage of time in role-jugglers' lives indicates the frantic pace of these women's days. Perhaps it is reasonable to assume that such pressure would take its toll on women's health. As women break away from their traditional roles and begin to compete in the work force, there is concern that they are increasingly risking their health. Possibly women are becoming equal to men, not only in the workplace, but in mortality rates and serious illness as well.

At first glance, some statistics seem to support the idea that women are, literally, dying for equality. Consider myocardial infarctions (heart-attacks). Until recently, heart attacks have been more frequent and more serious among men than among women. But in the last couple of decades, the gender gap has narrowed. Just as women have been joining the boardrooms, women have also been increasingly present in the cardiac intensive care units. Could there be a connection?

One study conducted by the National Heart, Lung and Blood Institute seemed at first to suggest a strong and direct connection. In data from the famous Framingham heart study, the investigators found that among women with three or more children in the town of Framingham, Massachusetts, 11% of those who worked outside the home developed coronary heart disease compared with only 4.4% of housewives (Haynes & Feinleib, 1980). At first blush, the attempt to "do it all" seemed to be jeopardizing women's lives.

Closer analysis of the data revealed quite a different story. When they scrutinized the figures, the investigators discovered that the health risk to women occurred only among working-class clerical employees who combined heavy family responsibilities with work outside the home. Women in professional occupations or clerical workers married to men with white-collar jobs showed no such pattern. Thus it was apparently the lack of money in the women's lives, not the presence of employment that was creating the health hazard (Haynes & Feinleib, 1980).

Similar reappraisal of aggregate data on the gender gap in fatalities from coronary disease also showed that initial impressions had been misleading. The women who have been dying of heart trouble are not the young and middle-aged women who are attempting to juggle home and work responsibilities. Rather, they are old and very old women, more of whom are present in our society than ever before. The increase in the proportion of coronary disease patients who are female is, in fact, a statistical artifact—it results from the ever-increasing longevity advantage that women have enjoyed, relative to men, since 1900 (Strickland, 1988). Far from killing women, breaking down the walls of the traditional sex-role prison has resulted in women staying alive even longer than before.

Other studies have shown that, across the adult years, employed women are physically healthier or more robust than women who are at home and out of the paid labor force (Amatea & Fong, 1991; Helson, Elliott, & Leigh, 1990). Whether health follows from or precedes employment is not entirely clear; but it is clear that employment does not interfere with health.

Mistaken impressions can also be found concerning role-jugglers and a specific aspect of health behavior: the risk of substance abuse. Both the popular "wisdom" and some past research have envisioned working women as more susceptible to drugs and alcohol than traditional homemakers. More recent studies in the area of alcohol use have not supported the stereotype (Driscoll, 1991). Indeed, it seems that women who combine roles are less likely to be abusive drinkers than are other women. A 1981 national survey (Wilsnack, Wilsnack, & Klassen, 1984) reported that 49% of women employed full time who had never married, were rated as moderate or heavy drinkers. In comparison, only 28% of married women employed full time were estimated as being heavy or moderate drinkers.

The media and some scholars have warned women that they will jeopardize their health by trying to "do it all." Some health statistics appear, at first glance, to add credence to the warning. At second glance, the statistics show no connection between role combination and ill health and, indeed, suggest the opposite relationship.

Empirical Data Challenge the Plausible Link Between Role Juggling and Stress

Women who juggle roles do experience stress, in the form of being hurried and starved for leisure. Of this there is no question. But the simple observation that women who juggle roles experience stress does not indicate whether the time pressure results from role combination, from being a woman, or from the unique constellation of being a woman who combines roles.

Could the stress come from being a woman? Yes, it could. The published comparisons, reviewed above, show that women are more desperate for time than are men. The gender discrepancy may be particularly marked among married, working parents. Indeed, men have traditionally combined the roles of worker, parent, and spouse with beneficial results for their physical and mental health (Coleman, Antonucci, & Adelmann, 1987).

It is important to note that comparisons of women who juggle roles to men who combine similar life roles is not the optimum way to analyze the effects of role combination and stress in women. Research findings that women experience greater role strain than men should not lead one to the conclusion that women who combine different life roles experience more stress than other women (Greenberger, Goldberg, Hamill, O'Neil, & Payne, 1989). Only research comparing the levels of stress experienced by (a) women who combine roles and (b) women with fewer life roles can accurately assess the effects of role juggling on women.

Such comparisons were attempted by Crosby (1991) and her research team. They were unable to locate any studies that compared women with different role constellations in terms of how pressed, hurried, or starved for minutes they felt themselves to be. There are no studies to show whether it is motherhood, marriage, work, or some combination of these roles that makes contemporary American women victims of frequent time crunches. Anecdotal evidence suggests that at-home mothers feel the same thirst for personal time that employed mothers feel; but no one has yet conducted systematic research.

On the issue of psychological stress, as opposed to time starvation, Crosby (1991) and her team did locate some studies. They found no compelling evidence to suggest that role-jugglers experience more stress than housewives or other women with fewer roles. The evidence was rather slim and inconsistent. Between 1975 and 1987, there were 13 studies, 8 of which showed no difference between role-jugglers and other women in the levels of stress. Three studies found that role-jugglers experienced greater amounts of stress than other women (e.g., Gerson, 1985). Two other studies reported the opposite results, indicating that role-jugglers experience less stress than other women (e.g., Cumming, Lazer, & Chisholm, 1975).

Since the completion of Crosby's (1991) review, two more studies have been published. A longitudinal survey of female college graduates over a 23-year period examined the relationship between the number of roles (spouse, parent, paid worker) the women played and their psychological as well as physical health (Helson et al., 1990). Psychological health was assessed with the California Personality Inventory (CPI) well-being scale. The authors found that women with more than one role were more likely than other women to experience good mental health.

In another study, interviews with 117 women employed by a large southern university led Amatea and Fong (1991) to conclude that the number of roles was negatively related to psychological (as well as physical) symptoms of stress. The fewer the roles, the greater the signs of strain.

Not all emotional distress manifests itself as stress. A related but quite distinct symptom is depression. The depressed person lacks energy and has a low appetite for life, and often experiences feelings of personal worthlessness. Depression is one of the most common psychological disorders among women, and women are more prone to depression than are men (Nolen-Hoeksema, 1990). Some of the gender difference in rates of depression may be traced to biology, but the fact that gender differences disappear in studies that control for income and for role constellation points to social roles as the primary explanation of why females predominate among the depressed (Repetti & Crosby, 1984).

As early as 1972, Walter Gove proposed that depression occurred more often and more severely in women than in men because women were typically forced to choose between employment and domesticity whereas men were typically expected to occupy a number of different roles. Reviewing data from a national study, Gove proposed that multiple role occupancy allowed people multiple sources of gratification and thus buffered them against disappointments in any one role. In other words, for both men and women, the more roles, the better.

Since Gove first articulated his theory, data from a number of studies have supported it. Early on, Mostow and Newberry (1975) discovered that employed married women were more likely than other women to recover rapidly from major life traumas of the kind that often produce depression. Soon after, some other researchers noted that wives are more likely to experience depression than their husbands, but only in households where the man is the single income-earner (Kessler & McRae, 1981).

Of course, there is more to consider than simply the number of different roles. The quality of the roles matters, too (Kibria, Barnett, Baruch, Marshall, & Pleck, 1990). Adding a difficult, unsatisfying, or degrading role to a life that is already well stocked in misery will not remedy a person's discontent (Belle, 1990).

Conversely, the cumulative effect of especially satisfying life roles is greater than the effect of roles that bring only moderate satisfaction. Baruch and Barnett (1987) questioned more than 200 women about their experiences in the roles of wife, mother, and worker. The women's psychological well-being was measured in the areas of depression, self-esteem, and pleasure. The most important role in determining well-being was the satisfaction derived in the role of wife. The higher the quality of the wife role, the greater a woman's feelings of self-esteem and pleasure and the less her risk of depression. The quality of both the mother and the worker roles was also strongly related to well-being on all measures. Baruch and Barnett also found that, although they could reliably predict well-being from the number of roles occupied (the more, the better), the quality of women's life roles explained a greater share of the variance than did the sheer number of roles.

Closely related to role quality is the commitment a person feels to a life role. Ellen Greenberger and Robin O'Neil (in press) surveyed 102 men and 194 women in dual-career families with preschool-age children, all living in California and all in the 30-something age range. The study examined, among other factors, the respondents' degree of commitment to the roles of spouse, parent, and worker, and how this commitment correlated to depression. Results indicated that among the female respondents of the survey, greater time devoted to work and work-related activities was associated with fewer symptoms of depression. Surprisingly, however, a greater commitment to parenting was positively related to more depressive symptoms. The researchers theorized that the relationship of parental commitment and depression was influenced by the degree of parental satisfaction, because women who believed they were doing well in the role of mother reported fewer symptoms of anxiety. Thus, in this survey, the potential threat to women's well-being was not devotion to the role of paid worker, which is frequently cited as being the most harmful and unnatural for women, but rather, a higher level of commitment to the role of mother.

Although the statistics on how role-jugglers are starved for time make it seem intuitively plausible that combining roles causes stress, the empirical evidence fails to show that association. There are no data on whether role-jugglers feel more rushed than other mothers, but there are data that show that role-jugglers are *not* more stressed than other women. Multiple role occupancy, furthermore, appears to insulate women (and men) against depression.

Focusing on the Harried Juggler
Entails Many Blind Spots

One thing that scholars have learned in the postmodern era, is to listen for silences (Hare-Mustin & Maracek, 1988). A great problem with the notion that juggling causes stress in women is that the connection appears to be true only if we ignore and distort women's sense of accomplishment and women's capacity for coping.

Listening for the joy. That women often experience a sense of exhilaration as they successfully manage home life and employment has been asserted by Cynthia Epstein (1987) on the basis of hundreds of interviews with women lawyers and judges. Feelings of well-being and fulfillment on the part of contemporary women stand out in the quotations included in several recent accounts of dual-career marriages (Hertz, 1986).

Curious about the balance between exhaustion and exhilaration, Crosby (1991) interviewed 20 middle-class employed women with school-age children. The interview started by asking about the shortage of time and moved to stresses and problems and then to the benefits of playing many roles. At the end of the interview, each woman was asked whether she felt the experience of juggling roles was, on the whole, more stressful or more beneficial to her life. Three women felt combining roles was more negative than positive, 2 women felt the negatives and positives were equal, and the remaining 15 women felt the benefits were greater than the stress. Thus 75% of the women interviewed—all of whom had been eloquent on the issues of time shortage and problems within each role—felt the rewards of juggling definitely outweighed the costs.

To explain why the pleasures of multiple roles outweigh the costs is not difficult. According to Crosby (1991), the link between multiple role occupancy, on the one hand, and health and zest, on the other, can be accounted for by variety, buffering, and amplification. First consider variety: By participating in many life roles, women are exposed to changes and allowed to experience many viewpoints. Researchers have found that a change of scene is often mentioned by women as an important factor in balancing their career and home life (Chambers, 1989). Not only is a change of scene cheering; so is a change in one's mode of operation. Bakan (1966) has described two modes of being that varied life roles allow people to experience: agency and communion. Agency refers to involvement in accomplishing one's individual goals and mastering tasks. In communion, a person lets go of goals, lives in the moment, and can be at one with others. By participating in both work and family life, and the different roles each area brings, women are able to benefit from involvement in both modes of being and more fully exercise the different aspects of their personality (Stewart & Malley, 1987).

Another important benefit of multiple roles is the buffering that any one role provides when a person experiences reversals or dissatisfactions in another. As a concrete example in one study, the degree of depression produced by marital dissatisfaction was attenuated in women who worked outside the home, as compared to housewives (Repetti & Crosby, 1984).

A final benefit of numerous life roles, which makes role-jugglers feel happy and alive, is the experience of amplification. Different life roles can bring a person into contact with very different groups of people, each of which can act as an audience for disclosure of events in the other life roles. By being able to recount—without fear of jealousy—important and happy stories in one's life, one is able to relive, and thus to amplify, joyous moments in one's life. Alternately, she or he can receive sympathy and advice from more than one group of people when discussing life's painful moments.

Acknowledging coping. Where there is stress, look for coping. Almost since the earliest treatises on "role strain" (Goode, 1960), sociologists and psychologists have also given accounts of how well women have coped with the problems facing them. To quote again from Cynthia Epstein (1987):

> My interviews with women in the 1970s who held demanding jobs in law, business, and academia gave me a new perspective on the problem of role strain, one also held by other researchers on women who work. . . . The most successful women lawyers I interviewed turned out to have the most to do. . . . When I asked one woman, who had attained partnership early in a large corporate law firm, about the problems she faced in reconciling her roles as a Wall Street partner with three children under the age of twelve, she answered: "No problems," and then qualified herself: "Well, not no problems, but none I can't deal with." That sort of answer was common for women at the top. (pp. 27-28)

Other studies (e.g., Cooke & Rousseau, 1984) summarized elsewhere (Crosby, 1991, chap. 2) have confirmed the observation that women who juggle high-stress occupations with family life do not wallow in self-pity, but rather take pride in how well they cope.

Recently, a number of studies have demonstrated the link between effective coping and social support. Amatea and Fong's (1991) previously cited study of women employed by a large southern university measured social support for each respondent on a 5-point scale of strength of agreement or disagreement with statements such as "I have one or more friends to confide in about personal matters." Symptoms of strain were measured on a 22-item index consisting of 17 physical symptoms and 5 psychological symptoms. The authors found an inverse relationship between social support and stress symptoms.

Less clear-cut associations were found in a survey of 200 married career women with small children that measured the effects of social support on reported levels of strain (Reifman, Biernat, & Lang, 1991). Symptoms of strain were measured on a 22-part index of stress covering areas such as work and family. The women in the survey were divided into either high levels of strain or low levels of strain in each area. Social support was measured in the degrees of assistance provided, both in terms of practical information and advice, as well as encouragement and reassurance. Contrary to their predictions, Reifman et al. (1991) found that social support in each role benefited women under low levels of strain but not women under high levels of strain. For example, a woman whose work did not impose on relaxation benefited from having friends at work. But for the woman whose work did impose on her relaxation, the more friends at work, the greater the felt strain.

Perhaps one reason that Reifman et al. found complicated results was that they asked, all together, about friends and colleagues and spouses. More straightforward results have been found by researchers looking at the effect of husbands' supportiveness on how well role-juggling wives function. The survey by Gray et al. (1990) on husbands' participation in household tasks in families with infants also asked the women in the study about life satisfaction, stress, and coping, and about the husbands' practical and emotional support. More than any other factor, including problems with child care, the degree of spousal support was the critical determinant of a woman's ability to cope. Those women who reported that their husband expressed high levels of understanding about his wife's career obligations and a high degree of practical support also displayed greater marital satisfaction and freedom from the symptoms of role strain.

Ideologies Revealed

We have seen that the conclusion that women are suffering from interrole conflict appears reasonable; but it is not supported by data and it runs counter to reliable research findings. Why do so many members of the media and so many scholars persist in treating the conclusion as justified? The reason the false conclusion has proven so resistant to modification in the face of facts is that the conclusion reinforces the status quo. As long as people accept the notion that contemporary American women experience strain from the effort to combine roles, they are spared from looking *within* each of women's life roles for the root source of difficulties. If we were to look within the roles, we would see problems that our society is ill prepared to remedy. Why are we not prepared to remedy the problems? Because to do so would disrupt our sexist and individualistic assumptions about the world.

Sexism and Sex Discrimination

America did not invent misogyny, but we certainly have not refused it entry at our shores. One does not need a certificate in women's studies to know that females have not been treated as well as males in the United States (Bergmann, 1986). Similarly, there is clear evidence that we have traditionally stereotyped males and females (Basow, 1992).

Since World War II, the country has experienced a radical change in attitudes on women's issues (Fleming, 1988). In 1936, for example, less than one American in five thought a married woman should be in the work force. Forty years later, the percentage was 68% (Kahn & Crosby, 1985). In 1988, more than half of the young women graduating from colleges in the New Haven, Connecticut, area labeled themselves as feminists (Crosby, 1991, p. 186).

The shift in attitudes has not signaled an equal change in our underlying preconceptions about women and men. As Carol Tavris (1992) argues convincingly, Americans are still deeply committed to the "mismeasurement of women." Many apparent friends of highly accomplished women give expression, without much self-awareness, to antifemale hostility. Joanne Martin (1990) described how the president of a multinational company saw himself as doing a great favor to one of his young female executives when he rescheduled a product presentation so that she could broadcast the presentation on closed circuit television. As for the woman, she "arranged to have her Caesarean yesterday in order to be prepared for this event." Would the president have seen his actions as being so benign if the medical procedure did not involve a young woman giving birth but rather involved a young man undergoing open-heart surgery. How ridiculous it would have been, Martin pointed out, for the president to say, "We are so kind that we have consented to allow the young man to keep our profits up rather than letting his heart heal" (p. 359).

Given the pervasiveness and depth of sexual prejudice, it seems wise to view with a jaundiced eye some of the "sympathy" with which commentators discuss the plight of women who juggle work and family roles. Much of the alleged sympathy derives from the assumption that women cannot and should not be providers of material goods for the family and that men cannot and should not attempt to nurture. Indeed, as Rose Coser and Gerald Rokoff (1971) pointed out nearly a generation ago, much of the concern over women's situation in the world of work—a concern that often comes into play only when women are on the verge of professional advance and not when women are confined to the workhouse—becomes manifestly illogical and nonsensical when scrutinized closely. As noted elsewhere (Crosby, 1987):

> The real reason that professional work and family cannot mix for women in our culture, according to Coser and Rokoff, is that a married woman is supposed to derive her status in the world from her husband. By engaging in a career of her own, the woman automatically develops an independent status and thereby threatens the social order. (p. xi)

Once we begin to view contemporary expressions of concern for the harried role-juggler with skepticism, it is easy to see the parallel between the anxieties expressed by some observers today about the health threat of juggling, and the laments voiced 80 years ago by Maudsley in England and by G. Stanley Hall in America about what higher education would do to the health of young women (Sayers, 1982). In hindsight, Maudsley's and Hall's concerns, centered as they were on the supposed negative effects of arduous mental activity on women's reproductive systems and especially on their mammary functioning, seem like nothing more than thinly veiled attempts to keep women in their place—under man's foot. How long will it take before everyone, and not just the insightful few, easily see the wisdom of Cynthia Epstein's observation?

> The current focus on role strain no doubt results in part from an honest recognition of the difficulties of meeting conflicting demands. But, in my view, it also results from the fact that some people feel threatened by the vitality and productivity of women with accomplishments in different life roles. (Epstein, 1987, p. 23)

Keeping the focus on the conflict between roles, furthermore, is a tactic that diverts attention away from the real source of the problems: what goes on *within* each role (Crosby, 1991). When we look clearly at the stresses that women encounter within the role of worker, we soon see a host of problems that face women more than men. Women are more often unemployed and underemployed than comparably qualified men; once hired, women are paid less than comparable men, promoted less frequently and less rapidly than comparable men, fired more frequently than comparable men, and harassed on the job much more frequently than comparable men. Adding it all up, sex discrimination is more potent (if more subtle, too) than one would expect given our society's sex-egalitarian attitudes (Faludi, 1991).

Individualism and the Nuclear Family

If examining the stresses that face women at work is uncomfortable, so is acknowledging the stresses that face women at home. Not only does a clear-headed look at families make us confront the unhealthiness of some of our gender-role stereotypes; it also makes us aware of the absurdity of some of our myths about the nuclear family. The time has come to replace our devotion to rugged individualism with a stronger sense of community (Sampson, 1977).

That ideology has been clouding our vision of family life is evident as soon as we look for issues not discussed and listen again for silences. Why have we shouted about the conflict between the worker role and the mothering role while remaining silent about potential conflicts between the worker role and the fathering role? Why have we asked only about conflicts and not about the ways in which the worker role might enhance the parenting role and vice versa? And why have we not worried about discontinuities and strains between either the worker role or the parenting role, on the one hand, and the role of spouse, on the other?

To be a mother and a worker, simultaneously, may pose less of a challenge for most women than to be a spouse and a parent or a spouse and a worker. Such was the intriguing implication of a survey of university employees (Frone & Rice, 1987). Investigating people's psychological commitment to their jobs, marriages, and roles as parents, Frone and Rice hypothesized that women who were very involved in both their work and parenting would experience interrole conflict. However, this was not what they found. Being committed to work did not conflict with parental involvement for the women; it conflicted instead with women's investment in being a good wife! Similarly, Gray et al. (1990) found that more than half of the women in their survey confessed that having a job led to some marital strain.

Although being a good wife in today's America may be no easy task, being a good mother seems a task of Herculean proportion—whether or not a woman works outside the home. To start, there is the shock that comes to most new mothers as they discover the realities of life with baby. Our media continue to present us with bowdlerized views of young motherhood as the ideal for women. The popular images of motherhood rarely prepare women for the sleepless nights, the continuous laundry cycle, the fears for the baby's health, the exasperations and the boredom that almost invariably accompany the isolated life of first-time mothers. No wonder mothers of young children are at risk for depression and feelings of low self-esteem (Bassof, 1984; Crosby, 1991, chap. 3) and for the sometimes intense feelings of loneliness (Fischer & Oliker, 1983).

The experiences of mothering are made especially stressful for women by the emphasis placed on individual responsibility and independence in our culture (Sampson, 1977). Our society teaches us that we should not rely on others beyond ourselves or our immediate families and that such dependence is an admission of failure and incompetence. The ethic of rugged individualism, linked with the standard division of family responsibilities along gender lines, creates a psychologically untenable situation in which isolated adults—almost invariably women—are expected to remain both vigilant and calm for extended periods of time with no relief and no support from other adults. The mother of a young child in the atomized family of contemporary America is like the soldier who goes on a solo watch lasting 24 hours a day. And yet we are surprised when mothers show signs of battle fatigue or when families begin to shatter under stress (Barnett & Baruch, 1987).

In our addiction to individualism, we are likely to confuse the sharing of responsibility and the abdication of responsibility. It takes a village to raise a child, and the parents who rely on the resources of their neighborhoods and schools are not necessarily less involved in the task of raising their children than are the parents who are too proud, too shy, too unconcerned, or too overwhelmed to ask for "outside" involvement (Ehrensaft, 1987). If we understood that individuals can fulfill their responsibilities by acting collectively for the good of all children, including their own, then we would see why it is a disgrace that the United States remains the only industrialized nation without a job-protected maternity leave policy, why much more and better day care is needed, and why community-based after-school and before-school programs should be a national priority. Although the new right talks about protecting "family values," each American family is left to reinvent solutions (Silberstein, 1992), and as many as 70% of American children are left to care for themselves during some part of the day (Wellesley College Center for Research on Women, 1990). The time has come for structural change.

Conclusion

As researchers who are also citizens, we should all reflect on the stories we tell and on the silences we keep and consider how our accounts help to bolster or dismantle the status quo. Some observations are both evident and true. Others are false but appear true because they accord well with our preconceptions and private beliefs of how the world can and should operate. Still other observations—such as the need for structural change—can remain obscure unless we make a concerted effort to bring them into consciousness.

For a long time the focus in the research literature has been on the overburdened woman. The literature has given the impression that women cannot balance work and home commitments. We have argued that the image of the hassled role-juggler is both false and dangerous. The real stresses for women who have responsibilities both at home and outside it do not come from trying to combine responsibilities; rather they come mostly from being a woman in our society.

One final word is in order. Role combination has been framed as a women's issue. But ultimately there are no women's issues. When we as a society set about solving the problems facing women who balance work and home, we will benefit not only women but also all those who have a regular and sustained contact with women, which is to say everyone.

References

Amatea, E. S., & Fong, M. L. (1991). The impact of role stressors and personal resources on the stress experience of professional women. *Psychology of Women Quarterly, 15,* 419-430.

Bakan, D. (1966). *The duality of human experience.* Boston: Beacon.

Barnett, R. C., & Baruch, G. K. (1987). Mothers' participation in childcare: Patterns and consequences. In F. J. Crosby (Ed.), *Spouse, parent, worker: On gender and multiple roles* (91-108). New Haven, CT: Yale University Press.

Baruch, G. K., & Barnett, R. C. (1987). Role quality and psychological well-being. In F. J. Crosby (Ed.), *Spouse, parent, worker: On gender and multiple roles* (pp. 63-72). New Haven, CT: Yale University Press.

Basow, S. (1992). *Gender stereotypes and roles* (3rd ed.). Pacific Grove, CA: Brooks/ Cole.

Bassof, E. S. (1984). Relationship of sex-role characteristics and psychological adjustment in new mothers. *Journal of Marriage and the Family, 46,* 449-454.

Beckett, J., & Smith, A. (1981). Work and family roles: Egalitarian marriage in black and white families. *Social Service Review, 55,* 314-326.

Belle, D. (1990). Poverty and women's mental health. *American Psychologist, 45,* 385-389.

Belsky, J., & Volling, B. L. (1987). Mothering, fathering, and marital interaction in the family triad during infancy. In P. W. Berman & F. A. Pedersen (Eds.), *Men's transitions to parenthood: Longitudinal studies of early family experience* (pp. 37-63). Hillsdale, NJ: Lawrence Erlbaum.

Bergmann, B. (1986). *The economic emergence of women.* New York: Basic Books.

Berk, S. F. (1985). *The gender factory. The apportionment of work in American households.* New York: Plenum.

Biernat, M., & Wortman, C. (1991). Sharing of home responsibilities between professionally employed women and their husbands. *Journal of Personality and Social Psychology, 60,* 844-860.

Chambers, D. L. (1989). Accommodation and satisfaction: Women and men lawyers and the balance of work and family. *Law and Social Inquiry, 14,* 251-287.

Coleman, L. M., Antonucci, T. C., & Adelmann, P. K. (1987). Role involvement, gender, and well-being. In F. J. Crosby (Ed.), *Spouse, parent, worker: On gender and multiple roles* (pp. 138-153). New Haven, CT: Yale University Press.

Cooke, R. A., & Rousseau, D. M. (1984). Stress and strain from family roles and work-role expectations. *Journal of Applied Psychology, 69,* 252-260.

Coser, R., & Rokoff, G. (1971). Women in the occupational world: Social disruption and conflict. *Social Problems, 18,* 535-554.

Coverman, S., & Sheley, J. (1986). Change in men's housework and child-care time, 1965-1975. *Journal of Marriage and the Family, 48,* 413-422.

Crosby, F. J. (1982). *Relative deprivation and working women.* New York: Oxford University Press.

Crosby, F. J. (1987). Preface. In F. J. Crosby (Ed.), *Spouse, parent, worker: On gender and multiple roles* (pp. ix-xiii). New Haven, CT: Yale University Press.

Crosby, F. J. (1991). *Juggling: The unexpected advantages of balancing a career and home for women and their families.* New York: Free Press.

Cumming, E., Lazer, C., & Chisholm, L. (1975). Suicide as an index of role strain among employed and not employed married women in British Columbia. *Canadian Review of Sociology and Anthropology, 12,* 462-470.

Douhitt, R. (1989). The division of labor within the home: Have gender roles changed? *Sex Roles, 20,* 693-704.

Driscoll, J. (1991). *Women's drinking as a function of multiple roles.* Unpublished paper, The Wright Graduate School of Psychology.

Ehrensaft, D. (1987). *Parenting together.* New York: Free Press.

Epstein, C. F. (1987). Multiple demands and multiple roles: The conditions of successful management. In F. J. Crosby (Ed.), *Spouse, parent, worker: On gender and multiple roles* (pp. 23-35). New Haven, CT: Yale University Press.

Faludi, S. (1991). *Backlash.* New York: Crown Publishers.

Fischer, C. S., & Oliker, S. J. (1983). A research note on friendship, gender, and the life cycles. *Social Forces, 62,* 124-133.

Fleming, J. J. (1988). Public opinion on change in women's rights and roles. In S. M. Dornbush & M. H. Strobes (Eds.), *Feminism, children, and the new families* (pp. 47-66). New York: Guilford Press.

Fowlkes, M. R. (1987). Role combinations and role conflict: Introductory perspective. In F. J. Crosby (Ed.), *Spouse, parent, worker: On gender and multiple roles* (pp. 3-10). New Haven, CT: Yale University Press.

Frone, M. R., & Rice, R. W. (1987). Work-family conflict: The effect of job and family involvement. *Journal of Occupational Behavior, 8,* 45-53.

Gerson, J. M. (1985). Women returning to school: The consequences of multiple roles. *Sex Roles, 13,* 77-91.

Gilbert, L. A. (1985). *Men in dual-career families: Current realities and future prospects.* Hillsdale, NJ: Lawrence Erlbaum.

Goode, W. J. (1960). A theory of role strain. *American Sociological Review, 25,* 483-496.

Gove, W. (1972). Sex, marital status, and mental illness. *Social Forces, 51,* 34-55.

Gray, E. B., Lovejoy, M. C., Piotrkowski, C. S., & Bond, J. T. (1990). Husband supportiveness and the well-being of employed mothers of infants. *Families in Society, 71,* 332-341.

Greenberger, E., Goldberg, W. A., Hamill, S., O'Neil, R., & Payne, C. K. (1989). Contributions of a supportive work environment to parents' well-being and orientation to work. *American Journal of Community Psychology, 17,* 755-783.

Greenberger, E., & O'Neil, R. (in press). Spouse, parent, worker: Role-related experiences in the construction of adult's well-being. *Developmental Psychology.*

Hare-Mustin, R. T., & Maracek, J. (1988). The meaning of difference. Gender theory, postmodernism, and psychology. *American Psychologist, 43,* 455-464.

Hayge, H. V. (1990). Family members in the workforce. *U.S. Bureau of Labor Statistics: Monthly Labor Review, 113,* 14-19.

Haynes, S., & Feinleib, M. (1980). Women, work, and coronary heart disease: Prospective findings from the Framingham Heart Study. *American Journal of Public Health, 70,* 133-141.

Helson, R., Elliott, T., & Leigh, J. (1990). Number and quality of roles. *Psychology of Women Quarterly, 14,* 83-101.

Hertz, R. (1986). *More equal than others: Women and men in dual career marriages.* Berkeley: University of California Press.

Hochschild, A., with Machung, A. (1989). *The second shift: Working parents and the revolution at home.* New York: Viking.

Jacobs, E., Shipp, S., & Brown, G. (1989). Families of working wives spending more on services and nondurables. *U.S. Bureau of Labor Statistics: Monthly Labor Review, 112,* 15-23.

Kahn, W., & Crosby, F. J. (1985). Change and stasis: Discriminating between attitudes and discriminatory behavior. In L. Larwood, B. A. Gutek, & A. H. Stromberg (Eds.), *Women and work: An annual review* (Vol. 1, pp. 215-238). Beverly Hills, CA: Sage.

Kessler, R., & McRae, J. M. (1981). Trends on the relationship between sex and psychological distress, 1957-1976. *American Sociological Review, 46,* 443-452.

Kibria, N., Barnett, R. C., Baruch, G. K., Marshall, N. L., & Pleck, J. H. (1990). Homemaking role quality and the psychological well-being and distress of employed women. *Sex Roles, 22,* 327-345.

Kilty, K., & Richardson, V. (1985). The impact of gender on productive and social activities. *Journal of Sociology and Social Welfare, 12,* 162-185.

Martin, J. (1990). Deconstructing organizational taboos: The suppression of gender conflict in organizations. *Organizational Science, 1,* 339-359.

Mostow, E., & Newberry, P. (1975). Work role and depression in women: A comparison of workers and housewives in treatment. *American Journal of Orthopsychiatry, 45,* 538-548.

The New York Times. (1989, August 21, p. A14).

Nolen-Hoeksema, S. (1990). *Sex differences in depression.* Stanford, CA: Stanford University Press.

Nyquist, L., Slivken, K., Spence, J. T., & Helmreich, R. L. (1985). Household responsibilities in middle-class couples: The contribution of demographic and personality variables." *Sex Roles, 12,* 15-34.

Pleck, J. H. (1985). *Working wives/working husbands.* Beverly Hills, CA: Sage.

Reifman, A., Biernat, M., & Lang, E. L. (1991). Stress, social support and health in married professional women with small children. *Psychology of Women Quarterly, 15,* 431-445.

Repetti, R. L., & Crosby, F. (1984). Gender and depression: Exploring the adult-role explanation. *Journal of Social and Clinical Psychology, 2,* 57-70.

Sampson, E. (1977). Psychology and the American ideal. *Journal of Personality and Social Psychology, 35,* 767-782.

Sayers, J. (1982). *Biological politics: Feminist and anti-feminist perspectives.* New York: Tavistock.

Schafran, L. (1992, February 19). *Women's lives.* Panel discussion at Smith College, Northampton, MA.

Shank, S. E. (1988). Women and the labor market: The link grows stronger. *U.S. Bureau of Labor Statistics: Monthly Labor Review, 111,* 3-8.

Silberstein, L. (1992). *The dual-career marriage: A system in transition.* Hillsdale, NJ: Lawrence Erlbaum.

Steil, J. (in press). Justice issues in the home. In M. Lerner & G. Mikula (Eds.), *Entitlements and the affectional bond.* New York: Plenum.

Stewart, A. J., & Malley, J. E. (1987). Role combination in women: Mitigating agency and communion. In F. J. Crosby (Ed.), *Spouse, parent, worker: On gender and multiple roles* (pp. 44-73). New Haven, CT: Yale University Press.

Strickland, B. (1988). Sex-related differences in health and illness. *Psychology of Women Quarterly, 12,* 381-399.

Tavris, C. (1992). *The mismeasure of woman.* New York: Simon & Schuster.

Thoits, P. A. (1987). Negotiating roles. In F. J. Crosby (Ed.), *Spouse, parent, worker: On gender and multiple roles* (pp. 11-22). New Haven, CT: Yale University Press.

Wellesley College Center for Research on Women. (1990). *Research Report, 9* (no. 2)1.

Wilsnack, R. W., Wilsnack, S. C., & Klassen, A. D. (1984). Women's drinking and drinking problems: Patterns from a 1981 national survey. *American Journal of Public Health, 74,* 1231-1237.

Wilson, M., Tolson, T., Hinton, I., & Kiernan, M. (1990). Flexibility and sharing of childcare duties in black families. *Sex Roles, 22,* 409-424.

Yogev, S. (1981). Do professional women have egalitarian marital relationships? *Journal of Marriage and the Family, 43,* 865-871.

8

What's So Special About Sex?[1] Gender Stereotyping and Discrimination

SUSAN T. FISKE
LAURA E. STEVENS

> The Expert Witness: There are general stereotypes of what people particularly expect men to be like and typically expect women to be like. People typically expect women to be strong on the social dimensions. Women are generally expected to be more tender and understanding and concerned about other people, and soft.
> The Court: You say that of people who have dealt with women expect that? People who have dealt with women in the business context expect that, or are you talking about people out on the farm?
> —*Price Waterhouse v. Hopkins*, 1989, p. 543

People all have their own opinions about gender stereotypes. Consequently, a social psychologist explaining the well-established research literature may find herself in the awkward position

AUTHORS' NOTE: Portions of this chapter were presented at the meetings of the American Psychological Society (June 1991), the American Psychological Association (August 1992), and at Tulane University (October 1992).

of disputing or at least elaborating the audience's commonsense judgments. Although common sense is the natural foil for all of social psychology given its domain (Kelley, 1992), it is particularly a problem in the field of gender stereotypes and discrimination, because of the special status of gender. This chapter addresses what makes sex special, that is, what makes gender-based responses more vulnerable to commonsense psychologizing than other types of category-based responses, stemming, for example, from race, age, or disability.

We will argue that gender is special (and especially awkward to evaluate in commonsense terms) because of (a) the heavily prescriptive aspects of gender stereotypes, (b) the inherent power asymmetries implied by gender differences in social status and average physical size, (c) the intimate communal relationships between members of the two groups, (d) the sexual and biological context of interpersonal interactions, and (e) the rapid historical change in the expression of sexism. As an illustration of these points let's begin with two case studies, drawn from the first author's experience as an expert witness. These cases depict superficially different but fundamentally similar cases of gender stereotyping and discrimination.

Tales of Two Women

Lois Robinson worked as a welder in a certain Jacksonville, Florida, shipyard. Jacksonville Shipyards, Inc. (JSI) repairs U.S. Navy and commercial ships in dry dock in what is tough, sometimes dangerous work. The enterprise includes a wide variety of skilled craftworkers: welders, shipfitters, carpenters, electricians, machinists, boilermakers, sheetmetal workers, and more. The atmosphere is heavily identified with the Navy; many of the management had Navy careers before moving to the private sector. Women are less than 5% of the JSI work force, and less than half of 1% of the skilled craftworkers. What this means from a practical point of view is that there are typically no or few women on any given shift, a minimum of none if business is slow, and a maximum of 8 to 10 out of 150 workers on a busy shift. Most often, there are 1 or 2 women out of 50 to 100 workers on shift, so a woman is likely to be the only woman in the crowd getting on the shipyard buses or at the time clock.

The JSI shipyard has been described as a boy's club, a man's world, and someone even painted "Men Only" on one of the work trailers. (When someone else complained, the sign was painted over, but in a cursory way.) It is perhaps best summarized as an atmosphere with a lot of joking and messing around. For example, one worker put a flashlight in his pants to show how well-endowed horses are; another carved the handle of a tool to resemble a penis, waving it in the faces of the women. There is open hostility to women on the part of a few men: "there's nothing worse than having to work around women; women are only fit company for something that howls." More often, there is simply a great deal of off-color joking (including one often-repeated joke about death by rape). Obscenity and profanity are routine.

Prominent in the visual environment (according to depositions, "every craft, every shop") are many calendars showing women in various states of undress and sexually explicit poses. Comparable magazines are widely shared, and pinups are torn out and posted spontaneously. Decorating various public walls are graffiti, both words and cartoons, with explicit sexual content depicting women. Note that there are of course no pictures, graffiti, or magazines depicting naked men. Note also that the workers are not allowed to bring other magazines on the job, and they are not allowed to post other material that is not work-related.

The few women workers are typically called by demeaning or sexually explicit names (honey, dear, baby, sugar, mamma, pussy, cunt, etc.). They are constantly teased, touched, humiliated, sexually evaluated, and propositioned; the incidents occur "every day all day" involving "all crafts," according to depositions.

Lois Robinson complained about the magazines and calendars, but she was brushed off, all the way up to the highest levels. A manager even pointed out that he had his own pinups. She eventually brought a lawsuit alleging sex discrimination due to sexual harassment in a hostile work environment; she won her case at the trial court level. An appeal by JSI is pending.

Let's move to the boardrooms of a Big Eight accounting firm, Price Waterhouse (PW), where one of the top managers brought in millions of dollars in accounts, worked more billable hours than anyone in that cohort, was well-liked by clients, and was described as aggressive, hard-driving, ambitious. But this exemplary manager was denied partnership because she was not feminine enough. Ann Hopkins was not accepted for partner because of "interpersonal skills problems" that would be corrected, a supporter informed her, by walking, talking, and dressing more femininely.

Although the setting was not exactly Jacksonville Shipyards, Inc., it encouraged stereotyping of women in several ways. First, Hopkins was in a firm that had about 1% female partners (7 of 662), and she was the only woman out of 88 people proposed for partner that year. The few women managers certainly stood out as women. Second, being a manager in a Big Eight firm is a stereotypically masculine job, calling for tough, aggressive behavior; consequently people think there is a lack of fit between being a woman and being a manager (Heilman, 1983). Third, gender stereotypes are more free to operate on ambiguous criteria, such as judgments of interpersonal skills, than they are on unambiguous counting criteria, such as number of billable hours. PW failed to guard against bias in these subjective judgments by even so minimal an effort as having a written policy against gender-based discrimination. And there were considerable differences of opinion about how to interpret Hopkins's hard-driving managerial behavior. Fourth, the partnership evaluations were based on ambiguous and scant information in many cases; hearsay and casual opinions were given substantial weight. Finally, the firm had no explicit policy against gender discrimination, although it did prohibit discrimination on the basis of age or health in partnership decisions (American Psychological Association [APA], 1989, details these points.)

Ann Hopkins also filed a lawsuit alleging sex discrimination, which she won, even though PW appealed it all the way to the Supreme Court.

What's So Special About Gender in These Cases?

Could such cases have been brought by a plaintiff who was not a woman (for example, by a man or by a person of color)? The answer is "probably not," and explaining it provides some insight into what is so special about gender. After playing out several alternative scenarios, later sections of the chapter will elaborate the conceptual analysis and provide relevant references. For the moment, simply consider the overall argument.

Imagine the alternative scenario that the Robinson case had been brought by a man of color, alleging racial harassment in a hostile work environment. Legal issues aside, the character of the harassment would have been rather different in several ways, each of which we will spend the rest of the chapter elaborating:

1. The harassment would not have such a prescriptive element. "Be more sexually available," said to a woman, is a more plausible message than "be more musical" or "be more hip," said to an African American.

2. It would not have the same type of power dynamics. Although in both the actual and the hypothetical instance, the target would be vastly outnumbered and perhaps feel physically threatened on that account, there are two important differences: the individual male, white or black, is on average evenly matched on physical power. And the social power is at least theoretically equivalent; an apologist might dismiss sexual harassment as harmless by saying "boys will be boys," but it would be less normative to defend racial hostility by saying "white guys will be white guys." (This is not to say that racial harassment is not often dismissed or minimized as harmless using other stratagems.)

3. Another difference is that the sexual harassers have knowledge and expectations based on their wives, girlfriends, mothers, and daughters, whereas racial harassers are less likely to have intimates or relatives who are members of the targeted group.

4. Yet another major difference lies in the (overt at least) goal of sexual harassment, which supposedly is sexual favors. (Hostility is another possible agenda, shared with other types of harassment.) The double message of sexual harassment is clear: "I am sexually interested in you but I am ignoring your refusal."

5. Finally, the norms against expressing sexism are not the same as the norms against expressing racism. The presence of pictures and messages demeaning to women is far more common than comparable materials demeaning to other groups. People are more defensive about appearing racist than sexist (people react more strongly to being called a racist than a sexist), giving rise to all kinds of subtleties in the expression of racism that do not operate identically in sexism, as we will elaborate later. Thus a charge of racial harassment in the Robinson case probably would have looked quite different in several respects.[2]

Consider the Robinson case again, now from the perspective of a man alleging sexual harassment by women (leaving aside the possibility of sexual harassment by other men). Everything here hinges on power differences, both physical and social. There are three main reasons female sexual harassment is not likely to be as threatening: (a) The average physical size difference favors men. (b) The nature of male and female genital physiology makes it far more plausible for men to genitally rape an unwilling woman than for women to genitally rape an unwilling man. (c) Men have more power in society generally, so they have a broader background of power, against which any particular interaction is set. In short, although a man or a person of color could clearly be harassed on the basis of sexual or racial categories, the nature of the harassment would differ dramatically from sexual harassment because of fundamental features of gender stereotyping. These differences form the themes of our discussion in this chapter.

The dramatically different case of Ann Hopkins also highlights what is so special about gender, but in a superficially quite different setting. Consider the Hopkins case if it were brought by a man of color, praised for his competence but faulted for his interpersonal skills problems. To be comparable, the situation would have to entail a job requiring behavior considered antithetical to the stereotypic expectations (e.g., international sophistication for a stereotypic African American or social improvisation for a stereotypic Japanese American). At the same time, strong social prescriptions would require that the person not display such career-enhancing behavior, at the risk of making the decision makers personally uncomfortable. The tension between job requirements and stereotypic prescriptions would result in the career-oriented target being blamed for interpersonal difficulties. The main issue here is that the prescriptive aspect of racial stereotypes is less salient than that for gender stereotypes, so the racial version of *Hopkins* is less plausible. We will elaborate in a later section.

Finally, consider the Hopkins case from the perspective of a man alleging sex discrimination on the basis of stereotyping of his interpersonal skills. Suppose that he behaved in a "feminine" manner that was suited to his job but not suited to the tastes of his employers. Certainly, the prescriptions are strong against men behaving in stereotypically feminine ways. It is possible to imagine a male nurse, for example, faulted for being a mother hen. But the difference is that most stereotypically feminine behavior is not adaptive in most task settings; it is simply not competent behavior to be stereotypically feminine: emotional, passive, vulnerable, and dependent. Hence the configuration of female gender stereotypic behavior is not valued in the workplace, so few employees aspire to it. Essentially, this brings up the power dimension in yet another form; that is, the workplace values "masculine" traits but suppresses them in women.

The Robinson and Hopkins cases and their hypothetical alternative scenarios illustrate some central features of gender stereotyping that set it apart from other kinds of stereotyping. The next sections address each feature in turn.

Gender Stereotypes Are Heavily Prescriptive

A stereotype has both a descriptive component and a prescriptive component. The descriptive component is composed of the attributes that constitute what people believe the typical group member to be like. For instance, the descriptive component of the female stereotype includes the following attributes: emotional, weak, dependent, passive, uncompetitive, and unconfident (Fiske, Bersoff, Borgida, Deaux, & Heilman, 1991). The prescriptive component of a stereotype is composed of the behaviors deemed suitable for the target group. In other words, prescriptions indicate how a member of the target group "should" behave. For example, the female stereotype includes the following prescriptions: A woman should have good interpersonal skills, she should be passive and docile, and she should cooperate with others.

Although all stereotypes include both descriptive aspects and prescriptive aspects, gender stereotypes are more prescriptive than other stereotypes. The many prescriptions characteristic of gender stereotypes are due in part to the amount of exposure people have to members of both gender categories. While observing and interacting with others, people develop a multitude of complex ideas about how members of each gender category actually do behave and how they would ideally behave. People are then able to incorporate these actual and ideal behaviors and formulate prescriptions or "shoulds" for each gender. These "shoulds" define behavior that is appropriate for members of each gender category (e.g., Terborg, 1977).

On the other hand, many people do not have much experience with the behavior of people in other categories. For example, many

European-American people have not observed or interacted with African Americans often enough to have significant knowledge of their behavior. Thus it would be difficult for these people to develop shoulds. However, they could still subscribe to the general descriptive aspect of the African-American stereotype: Blacks are athletic, talkative, religious, and musical (Dovidio & Gaertner, 1986; Stephan & Rosenfield, 1982). The descriptive aspect of a stereotype is more cognitive and could be easily learned from other people (think of all the people who endorse stereotypic descriptions about a category of people with whom they have never interacted). We would argue, however, that the prescriptive aspect of a stereotype is centrally based on experience with the target group.

Not only do people have more experience with gender categories than other categories, people also learn gender categories earlier than other categories. Though children only 24 months old have shown gender stereotyping of objects (Thompson, 1975), simple racial classification of black and white dolls does not emerge until around the age of 5 (Williams & Morland, 1976). In terms of gender stereotypes, by the time children are in preschool and kindergarten they ascribe gender stereotypic labels to toys, activities, and occupations without making many "errors." However, children do not seem to acquire knowledge of gender stereotypic descriptive traits until they are around 8 years old. Thus children apparently acquire knowledge of gender roles (i.e., stereotypic prescriptions) before they acquire knowledge of gender attributes (i.e., stereotypic descriptions) (Ruble & Ruble, 1982). Because the prescriptions people develop as a child are held for such a long time, it is likely that they are very strong.

The strength and complexity of the prescriptive aspects of gender stereotypes contribute to their saliency. Overall, gender is a more salient category than other categories. For instance, Fiske, Haslam, and Fiske (1991) found that people are more likely to confuse individuals of the same gender than individuals of the same age, race, role, or name. In addition, Stangor, Lynch, Duan, and Glass (1992) found people were more likely to categorize people according to their sex than their race. Because gender is such a salient category and the many prescriptive aspects are very strong, it follows that the prescriptive aspects of gender stereotypes will be more salient than the weaker prescriptive aspects of less salient categories. Therefore, people should be more likely to notice when a woman breaks with a stereotypic prescription than when, for example, a person fails to "act his or her age," thereby breaking with a stereotypic prescription.

Well-developed gender stereotypic prescriptions or shoulds limit both men's and women's behavior and, when the prescriptions are broken, it is particularly salient to observers. In addition, any behavior that violates gender prescriptions is generally negatively evaluated by others (Nieva & Gutek, 1980). This poses an especially difficult situation for working women. People will notice when working women do not meet the prescriptive demands of the female stereotype. Yet, as noted, these prescriptions are not usually adaptive for women in work settings (Bardwick & Donovan, 1971; Heilman, 1983). For example, if a female lawyer could not make up her mind, tended to behave in a passive and uncompetitive manner with her peers, and had publicly emotional reactions to both professional and personal experiences, she probably would not advance her career. Women are thus in a double bind. Do they behave in a way that will meet the sex stereotypic prescriptive demands to be feminine? Or, do they act competently and aggressively in order to fill job-specific demands? If they work to fill the job-specific demands, they run the risk of being evaluated negatively for displaying behavior antithetical to the stereotypic expectation for women. On the other hand, if they fill the gender-prescriptive demands, they run the risk of being viewed as incapable of having a successful career. Interestingly, both of these scenarios could result in sexual discrimination. In one case, discrimination would result from not behaving like a woman should and, in the other case, from behaving too much like a woman.

In sum, the prescriptive aspects of stereotypes are more central to gender stereotypes than they are to other stereotypes for a number of different reasons. First, people have more experience with members of each gender category than with members of other categories. This experience allows people to develop many complex prescriptions for gender. Second, people begin learning gender prescriptions at a very young age. These prescriptions are strong because they have been with people for so long. Finally, gender prescriptions are more salient than the prescriptions for other social categories. Unfortunately, the centrality and strength of gender prescriptions places working women in a sensitive situation that easily results in sexual discrimination.

Gender Stereotypes Are Based
on Dramatic Power Differences

The illustrative hypothetical scenarios presented earlier in the chapter suggested the culturally unusual notion of a man bringing a sexual harassment suit, or a man wanting to behave in a feminine fashion to keep a job, but being prevented from doing so by female colleagues. Power is a core issue defining the implausibility of both hypotheticals. If we define *power* as the asymmetrical control over another person's outcomes (Dépret & Fiske, in press), then because men control a disproportionate share of outcomes valued in society (or at least in the workplace), men have power. It is common wisdom that this is so (e.g., Rohrbaugh, 1979), supported by sample statistics, such as the fact that women comprise a mere 3% of the top executive positions, with no increase over the last decade, and earning 72 cents for every dollar earned by men, with wage gaps even in female-dominated professions (Saltzman, 1991).

Sociologists have recognized these phenomena and their impact on gender differences, described in status theories such as expectation states theory (Berger, Conner, & Fisek, 1974; Berger, Fisek, Norman, & Zelditch, 1977). The basic premise is that expected performance (i.e., perceived competence) ranks people in interactions, such that some people's contributions are expected to be more valuable than others. Those higher ranked people (e.g., men, European Americans) are then given more opportunities to contribute, receive deference, and so on (for a recent review and analysis, see Ridgeway & Diekema, 1992). Although this theory is designed to explain gender differences in communication styles, both verbal (Aries, 1987; Smith-Lovin & Robinson, 1992; Wood & Rhodes, 1992) and nonverbal (Ellyson, Dovidio, & Brown, 1992; Hall, 1987; Hall & Veccia, 1992), it also may be expanded to help us understand gender stereotyping.

The higher status of men in general leads to expectations that they will be more competent in general than women. But more specifically, the power and status differences can account for the differential valuing of male stereotypic traits (the competency cluster) and devaluing of female stereotypic traits (the social-emotional cluster), at least in task settings. In fact, the power itself may enable those people in power to define which traits are valuable. Because men have more status and power, their stereotypic traits are viewed as more deserving of respect. Which came first is unclear, but at least some of the variance is due to the power → respect sequence. This is not to say that people do not feel fond of others who display the social-emotional cluster stereotypic of women (Eagly & Mladinic, 1989). They often do, but this fondness may be accompanied by contempt (Kirchler, 1992). Fiske and Ruscher (in press) have argued that people seem to view women simultaneously as likable but also as unworthy of much respect (also see Freeman, 1971). Respect, which translates into rewards in the public marketplace, is differentially awarded to male stereotypic traits precisely because of their association with the group having more power and prestige.

The power and prestige asymmetry can also explain the prescription that women, the stereotypically less competent group, should limit themselves to their stereotypic (less valued) domains of expertise. And, clearly, it explains why men traditionally would not aspire to "feminine" traits, the devalued alternative. Indeed, as more women move into a given field, the status of the field may decline (Touhey, 1974).

In contrast to the status-and-power-differences argument, there is the role theory explanation of gender differences. Eagly (1987) argues that women take on the communal characteristics needed for their traditional roles at home, and men conversely take on the agentic characteristics needed for their traditional roles in the work world. In effect, people are what they do and what other people expect them to be. Both individual and social experience contribute to gender differences. In this analysis, gender roles cause gender differences in behavior, and stereotypes reflect this process. However, this analysis does not account for the devaluing of women more generally in marketplace terms. Role theory does focus squarely on face-to-face interactions as people enact their traditional or nontraditional roles, and the more sociological status theory explanations are incorporating this level of analysis as well (Ridgeway & Diekema, 1992). Power dynamics in specific organizational settings are also important determinants of the extent of stereotyping. So, for example, solo status in an organization encourages stereotyping of individuals from the rare group (B. Mullen, personal communication, May 1992). This is consistent with a power-based explanation, whereby the outnumbered group has less power, and so it is not able to control as many resources. The lack of rewards available from the smaller group in turn decreases the motivation of the larger group to go beyond their initial stereotypes, and it also limits the power of the outnumbered group to alter those stereotypes. The larger, more powerful group in effect defines the norms (Kanter, 1977). Maccoby (1990) suggests that this may cause the disadvantaged group, that is, little girls, to withdraw and create their own subculture.

A final source of power differences results from relative physical size of men and women on average. For example, Dutton (1988) uses this as one among several explanations for the greater seriousness of wife assault than husband assault. This argument of course extends to other types of violence against women by men. It is important to note the physical size issue's contribution to male-female power asymmetries.

Power differences between men and women, then, are based on relative status, expected competence, common roles, relative numbers in the workplace, and average physical size.

Gender Stereotypes Derive Complexity From Close Contacts

Another characteristic of gender stereotypes that separates them from other category-based responses is their complexity. This complexity is derived from the numerous communal relationships between men and women. People have relationships with members of the "opposite" sex every day. Even if people do not have friends or co-workers of the other sex, members of their family are of the other sex. Women have fathers, boyfriends, husbands, and sons; men have mothers, girlfriends, wives, and daughters. Members of no other "minority group" have such routinely close relationships outside their group (Hacker, 1951). The mix of intimacy and discrimination can create profound ambivalence.

Furthermore, people generally have a great deal of time and effort invested in these personal relationships. In fact, some people may consider the behavior of their close friends, family members, and intimates to be the prototypical behavior for other members of the same gender category. They therefore derive expectations for members of the other sex from their personal experiences with these people. Some support for this lies in the fact that men in more egalitarian relationships have less traditional stereotypes of women than men in more traditional relationships (Peplau & Campbell, 1989). Even though these egalitarian partners may have chosen one another because they were each somewhat egalitarian, once in the relationship the expectations of the partners, in particular the male partners, also may have changed to become even more egalitarian.

This variety of close contact with family members, intimates, and friends of the other sex not only affects people's expectations for members of the other sex. It also increases the complexity of gender stereotypes by promoting the use of subtypes. *Subtypes* are "subcategories develop[ed] in response to isolated cases that disconfirm [a stereotype]" (Fiske & Taylor, 1991). For example, a man may have a female cousin who is a very aggressive and competent brain surgeon. She does not fit his female stereotype in many ways. Therefore, he may develop a subtype: female doctors. In essence, he has "fenced off" (Allport, 1954) this family member who disconfirms his more global stereotype of women. In fact, this subtype gives him more information regarding his cousin's dispositions than would the other, broader category (Stangor et al., 1992).

The process of subtyping women is not a recent phenomenon. Women have been subtyped throughout history. Subtypes of women have ranged from love goddesses (e.g., the chivalric notion of the woman on the pedestal) to wholesome mother figures (e.g., the Christian ideal of Mother Mary) to inferior and evil creatures (e.g., the Chinese conception of the feminine nature, the Yin, which is evil and dark) (Rohrbaugh, 1979; Ruble & Ruble, 1982). In the 1970s, research began to address directly these more specific gender subtypes. For instance, Clifton, McGrath, and Wick (1976) discussed two different female stereotypes: "housewife" and "bunny." More recently, Deaux and her colleagues (Deaux, Kite, & Lewis, 1985; Deaux & Lewis, 1984) have also noted specific types of women, many based on job categories.

On the surface, subtyping may appear to be a good process, one that reduces stereotyping. After all, by subtyping, people are recognizing that not all people in a category are the same. For example, there are female doctors, female bunnies, and female leaders. Each of these subtypes has unique characteristics that separate it from the others and, to some degree, from the overall female stereotype. As promising as this line of thinking appears to be, however, it has not proven to be beneficial.

Subtyping or "fencing off" actually allows people to keep their overall stereotype intact (Hewstone, Hopkins, & Routh, 1992; Hewstone, Johnston, & Aird, 1992; Johnston & Hewstone, 1992). By separating people who disconfirm a stereotype into a subtype, people brand these disconfirmatory cases as atypical. If these disconfirmatory cases are considered atypical, they will not affect the overall stereotype because the overall stereotype describes people who are *typical* members of the category.

Interestingly, even the subtypes people form to account for women who disconfirm the stereotype still incorporate gender. Women are not simply doctors or professors. They are *female* doctors or *female* professors. These category labels imply that there is something about being female that is relevant to role performance. One rarely says "male doctor" or "male professor." Moreover, one would think that gender would not be a part of the label of a category developed to classify women who disconfirm the gender stereotype.

So, what would be the best way to disconfirm and, subsequently, to change a stereotype that has a propensity for subtyping? Rothbart and John (1985) argue that disconfirming behaviors will only alter stereotypes if they are associated with people who are otherwise typical group members. In this way the overall category is activated and it is more difficult to subtype. The female fighter pilot who also has a husband, two children, and a big kitchen probably does more to counteract stereotypes than the unmarried female fighter pilot who hates to cook. Change of stereotypes is also promoted if the disconfirming behavior displayed by otherwise typical group members occurs repeatedly in many different settings. This reduces the chance that the disconfirming behavior will be attributed to environmental conditions. Women who are fighter pilots, rock climbers, and construction workers have undermined the old stereotype that women cannot do tough, demanding work. More recently, Hewstone and his colleagues have found support for the idea that dispersed inconsistent information promotes more stereotype change than does concentrated inconsistent information (Hewstone et al., 1992; Johnston & Hewstone, 1992).

One would think, with all the experiences shared between members of the two genders, that gender stereotypes would have changed. In particular, in recent years many American women have entered the work force and disconfirmed a number of stereotypic beliefs about women. Yet the basic, core contents of the female stereotype have not changed to any great degree over centuries (for a recent reference, see Eagly & Mladinic, 1989; for a review, see Ruble & Ruble, 1982).

Perhaps men who subscribe to the traditional female stereotype think they are "experts" on women's behavior because they have had first-hand experience and they "know" how women should and do act. In other words, these men may have their own prescriptions and descriptions for women's behavior that they think must be appropriate and accurate because they have had many experiences that confirm their ideas. This poses two problems for stereotype change. First, the "experts" may simply refuse to accept that their stereotypes are inaccurate. Second, the group that believes it is an expert on the other group may have a sense of superior status and many studies on intergroup contact have indicated that stereotypes are not likely to change unless the two groups experience contact with one another under conditions of equal status (Stephan & Brigham, 1985).

Finally, the expectations sexual harassers have for people of the opposite sex, which are based on their friends, family members, and intimates, are complex and hard to change. Even sexual harassers who treat their female intimates respectfully are aware of both the more positive aspects of the female stereotype, which may lead to respect, and the more traditional aspects of the stereotype, which may promote harassing behavior in the workplace. Thus, because they have extremely complex and subtyped stereotypes of women, it may be even more difficult to change the stereotypes of "respectful" harassers than those of "consistent" harassers who have less complex and subtyped stereotypes.

On the other hand, racial harassers are less likely to have intimates who are members of the targeted group. Therefore, racial harassers' stereotypes should be less defined and less complex. Thus it may even be simpler to change racial harassers' stereotypes because they do not have a large number of subtypes that would need to be incorporated into the global stereotype. Of course, the problem of promoting equal status between the two groups would still exist.

In sum, gender stereotypes seem more complex than other stereotypes. The two genders share many experiences with one another. These experiences allow people to develop complex expectations for members of the other gender. In addition, this interaction promotes the use of subtypes. Unfortunately, stereotype change for gender stereotypes seems more difficult than for other categories because people have many subtypes for gender categories that would need to be integrated for change to occur.

Gender Stereotypes
Derive Universality From Biology

Men and women are biologically fated to intertwined lives. Nevertheless, that very same biology suggests that men and women may want different things from each other, and this is likely to affect their mutual perceptions. The potential impact of sexual biology tells us mostly about the evolution of our ancestors rather than about the social developments since that time or to come in the future. Social change is also part of the evolution of the species. Nevertheless, some evolutionary biological background sheds light on the near universality—but not inevitability—of certain cultural forms, including gender stereotypes.

From this standpoint, men and women regard each other primarily as potential mates, and sex differences in mate preferences suggest some important mismatched goals and stereotypes. Starting from the biological premise that females have more physical investment in each individual child than males do, females should value males who show signs of ability and willingness to invest in joint offspring (Buss, 1988, 1989). This suggests that women will look for men with financial resources. On the other hand, males can maximize their reproductive capability by finding fertile and nurturing females, and this suggests to sociobiologically oriented psychologists that men should value women who appear young and healthy. Other evolutionary sex differences can be similarly analyzed, but the basic contrast lies in women looking for mates showing evidence of resource acquisition and men looking for mates showing evidence of reproductive capacity (Buss, 1988; for a similar analysis, see Kenrick, 1989). Some of these preferences have been confirmed in samples from 37 different cultures (Buss, 1989).

Whatever the merits of the evolutionary argument, it certainly fits with the division of male and female prescriptive stereotypes into a competency cluster for men (indicating the means to resource acquisition) and an attractiveness-nurturance cluster for women (signs of reproductive capacity). If the men in the Jacksonville Shipyard had only appreciated aspects of the women workers other than their reproductive readiness, and if the men at Price Waterhouse had only appreciated other aspects of Ann Hopkins than her apparent lack of nurturance, both environments would have been much more civilized. The women were foolish enough to believe that work was what mattered in the workplace; fortunately, the courts agreed with them, despite human evolutionary proclivities.

Gender Stereotypes
Are Historically Situated

Reviewing two decades of research on gender stereotypes (an enterprise not intended here, but see Deaux, 1985; Ruble & Ruble, 1982), one would see a sea-change in the message of the literature then and now. Either our research subjects or our psychological colleagues or both are changing their minds about the content and scope of gender stereotypes. The historical context has shifted from men and women being perceived as opposite sexes to men and women being perceived as overlapping on multiple dimensions and gender stereotypes being fleshed out in multiple subtypes. Whether we or our subjects are becoming more sophisticated almost does not matter, for some change is accomplished. (Perhaps our biology is not so fixed after all?)

One index of the change is the citation frequency of the classic article by Broverman, Vogel, Broverman, Clarkson, and Rosenkrantz (1972) documenting the content of gender stereotypes. From a steady buildup from 1972 to 1980, with a peak of nearly 80 citations in 1980, the citations dropped to less than half that in 1990 (according to citations listed in the *Social Science Citation Index*). Any article has a similar citation profile, assuming it is cited at all, but this article, as one of the catalysts of the research literature, is intrinsically diagnostic. Although there have been no replications of Broverman et al. (1972), there is evidence that people still endorse these gender stereotypes (e.g., Martin, 1987).

Another gender stereotype classic, the Goldberg (1968) study, illustrates the change in the overall message over time. Although the 1968 study seemed to demonstrate that the same work product was evaluated more favorably when attributed to a man than to a woman, the message has become more complex over time (Swim, Borgida, Maruyama, & Myers, 1989). The effect size was larger in studies published during 1968-1973, but not huge even then. Essentially the current message is that stereotyping is a function of many moderator variables, most of which have not been examined in enough detail to conduct a meta-analysis on the moderators. Swim et al. suggested several plausible moderators: particular subtypes activated, perceived diagnosticity of information, interaction between stereotype and information, goals or motives of the subject, and task demands.

When one collapses over various moderators, of course, one is averaging over (a) control conditions designed to show the baseline discriminatory effect (i.e., women are evaluated less favorably than comparable men) and (b) experimental conditions designed to eliminate the effect (i.e., the effect goes away if people are motivated to be more careful). It is not surprising then that an overall meta-analysis of the main effect concluded that the effect is small (Fiske, Bersoff, Borgida, Deaux, & Heilman, 1991). The interactions between the basic effect and the proposed moderator variables are being ignored.

One might examine the small main effects for gender and conclude that gender stereotyping has nearly vanished. Some textbook writers indeed are beginning to conclude that gender stereotyping is less of a problem than it used to be. Compare one of the best-selling social psychology texts in 1981: "As we have seen throughout this discussion, sexual stereotypes, and the discriminatory behaviors that accompany them, certainly persist at the present time" (Baron & Byrne, 1981, p. 182); and a decade later: "Together, all these findings point to substantial shifts toward a reduced incidence of sex discrimination in the world of work" (Baron & Byrne, 1991, p. 219). There is clearly some room for optimism at present; however, the experimental research is not an indicator of incidence per se, not being a representative sample survey, but rather having been designed to study moderators and mediators of effects. In other words, current experiments show that stereotyping is a complex process but say little about how frequently it occurs.

An illustration of the role of subtypes in stereotyping serves to indicate the complexity of modern sexism. Ann Hopkins was a victim of gender stereotypes, but certainly not the stereotype that she was passive, incompetent, and emotional. Quite the contrary. And a recent meta-analysis bears (Eagly, Makhijani, & Klonsky, 1992) out the conclusions of the American Psychological Association's amicus brief (APA, 1989) and the Supreme Court:

> Women in leadership positions were devalued relative to their male counterparts when leadership was carried out in stereotypically masculine styles, particularly when this style was autocratic or directive. In

addition, the devaluation of women was greater when leaders occupied male-dominated roles and when the evaluators were men. (Eagly, Makhijani, & Klonsky, 1992, p. 3)

In short, one would not expect a main effect such that all women are universally devalued; rather, certain women are devalued when gender-based subtypes interact with the features of a particular work environment.

Elsewhere, Fiske (1989) has argued that these people, who do not match widespread descriptive stereotypes, are faulted on subjective grounds because they make us uncomfortable by violating our notions of how such people should behave. This gives rise to the perception that one is dealing with a "difficult" person, someone who simply does not fit in. The point is that such people are stereotyped and the blame for their problems is laid at the door of their own personal attributes. Hopkins was certainly seen as a difficult person, and Lois Robinson also was faulted for not going along with the locker-room atmosphere. Both were perceived as difficult people.

Besides the increasing complexity of subtypes, gender stereotyping has the potential for another major historical shift. Such a shift has already occurred in the literature on racism, along with changing historical norms. Whereas early research indicated overt, old-fashioned racism (claiming blacks are inferior to whites), more recent efforts have tackled modern racism in several forms (see Pettigrew, 1985, for a review). For example, Sears and his colleagues (Sears, Hensler, & Speer, 1979) argued that people do not want to feel racist, so instead they attack issues symbolic of the out-group; thus, opposing all policies related to busing, affirmative action, welfare, and the like, would indicate symbolic racism. Similarly, Gaertner and Dovidio (1986) described aversive racism: the person's racism is aversive to his or her self-image, so the person behaves in a nondiscriminatory, even reverse discriminatory way, except when the behavior is covert or when there is an acceptable alternative explanation (an excuse) for the discriminatory behavior that would make it appear nonracist. Also, Katz and his colleagues (Katz, Wackenhut, & Hass, 1986) discussed at length the ambivalence and response amplification that may result when people hold simultaneously sympathetic and rejecting attitudes toward an out-group. All of these dynamics seem to us to be plausible accounts of what is beginning to happen with sexism as well; it has not vanished, just become less acceptable in many circles, so it has gone underground.

Researchers need to pursue this parallel between modern racism and modern sexism.

Research topics go through a predictable development, and gender stereotyping research is no exception: from the heady days of first discoveries (the more counterintuitive or provocative, the better), to the replications and extensions, to the inevitable dissent, to the moderator variable stage. Gender stereotyping research has clearly arrived at the moderator variable stage. From there, research can fizzle if people decide "there is no there there" (too many contradictions, too many qualifications, too complicated, too limited to one paradigm; whatever the complaint, the result is the same). Alternatively, research at this stage can spin off new theoretical approaches that synthesize previous work. Given the importance and interest value of gender as an enduring feature of the human landscape, we expect that the future will bring synthesis rather than fizzle.

Summary

This chapter has argued that gender-based responses differ from other types of category-based responses in a variety of ways. First, gender stereotypes are heavily prescriptive. People acquire gender categories in the family, before they acquire other categories, and they therefore have more time to develop and motivation to invest in gender prescriptions. Second, gender stereotypes are based on dramatic power differences. Men are not only physically larger than women, but they also control a disproportionate share of the outcomes valued in society. Third, close contact between the two genders increases the complexity of gender stereotypes, and thus gender stereotypes may be characterized by more subtypes than other stereotypes. Fourth, gender stereotypes possess sexual and biological facets that other stereotypes do not have. And, finally, gender stereotypes change as a function of cultural change and scientific advance.

Every one of these distinctive characteristics of gender stereotypes has significant effects on interactions between people. As illustrated in the text of this chapter, they each affected the stereotyping of and discrimination against both Lois Robinson and Ann Hopkins. In addition, these characteristics influence the literature on gender. And, perhaps most importantly, they affect our everyday interactions with our friends, co-workers, relatives, and intimates.

Notes

1. Technically, this part of the title should read "What's So Special About Gender?" However, we opted for the more eye-catching "What's So Special About Sex?"

2. We are merely trying to illustrate how sexism is different from racism. We are not saying that sexism is more important or more serious.

References

Allport, G. W. (1954). *The nature of prejudice.* Reading, MA: Addison-Wesley.

American Psychological Association Brief for Amicus Curiae in Support of Respondent, *Price Waterhouse v. Hopkins,* 109 S. Ct. 1775 (1989).

Aries, E. (1987). Gender and communication. In P. Shaver & C. Hendrick (Eds.), *Review of personality and social psychology: Sex and gender* (Vol. 7, pp. 149-176). Newbury Park, CA: Sage.

Bardwick, J. M., & Donovan, E. (1971). Ambivalence: The socialization of women. In V. Gornick & B. K. Moran (Eds.), *Woman in sexist society* (pp. 147-159). New York: Basic Books. (Reprinted from J. M. Bardwick (Ed.), *Readings on the psychology of women* (pp. 52-58), Harper & Row, 1972)

Baron, R. A., & Byrne, D. (1981). *Social psychology: Understanding human interaction* (3rd ed.). Boston: Allyn & Bacon.

Baron, R. A., & Byrne, D. (1991). *Social psychology: Understanding human interaction* (6th ed.). Boston: Allyn & Bacon.

Berger, J., Conner, T. L., & Fisek, M. H. (1974). *Expectation states theory: A theoretical research program.* Cambridge, MA: Winthrop.

Berger, J., Fisek, M. H., Norman, R. Z., & Zelditch, M., Jr. (1977). *Status characteristics and social interaction.* New York: Elsevier.

Broverman, I. K., Vogel, S. R., Broverman, D. M., Clarkson, F. E., & Rosenkrantz, P. S. (1972). Sex-role stereotypes: A current appraisal. *Journal of Social Issues, 28*(2), 59-78.

Buss, D. M. (1988). Love acts: The evolutionary biology of love. In R. J. Sternberg & M. L. Barnes (Eds.), *The psychology of love* (pp. 100-118). New Haven, CT: Yale University Press.

Buss, D. M. (1989). Sex differences in human mate preferences: Evolutionary hypotheses tested in 37 cultures. *Behavioral and Brain Sciences, 12,* 1-49.

Clifton, A. K., McGrath, D., & Wick, B. (1976). Stereotypes of woman: A single category? *Sex Roles, 2,* 135-148.

Deaux, K. (1985). Sex and gender. *Annual Review of Psychology, 36,* 49-81.

Deaux, K., Kite, M. E., & Lewis, L. L. (1985). Clustering and gender schemata: An uncertain link. *Personality and Social Psychology Bulletin, 11,* 387-397.

Deaux, K., & Lewis, L. L. (1984). Structure of gender stereotypes: Interrelationships among components and gender label. *Journal of Personality and Social Psychology, 46,* 991-1004.

Dépret, E. F., & Fiske, S. T. (in press). Social cognition and power: Some cognitive consequences of social structure as a source of control deprivation. In G. Weary, F. Gleicher, & K. Marsh (Eds.), *Control motivation and social cognition.* New York: Springer.

Dovidio, J. F., & Gaertner, S. L. (1986). Prejudice, discrimination, and racism: Historical trends and contemporary approaches. In J. F. Dovidio & S. L. Gaertner (Eds.), *Prejudice, discrimination, and racism* (pp. 1-34). New York: Academic Press.

Dutton, D. G. (1988). Research advances in the study of wife assault etiology and prevention. *Law and Mental Health,* 161-219.

Eagly, A. H. (1987). *Sex differences in social behavior: A social-role interpretation.* Hillsdale, NJ: Lawrence Erlbaum.

Eagly, A. H., Makhijani, M. G., & Klonsky, B. G. (1992). Gender and the evaluation of leaders: A meta-analysis. *Psychological Bulletin, 111,* 3-22.

Eagly, A. H., & Mladinic, A. (1989). Gender stereotypes and attitudes toward women and men. *Personality and Social Psychology Bulletin, 15,* 534-558.

Ellyson, S. L., Dovidio, J. F., & Brown, C. E. (1992). The look of power: Gender differences and similarities in visual dominance behavior. In C. L. Ridgeway (Ed.), *Gender, interaction and inequality* (pp. 50-80). New York: Springer.

Fiske, A. P., Haslam, N., & Fiske, S. T. (1991). Confusing one person with another: What errors reveal about the elementary forms of social relations. *Journal of Personality and Social Psychology, 60,* 656-674.

Fiske, S. T. (1989, August). *Interdependence and stereotyping: From the laboratory to the Supreme Court (and back).* Invited address given at the 97th Annual Convention of the American Psychological Association, New Orleans.

Fiske, S. T., Bersoff, D. N., Borgida, E., Deaux, K., & Heilman, M. E. (1991). Social science research on trial: Use of sex stereotyping research in *Price Waterhouse v. Hopkins. American Psychologist, 46,* 1049-1060.

Fiske, S. T., & Ruscher, J. B. (in press). Negative interdependence and prejudice: Whence the affect? In D. M. Mackie & D. L. Hamilton (Eds.), *Affect, cognition, and stereotyping: Interactive processes in group perception.* New York: Academic Press.

Fiske, S. T., & Taylor, S. E. (1991). *Social cognition* (2nd ed.). New York: McGraw-Hill.

Freeman, J. (1971). Social construction of the second sex. In M. H. Garskof (Ed.), *Roles women play: Readings toward women's liberation* (pp. 123-141). Belmont, CA: Wadsworth.

Gaertner, S. L., & Dovidio, J. F. (1986). The aversive form of racism. In J. F. Dovidio & S. L. Gaertner (Eds.), *Prejudice, discrimination, and racism* (pp. 61-89). New York: Academic Press.

Goldberg, P. (1968). Are women prejudiced against women? *Transaction, 5,* 28-30.

Hacker, H. M. (1951). Women as a minority group. *Social Forces, 30,* 60-69.

Hall, J. A. (1987). On explaining gender differences: The case of nonverbal communication. In P. Shaver & C. Hendrick (Eds.), *Review of personality and social psychology: Sex and gender* (Vol. 7, pp. 177-200). Newbury Park, CA: Sage.

Hall, J. A., & Veccia, E. M. (1992). Touch asymmetry between the sexes. In C. L. Ridgeway (Ed.), *Gender, interaction, and inequality* (pp. 81-96). New York: Springer.

Heilman, M. E. (1983). Sex bias in work settings: The lack of fit model. *Research in Organizational Behavior, 5,* 269-298.

Hewstone, M., Hopkins, N., & Routh, D. A. (1992). Cognitive models of stereotype change: Generalization and subtyping in young people's views of the police. *European Journal of Social Psychology, 22,* 219-224.

Hewstone, M., Johnston, L., & Aird, P. (1992). Cognitive models of stereotype change: Perceptions of homogeneous and heterogeneous groups. *European Journal of Social Psychology, 22,* 235-250.

Johnston, L., & Hewstone, M. (1992). Cognitive models of stereotype change: Subtyping and the perceived typicality of disconfirming group members. *Journal of Experimental Social Psychology 28,* 260-386.

Kanter, R. M. (1977). *Men and women of the corporation.* New York: Basic Books.

Katz, I., Wackenhut, J., & Hass, R. G. (1986). Racial ambivalence, value duality, and behavior. In J. F. Dovidio & S. L. Gaertner (Eds.), *Prejudice, discrimination, and racism* (pp. 35-59). New York: Academic Press.

Kelley, H. H. (1992). Common-sense psychology and scientific psychology. *Annual Review of Psychology, 43,* 1-23.

Kenrick, D. T. (1989). A biosocial perspective on mates and traits: Reuniting personality and social psychology. In D. M. Buss & N. Cantor (Eds.), *Personality psychology: Recent trends and emerging directions* (pp. 308-319). New York: Springer.

Kirchler, E. (1992). Adorable woman, expert man: Changing gender images of women and men in management. *European Journal of Social Psychology, 22,* 363-373.

Maccoby, E. E. (1990). Gender and relationships. *American Psychologist, 45,* 513-520.

Martin, C. L. (1987). A ratio measure of sex stereotyping. *Journal of Personality and Social Psychology, 52,* 489-499.

Nieva, V. F., & Gutek, B. A. (1980). Sex effects on evaluation. *Academy of Management Review, 5,* 267-276.

Peplau, L. A., & Campbell, S. M. (1989). The balance of power in dating and marriage. In J. Freeman (Ed.), *Women: A feminist perspective* (pp. 121-137). Mountain View, CA: Mayfield.

Pettigrew, T. F. (1985). New black-white patterns: How best to conceptualize them? *Annual Review of Sociology, 11,* 329-346.

Price Waterhouse v. Hopkins, 109 S. Ct. 1775 (1989).

Ridgeway, C. L., & Diekema, D. (1992). Are gender differences status differences? In C. L. Ridgeway (Ed.), *Gender, interaction, and inequality* (pp. 157-180). New York: Springer.

Rohrbaugh, J. B. (1979). *Women: Psychology's puzzle.* New York: Basic Books.

Rothbart, M., & John, O. P. (1985). Social categorization and behavioral episodes: A cognitive analysis of the effects of intergroup contact. *Journal of Social Issues, 41*(3), 81-104.

Ruble, D. N., & Ruble, T. L. (1982). Sex stereotypes. In A. G. Miller (Ed.), *In the eye of the beholder: Contemporary issues in stereotyping* (pp. 188-252). New York: Praeger.

Saltzman, A. (1991, June 17). Trouble at the top. *U.S. News and World Report,* pp. 40-48.

Sears, D. O., Hensler, C. P., & Speer, L. K. (1979). Whites' opposition to busing: Self-interest or symbolic politics? *American Political Science Review, 73,* 369-384.

Smith-Lovin, L., & Robinson, D. T. (1992). Gender and conversational dynamics. In C. L. Ridgeway (Ed.), *Gender, interaction, and inequality* (pp. 122-156). New York: Springer.

Stangor, C., Lynch, L., Duan, C., & Glass, B. (1992). Categorization of individuals on the basis of multiple social features. *Journal of Personality and Social Psychology, 62,* 207-218.

Stephan, W. G., & Brigham, J. C. (1985). Intergroup contact: Introduction. *Journal of Social Issues, 41*(3), 1-8.

Stephan, W. G., & Rosenfield, D. (1982). Racial and ethnic stereotypes. In A. G. Miller (Ed.), *In the eye of the beholder: Contemporary issues in stereotyping* (pp. 92-136). New York: Praeger.

Swim, J., Borgida, E., Maruyama, G., & Myers, D. G. (1989). Joan McKay versus John McKay: Do gender stereotypes bias evaluations? *Psychological Bulletin, 105,* 409-429.

Terborg, J. R. (1977). Women in management: A research review. *Journal of Applied Psychology, 62,* 647-664.

Thompson, S. K (1975). Gender labels and early sex role development. *Child Development, 46,* 339-347.

Touhey, J. C. (1974). Effects of additional women professionals on ratings of occupational prestige and desirability. *Journal of Personality and Social Psychology, 29,* 86-89.

Williams, J. E., & Morland, K. J. (1976). *Race, color and the young child.* Chapel Hill: University of North Carolina Press.

Wood, W., & Rhodes, N. (1992). Sex differences in interaction style in task groups. In C. L. Ridgeway (Ed.), *Gender, interaction, and inequality* (pp. 97-121). New York: Springer.

9

Responses to Sexual Harassment

BARBARA A. GUTEK

Sexual harassment has been illegal in the United States since 1980. Over the past decade, many developments have occurred: A substantial amount of research has been conducted, the law has continued to evolve, and many mechanisms have been proposed both to handle sexual harassment when it occurs and to prevent it from occurring. Although in 1980 about 15% of workers had not heard the term *sexual harassment* (Gutek, 1985), it is a household word today as a result of several prominent allegations. The 1991 resignation and subsequent reinstatement of Stanford University neurosurgeon Frances Conley, which received considerable press, was soon overshadowed by allegations made by Professor Anita Hill during the Clarence Thomas Supreme Court confirmation hearings later in that year.

Despite noticeable progress on several fronts, sexual harassment is still a problem for many employed women and some men. This chapter focuses on the extent of the problem and the extent to which the developments that have already occurred are sufficient to eliminate sexual harassment as a workplace problem. This chapter first provides a short history of the discovery and documentation of sexual harassment. The prevalence of harassment and nonharassing sexual behavior at work are assessed as well as the reactions of victims of harassment. The chapter then turns to a case about one sexual harassment victim who took her grievance to court. The case illustrates some of the problems confronting the person who seeks legal redress for being sexually harassed. The chapter concludes with some thoughts about progress.

The Discovery of Sexual Harassment

Sexual harassment was "discovered" in the mid-1970s, and it was postulated to be relatively widespread and to have long-lasting, harmful effects on a significant number of working women. This "discovery" was somewhat counterintuitive, because some women were believed to benefit from seductive behavior and sexual behaviors at work, gaining unfair advantage and acquiring perks and privileges from their flirtatious and seductive behavior (Lipman-Blumen, 1976, 1984; Quinn, 1977).[1] The first accounts of sexual harassment were journalistic reports and case studies (Bernstein, 1976; Lindsey, 1977; Pogrebin, 1977; Rivers, 1978; Safran, 1976). Soon the topic was catapulted into public awareness through the publication of two important books. Farley's 1978 book, *Sexual Shakedown: The Sexual Harassment of Women on the Job,* aimed to bring sexual harassment to public attention, create a household word, and make people aware of harassment as a social problem. Providing a label and then a definition for sexual harassment was an important step in developing ways to measure the prevalence of sexual harassment. Similarly, MacKinnon wrote: "The unnamed should not be taken for the nonexistent" (1979, p. 28). MacKinnon's book, *Sexual Harassment of Working Women* (1979), built on the journalistic work of Farley. As a lawyer MacKinnon sought a legal mechanism for handling sexual harassment and compensating its victims. In a strong and compelling argument, she contended that sexual harassment was primarily a problem for women, that it rarely happened to men, and therefore that it should be viewed as a form of sex discrimination. Viewing sexual harassment as a form of sex discrimination would make available to victims the same legal protection available to victims of sex discrimination.

In 1980 the Equal Employment Opportunity Commission (EEOC) established guidelines consistent with MacKinnon's position and defined sexual harassment under Title VII of the 1964 Civil Rights Act as a form of unlawful sex-based discrimination. Several states have passed their own increasingly strong laws aimed at eliminating sexual harassment (see Pearman & Lebrato, 1984; Shullman & Watts, 1987), and legal scholars and practitioners have sought additional avenues to recover damages incurred from sexual harassment (Dworkin, Ginger, & Mallor, 1988; Estrich, 1991; Vermeulen, 1982). Various public and private agencies as well as the courts have recorded a steady if uneven increase in sexual harassment complaints since the early 1980s (see Livingston, 1982; National Council for Research on Women, 1991).

Current guidelines and regulations define sexual harassment broadly. For example, the EEOC (1980) guidelines, updated in a policy statement in 1984, state that unwelcome sexual advances, requests for sexual favors, and other verbal or physical conduct of a sexual nature constitute sexual harassment when (a) submission to such conduct is made either explicitly or implicitly a term or condition of an individual's employment or academic advancement, (b) submission to or rejection of such conduct by an individual is used as the basis for employment decisions or academic decisions affecting such an individual, or (c) such conduct has the purpose or effect of reasonably interfering with an individual's work or academic performance or creating an intimidating, hostile, or offensive working or academic environment.

Although the guidelines define the terms of sexual harassment, they are not explicit in providing examples. Unfortunately, the examples given in the media, in training materials, and in research are frequently rather sanitized versions of the experiences of real victims of harassment. This is true in part because the real experiences often cannot be, or are not, printed or discussed in public. Instances that eventuate in court cases often involve behavior that is not usually discussed in "polite company" and jokes, epithets, or comments that are not printable in magazines and newspapers. Thus women who take their sexual harassment case to court have often been addressed in derogatory sexually explicit language, have been pressured to engage in unusual sexual behavior, have been threatened with physical violence, and/or have been victims of cruel sexual pranks. The latter include finding "used" condoms or other sexual paraphernalia (e.g., dildos) in their desks or lockers, finding obscene and physically threatening messages posted in their workspaces, and regularly being addressed in a crude insulting manner (e.g., "dumb fucking cunt").

Research on Sexual Harassment

Researchers began serious study of sex at work only after Farley's and MacKinnon's books were published, two compendia of information on sexual harassment were in progress (Backhouse & Cohen, 1978; Neugarten & Shafritz, 1981), and generally after the EEOC had established guidelines in 1980. Not surprisingly, researchers were heavily influenced by these important developments in policy and law.

Frequency of Sexual Harassment at Work

One area of research that developed in response to legal and policy development was documentation of the forms and prevalence of harassment experienced by people. The research on frequency focuses heavily but not exclusively on heterosexual harassment (see U.S. Merit Systems Protection Board [USMSPB], 1981, 1987).

The research on prevalence shows a broad range of rates, depending in part on the time frame used. The U.S. Merit Systems Protection Board's (1981) study found that 42% of the women respondents reported experiencing sexual harassment on the job within the previous 2 years. When the study was repeated several years later (USMSPB, 1987), the figure remained the same. In a Seattle, Washington, study of city employees, more than one third of all respondents reported sexual harassment in the previous 24 months of city employment (Stringer-Moore, 1982). Dunwoody-Miller and Gutek (1985) found that 20% of California state civil service employees reported being sexually harassed at work in the previous 5 years. Reviewing the results from several different measures of prevalence she used, Gutek (1985) suggested that up to 53% of women had been harassed sometime in their working life. The figures are higher in the military—two thirds of women surveyed in a 1990 study said they have been sexually harassed (Women's Legal Defense Fund, 1991).

Other studies using purposive or convenience samples generally show higher rates of harassment. In these studies (Working Women's Institute, 1975; Safran, 1976; Schneider, 1982) the percentage of women reporting that they have been harassed varies from about 65% to 90%. Because of self-selection biases that exist in purposive or convenience samples, researchers assume that people who have been harassed may be more motivated to participate. Thus these incidence rates are likely to be somewhat inflated.

Although women of all ages, races, occupations, income levels, and marital statuses experience harassment (see Farley, 1978), research suggests that young and unmarried women are especially vulnerable (Gutek, Nakamura, Gahart, Handschumacher, & Russell, 1980; Schneider, 1982; Tangri, Burt, & Johnson, 1982). Not surprisingly, most women are harassed by men, not by women (Schneider, 1982; USMSPB, 1981). In addition, women in nontraditional jobs (e.g., truck driver, neurosurgeon, engineer, roofer) and in nontraditional fields such as the military and mining are more likely to experience harassment than are other women. These higher rates are over and above what is expected due to their high amount of work contact with men (Gutek & Morasch, 1982; Gutek, Cohen, & Konrad, 1990). On the basis of the set of studies done so far, it seems likely that overall, from one third to one half of all women have been sexually harassed at sometime in their working lives, although frequency rates in some types of work may be higher.

Sexual harassment at work has also been reported by men in several studies. The U.S. Merit Systems Protection Board study found 15% of the men to be harassed by male or female employees (Tangri, Burt, & Johnson, 1982). On the basis of men's reports of specific behavior, Gutek (1985) suggested that up to 9% of men could have been harassed by women sometime in their working lives. After a careful analysis of men's accounts of harassment, however, Gutek (1985) concluded that very few of the reported incidents were sexual harassment as it is legally defined, and some of the incidents might not have even been considered sexual if the same behavior had been initiated by a man or by another woman who was considered a less desirable sexual partner by the man. (See also Quina, 1990, for similar conclusions.)

Frequency of Other Sexual Behavior at Work

Several studies have also examined other kinds of sexual behavior at work—behavior that most people do not consider harassment—including comments or whistles intended to be compliments, quasi-sexual touching such as hugging or an arm around the shoulder, requests for a date or sexual activity often in a joking manner, and sexual jokes or comments that are not directed to a particular person (Brewer, 1982). These other "nonharassing," less serious, and presumably nonproblematic behaviors are considerably more common than harassment. For example, Gutek (1985) found that 61% of men and 68% of women said that they had received at least one sexual comment that was meant to be complimentary sometime in their working lives. In addition, 56% of men and 67% of women reported that they had been the recipient of at least one sexual look or gesture that was intended to be complimentary. About 8 out of every 10 workers have been recipients of some kind of sexual overture that was intended to be a compliment. Schneider (1982) found that 55% of a sample of heterosexual working women and 67% of a sample of lesbian working women reported that within the last year at work, someone had joked with them about their body or appearance. Other studies show similar findings. Dunwoody-Miller and Gutek (1985) reported that 76% of women and 55% of men indicated that as California state civil service employees, they had received complimentary comments of a sexual nature. Looks and gestures of a sexual nature that were meant as compliments were also common (reported by 67% of women and 47% of men).

Although men seem rarely to be harassed, the amount of sexual behavior reported by them at work is substantial. For example, Gutek (1985) found that men were more likely than women to say that they were sexually touched by an opposite-sex person on their job. According to Abbey (1982), Davies (1982), and Gottfried and Fasenfest (1984), men are more likely than women to perceive the world in sexual terms. Also, men are more likely than women to mistake friendliness for seduction (Abbey, 1982, 1987), and they find the office is a little too exciting with women around ("Sexual Tension," 1981). This seems consistent with the common stimulus-response view that women's presence elicits sexual behavior from men. Reports from men, however, suggest that attention to sex is common in many male-dominated workplaces, whether or not women are actually present (Gutek, 1985). This sexualized culture takes the forms of posters, jokes, sexual metaphors for work, comments, obscene language, and the like. The relationship seems to be quite straightforward: the more sexualized the workplace, the more likely the workplace is mostly male. The fact that much of this sexualization of work settings is degrading to women as well as sexual is what creates the "hostile" environment that government regulations aim to eliminate.

Taken together, the research on harassment and "nonharassment" shows that sexual behavior at work is very common; in many work settings, attention to sex permeates work. An equally important conclusion of this body of research is that legal sex-related behavior is considerably more common than illegal sexual harassment. This finding is not surprising, but it is important; when some people first hear about sexual harassment, they may confuse it with the more common legal behavior at work which they, themselves, have seen and experienced. This confusion of nonthreatening and legal behavior with sexual harassment can lead some incorrectly to denigrate women's complaints as prudish or overly sensitive.

Consequences of Sexual Behavior at Work

Any behavior that is as common as sexual harassment and sexual nonharassment at work is likely to have a wide variety of ramifications for the individuals involved. Most of the research has quite naturally focused on the consequences to women. Sexual harassment has a variety of negative consequences for women workers (Benson & Thompson, 1982; Crull & Cohen, 1984; Dunwoody-Miller & Gutek, 1985; Evans, 1978; Gutek, 1985; Gutek & Nakamura, 1982; Koss, 1990; Schneider, 1982; Tangri et al., 1982; USMSPB, 1981). In addition to the discomfort associated with the sexually harassing experiences and violation of physical privacy, women often find that their careers are interrupted (Hemming, 1985). Up to 10% of women have quit a job because of sexual harassment (Gutek, 1985; Gutek, Nakamura, Gahart, Handschumacher, & Russell, 1980). Others fear becoming victims of retaliation if they complain about the harassment, and some are asked to leave (Crull & Cohen, 1984). For example, Coles (1986) found that among 81 cases filed with the California Department of Fair Employment and Housing between 1979 and 1983, almost half of the complainants were fired and another quarter quit out of fear or frustration. Interestingly, this information can be interpreted in a different fashion. Although it can be interpreted as an indication of the negative effects of harassment, employers sometimes claim that it is only those who were legitimately fired and cannot find a comparable job who lodge complaints. That is, a person who cannot find a replacement job because of low skill or incompetence may try to claim harassment in order to extract money from their former employer or regain their former job.

Women who are harassed may experience lower productivity, less job satisfaction, reduced self-confidence, and a loss of motivation and commitment to their work and their employer (Gutek, 1985). They may avoid men who are known harassers, even though contact with those men is important for their work (see Benson & Thomson, 1982). Thus harassment constrains the potential for women to form friendships or work alliances with male workers (Schneider, 1982). Furthermore, women are likely to feel anger and resentment and even to exhibit self-blame (Jensen & Gutek, 1982), which leads to additional stress. Crull and Cohen (1984) also stated that although the implicit/covert types of harassment may not have the same direct repercussions as do the explicit/overt types, all types of sexual harassment at work create high stress levels and serve as a hidden occupational hazard. Finally, sexual harassment helps to maintain the sex segregation of work when it is used to coerce women out of nontraditional jobs (see Gutek, 1985; MacKinnon, 1979; O'Farrell & Harlan, 1982).

Besides affecting their work, sexual harassment affects women's personal lives in the form of physical and emotional illness and disruption of marriage or other relationships with men (see Dunwoody-Miller & Gutek, 1985). For example, Tangri et al. (1982) reported that 33% of women said their emotional or physical condition became worse, and Gutek (1985) found that 15% of women victims of harassment said their health was affected and another 15% said it damaged their relationships with men.

An intriguing finding is that nonharassing sexual behavior also has negative work-related consequences for women workers, although even the women themselves are not always aware of them. For example, Gutek (1985) found that the experience of all kinds of sexual behavior, including remarks intended to be complimentary, was associated with lower job satisfaction among women workers. In addition, women reported that they are not flattered, and in fact are insulted, by sexual overtures of all kinds from men (Carothers & Crull, 1984; Gutek, 1985; Littler-Bishop, Seidler-Feller, & Opaluch, 1982). In one study, 62% of women said they would be insulted by a sexual proposition from a man at work (Gutek, 1985). In addition, the office "affair" can have serious detrimental effects on a woman's credibility as well as her career, especially if the relationship is with a supervisor (Schneider, 1984).

Men seem to suffer virtually no work-related consequences of sexual behavior at work. Less than 1% of men reported that they quit a job because of sexual harassment, and in the course of discussing sexual incidents not one man said he lost a job as a consequence of a sexual overture or request from a woman at work (Gutek, 1985). In the same study, 67% of men said they would be flattered by sexual overtures from women (Gutek, 1985). In addition, many men view a certain amount of sexual behavior as appropriate to the work setting (Gutek, Morasch, & Cohen, 1983; Hearn, 1985), and, as noted above, they are less likely to consider any given behavior as sexual harassment. In one study, 51% of the men who received overtures from women said they themselves were at least somewhat responsible for the incident (Gutek, 1985). That men experience so few work-related consequences of sex at work is especially odd, because they report so much sexual behavior—both that directed at them by women and that which exists as part of the culture in some workplaces.

When men do report "consequences," they are personal rather than work-related impacts, and they are generally viewed in a positive manner. Most often, they report dating relationships or affairs that they find enjoyable; for instance, "There was this little blond who had the hots for me" or "I think she liked me. I was young and she was married. She wasn't very happy with her husband" (Gutek, 1985, Chapter 5).

A Response to Harassment: Going to Court

If people are asked what they would do if they were harassed (Dunwoody-Miller & Gutek, 1985), most people, perhaps naively, say they would tell the person to stop. But real victims rarely tell the harasser to stop. They are often inhibited or constrained from doing so by the situation (e.g., their supervisor is the harasser), or by their upbringing (e.g., "I was taught to be polite"). Their responses are varied; some are attempts to cope with the experience of harassment, some are attempts to stop the harassment, some are attempts to prevent it in the future, and others are attempts to seek restitution or redress for their experiences. In going to court, a person tries to do all of these.

Typically, workers who are harassed first try to ignore the harassment and explain it away. For example, some cite extenuating circumstances ("He is going through a divorce"; "He had too much to drink"). They may also try to avoid the harasser (Dunwoody-Miller & Gutek, 1985). Often, neither of these approaches is effective. Nevertheless, less than 20% of people who had experienced more serious harassment ever reported it to anyone in authority (Gutek, 1985). Only 5% of women victims in the 1987 U.S. Merit Systems Protection Board study either filed a formal complaint or requested an investigation. The Women's Legal Defense Fund (1991) concluded that between 1% and 7% of women who are harassed file a formal complaint or seek legal help.

Among lawyers who handle sexual harassment cases, many say they turn down more than 90% of the people who come to them. In some cases, the person may not have been harassed. More likely, it is not possible to make the case worth the attorney's while, the case is not winnable (for lack of evidence, etc.), or the lawyer judges that the complainant would not be able to, or would not want to, go through the considerable stresses of a court case.

Despite this rather high rate of rejecting potential clients, it is not easy to win a case of sexual harassment. Terpstra and Baker (1988) studied Illinois state EEOC cases and examined the factors associated with the outcomes of sexual harassment charges; only 31% of formal charges (20 of 65 cases) resulted in a settlement favorable to the complainant. In a subsequent study (Terpstra & Baker, 1992) they found that among court cases about 38% were won by the plaintiff. Thus taking a sexual harassment case to court is hardly a sure thing. Using the set of EEOC cases, Terpstra and Cook (1985) found that employment-related consequences experienced by the complainant were the most critical factor in filing a charge. Consequences did not, however, tip the verdict in favor of the plaintiff. Terpstra and Baker (1992) found that the factors that were associated with a favorable outcome for the plaintiff were the severity of the behavior, the presence of witnesses and supporting documents, informing the organization of the harassment, and failure of the organization to respond to it.

An Illustrative Case

Following is an example of what happens when one goes to court over sexual harassment. Although there is no typical case, this case is fairly representative of the cases on which I have worked as an expert witness. A law firm was willing to take the case and it had many of the characteristics of a good case, specifically, the sexual harassment seemed obvious, witnesses were willing to testify, the organization failed to take the appropriate steps to investigate and prevent harassment, and the complainant was willing to fight for redress of wrongs. The presenting conditions suggested that the defendant organization would settle out of court. They were, after all, a sophisticated and presumably reasonable firm.

The company being sued was the Boeing Corporation, a large, well-respected aerospace firm, highly regarded for its engineering expertise and superior products. The plaintiff in this case was a woman who worked supplying tools to various production units. Her work required her to walk through several buildings delivering tools. The plaintiff was terminated by Boeing when she failed to report back to work after illness and surgery. Plaintiff's physician had said that plaintiff could not return to her job because of the stress and harassment she experienced there; Boeing maintained that plaintiff must return to her job before she could be considered for another job. When she did not return to the job where she was being harassed, Boeing fired her.

A highly sexualized culture pervaded the Boeing workplace. The allegations included the following: (a) Many sexually explicit posters and pin-ups were displayed in public work areas and many of these were highly derogatory to women. These included one poster showing a dog licking a woman's genitals and an ad for an inflatable "female substitute" sex partner. (b) One of the male supervisors had made sexually explicit overtures to several of the women, including the plaintiff. In addition, he had previously had sexual relations with at least one direct subordinate. He was known informally as "rodeo rod" for his treatment of women. (c) Sexual slang terms were used for women, for example, the women's bathroom was called "the beaver pond." (d) After the plaintiff complained of sexist treatment, she experienced retaliatory treatment, including having her car smeared with feces and finding a condom filled with hand lotion in her coat pocket. Witnesses were available to verify many of the allegations.

All in all, it looked like a case that would be settled without going to court. Nevertheless, Boeing took the case to court and won. Unanimity among the jury was required in order to find Boeing guilty of sexual harassment, and they were not unanimous.

Rather than focus on the legal argument made in the case, the deliberations of the jury, or the reasons for the outcome, I want to focus here on some of the possible reasons why the case ended up in court and on some of the tribulations of the plaintiff who took the case to court. At least three factors may have motivated Boeing to take the case to court: the ability to (a) outspend the plaintiff, (b) discredit the plaintiff, and (c) discredit the plaintiff's expert and her base of expertise.

Boeing, of course, had "deep pockets" relative to the plaintiff. She and her husband were both hourly workers at Boeing before she was terminated. Not surprisingly, because the pay at Boeing is relatively high, at the time of the court case in February 1992, the plaintiff had not found another job that paid as well as the job she had held at Boeing. In addition, Boeing was represented by a large, established law firm. The plaintiff was represented by a relatively new, small law firm. It is possible that Boeing hoped to force the plaintiff to drop her case for lack of funds if the case was prolonged and taken to court.

Second, Boeing attacked the credibility of the plaintiff. Perhaps buoyed by recent events (e.g., the Clarence Thomas hearings, the William Kennedy Smith rape trial), Boeing attorneys realized the potential of discrediting the plaintiff. According to the *U.S.A. Today* polls, only one quarter of Americans and less than one quarter of men believed Anita Hill's testimony in fall, 1991.

In the Boeing case, the attack took the following forms. First, the plaintiff was alleged to be physically and emotionally unstable. This seems to be a common way of attempting to discredit a plaintiff; it is almost a by-product of one aspect of many court cases. In asserting that the sexual harassment was harmful to the plaintiff, it is commonplace to argue that the harassment caused physical or emotional damage that is evidenced in reports of physicians, psychiatrists, and clinical psychologists who treat the plaintiff and then testify in court. This testimony is one form of evidence showing that the work environment was intimidating and hostile to the plaintiff. But this line of reasoning leaves open another interpretation usually preferred by the defendant, namely that the plaintiff is and always has been an unstable person. The clinical reports say nothing about sexual harassment, defendant's attorneys will contend, but simply show that the plaintiff is unstable. Regardless of who prevails, the plaintiff is portrayed in an unflattering manner: She has been declared an unstable or ill person; the only issue is whether she always was sick and/or crazy or only became sick and/or crazy as a result of the harassment.

The second form of attack on the plaintiff took a more original form in the Boeing case. Boeing's attorneys contended that the plaintiff participated in and contributed to the sexualized culture at Boeing and therefore the environment could not possibly have been intimidating or hostile for her. They offered two forms of evidence for their argument. Plaintiff and her husband had been active bodybuilders. Plaintiff's husband apparently had a photograph of plaintiff showing her in a bodybuilding pose and clad in a bathing suit. In addition, he sometimes brought bodybuilding magazines to the workplace, the covers of which showed men and women in bathing suits in bodybuilding poses. Boeing attorneys implied that these materials were not significantly different from pictures and behaviors that were considered sexual harassment.

A second form of evidence they offered was the fact that plaintiff had had breast surgery after she quit bodybuilding. The surgery, which was apparently intended to regain a more traditional rather than muscular shape to her breasts, was described by Boeing attorneys as breast "augmentation" surgery and, Boeing attorneys suggested, was done to encourage overtures from male co-workers at Boeing.

Whether or not these factors affected the deliberations and decision of the jury is not clear and is not the issue here. The issue is the nature of the attack that defendant's attorneys can and will make against the plaintiff. The plaintiff probably knew ahead of time that her physical and emotional health would be discussed extensively, but it is unlikely that she expected her breasts to become a major topic of conversation in the trial.

The third reason Boeing may have decided to take this case to court was the potential for attacking the base of knowledge, and the expertise of the plaintiff's expert. In many court cases experts are called to testify; psychology is one of the fields from which experts are drawn, but most experts are clinical psychologists who diagnose individuals. As Loftus (1991) noted: "For years, clinically oriented psychologists have swum in legal waters, as they offered opinions on the mental competence of a particular defendant to stand trial or the likelihood of a defendant's insanity at the time a crime was committed." They do not, as social psychologists do, provide "social framework data" (Loftus, 1991; Monahan & Walker, 1988)—that is, "the use of general conclusions from social science research in determining factual issues in a specific case" (Loftus, 1991, p. 1046). Providing social framework data is not a new practice but is relatively rare as yet, especially when compared with clinical evidence. Such data are not always accepted in court, and experts who provide them may be disparaged in various ways (Loftus, 1991; Fiske, Bersoff, Borgida, Deaux, & Heilman, 1991). For example, in the widely discussed case of Ann Hopkins against Price Waterhouse, for which the American Psychological Association prepared an *amicus brief* on the psychology of sex stereotyping, and where social psychologist Susan Fiske served as an expert witness, both the base of knowledge and the expert were attacked by the defendant, Price Waterhouse.

> Throughout their briefs, they [Price Waterhouse] disparaged the psychology of stereotyping. They placed the term *expert* in quotation marks, in a belated effort to discredit the validity of research on stereotyping. In addition, they placed the term *sex stereotyping* within quotation marks, falsely implying that it is an unaccepted neologism, and they characterized as an *amorphous proposition* the appeals court finding that the employer discriminated against Ms. Hopkins because of "stereotypical attitudes" (Brief for petitioner Price Waterhouse, p. 15). They claimed that the finding was derived from "intuitions about unconscious sexism— discernible only through an "expert" judgment (p. 17). In addition to labeling Fiske's opinion as "gossamer evidence" and "intuitively divined" (p. 45), Price-Waterhouse claimed that Fiske's conclusions were faulty because she never met Hopkins and only reviewed the partners' evaluations of her. (Fiske et al., 1991, p. 1053)

Boeing employed a similar tactic in this case. Boeing sought to exclude the expert using three arguments. The first was to attack the base of knowledge, declaring expert testimony on sexual harassment to be "policy preferences."

> Dr. Gutek's testimony should be excluded. Her testimony is nothing more than a series of irrelevant policy statements concerning what she believes is sexual harassment and what "remedial steps" an employer can take for "handling and eliminating sexual harassment." The testimony . . . bears no relation whatsoever to the *legal* standards required of an employer (as opposed to the *policy* preferences of Dr. Gutek). Furthermore, Dr. Gutek's testimony would be grossly prejudicial—it would allow what are essentially the policy arguments of counsel to masquerade as expert testimony. (Boeing's motion to exclude expert testimony of Gutek, 1992, p. 2)

The second type of attack by Boeing's attorneys was directed at assumptions about psychologists who serve as expert witnesses. They wrote:

> Dr. Gutek has not done any psychological review of Chris Stapp. In fact, she does not do any clinical evaluations at all. Nor does she do any individual counseling on sexual harassment, or administration or interpretation of psychological assessment tools. (Boeing's motion to exclude expert testimony of Gutek, 1992, p. 4)

This is similar to Price Waterhouse's charge that Susan Fiske could not give expert testimony because she had not interviewed Ann Hopkins.

The third form of attack was directed at the expert's lack of knowledge of the law.

> Dr. Gutek is unfamiliar with Washington State Law Against Discrimination, and the Washington State Human Rights Commission's regulations on sexual harassment. She is not familiar with any case law interpreting RCW 49.60(74). (Boeing's motion to exclude expert testimony of Gutek, 1992, p. 3)

The assumption seems to be that legal knowledge about sexual harassment constitutes all the knowledge there is on the subject or all the knowledge that is necessary. It is unlikely that a physician testifying on the effects of an accident on her patient's ability to work or a clinical psychologist testifying on a defendant's ability to stand trial might be excluded from testifying because she was not familiar with details of the law under discussion in the case.

Despite these efforts by Boeing to exclude expert testimony, I was allowed to testify in this case, but in a limited way. However, as Loftus (1991) pointed out, often psychologists prepared to provide general conclusions from social science data have been excluded from testifying in court cases, and I have been excluded from testifying in other cases involving sexual harassment. Courts exhibit a noticeable capriciousness in accepting and rejecting expert testimony involving social framework data.

Needless to say, it is not a particularly enjoyable experience to serve as an expert when one's expertise will be dismissed as "mere speculation" (Fiske et al., 1991) or "irrelevant policy statements," and/or when one is expected to provide services (clinical assessment) or have knowledge (of Washington State Law on sexual harassment) that is clearly outside of the areas of one's intended testimony.[2] Yet these indignities are small compared to the indignities experienced by any plaintiff whose behavior, physical appearance, and physical features are likely to be a prime subject of discussion in an expensive and lengthy court action.

In the Boeing case, Boeing's attorneys were not able to force a withdrawal of the case, nor were they able to eliminate completely the testimony of an expert. They did appear to be quite successful in attacking the plaintiff. The "not guilty" verdict of the jury seems to have resulted from the jury's interpretation of the plaintiff's behavior and a misunderstanding of a legal ruling (Paul Delay, Thompson & Delay, plaintiff's attorney, personal communication, March 1992). The jury was instructed to use a "reasonable woman standard" in determining whether Boeing was guilty of sexual harassment, that is, they were asked to consider whether a reasonable woman would consider the work environment of Boeing a sufficiently hostile and abusive work environment to constitute sexual harassment. The jury, however, apparently focused on the plaintiff's behavior and judged whether or not she was a reasonable woman in dealing with the situation at Boeing. In short, as with Anita Hill's testimony where many observers focused on her behavior and motivations rather than on Clarence Thomas, the jury in this case focused not on the behavior of defendant Boeing and its representatives, but on the plaintiff's behavior. Critical of her behavior, they found Boeing not guilty of sexual harassment.[3]

Summary

Sexual harassment is a common occurrence in the American workplace. Illegal forms of harassment are much less common than less serious and inoffensive sexual overtures, innuendos, comments, and graphic material. Serious sexual harassment is against the law, yet achieving legal redress is difficult.

It is worth noting that sexual harassment is one of the few crimes where the focus of attention is on what the victim did to elicit the crime. We do not tell Porsche owners they deserved to have their car stolen because they did not buy a Hyundai instead. We do not ask homeowners who were burgled what they did to elicit the burglary—perhaps bought silverware or nice china or art work for their home, or failed to purchase a costly security system. We do not ask companies what they did to encourage employees to use drugs on the job or to take money from the till. But sexual harassment seems to be different. Standing up and declaring oneself to have been harassed is not likely to elicit either sympathy or justice in the court (as Terpstra & Baker's 1988 and 1992 research also shows). Even having witnesses or others who report similar experiences will not guarantee a verdict favoring the plaintiff. Expert knowledge may or may not be admissible in court. Although it is a clear sign of progress that sexual harassment is against the law and perpetrators can be taken to court, much more needs to be done before the burden shouldered by victims who go to court will be lifted. Whether the threat of going to court and the expense of a court case, successfully fought or otherwise, will encourage companies to work diligently to eliminate sexual harassment from their premises remains to be seen.

Notes

1. The belief that women use sexuality to obtain work-related goals is still prevalent in movies and films. For example, the recent film *Other People's Money* shows an attractive female lawyer openly engaging in seductive and flirtatious behavior to try to influence her client's opposition.

2. Despite Boeing attorneys' attempts to disparage my expertise and the negative verdict, my testimony was well-received by the local media. One report began: "A national expert testified yesterday that the Boeing plant in Auburn where a former female employee contends she was sexually harassed was a sexual harassment disaster area" (Lewis, 1992). I do not know how the jury reacted to my testimony.

3. In an editorial following the Boeing case, *The Seattle Post Intelligencer* wrote the following: "The Stapp case, as it unfolded in the courtroom, was far from a compelling, conclusive one. Sadly, her own troubles and her own behavior ultimately served to confuse the issue and blur the lines of responsibility for any humiliation she suffered" ("The Stapp Verdict," 1992).

References

Abbey, A. (1982). Sex differences in attribution for friendly behavior: Do males misperceive females' friendliness? *Journal of Personality and Social Psychology, 42*(5), 830-838.

Abbey, A. (1987). Misperceptions of friendly behavior as sexual interest. *Psychology of Women Quarterly, 11,* 173-195.

Backhouse, C., & Cohen, L. (1978). *The secret oppression: Sexual harassment of working women.* New York: Macmillan.

Benson, D. J., & Thomson, G. E. (1982). Sexual harassment on a university campus: The confluence of authority relations, sexual interest, and gender stratification. *Social Problems, 29*(3), 236-251.

Bernstein, P. (1976, August). Sexual harassment on the job. *Harper's Bazaar,* p. 33.

Boeing's motion in limine to exclude expert testimony of Gutek. (1992). *Christine C. Stapp and Stephen A. Stapp v. The Boeing Company, et al.* No. C90-1332Z.

Brewer, M. (1982). Further beyond nine to five: An integration and future directions. *Journal of Social Issues, 38*(4), 149-158.

Brief for petitioner Price Waterhouse. (1988, January). Petition for a writ of certiorari to the United States Court of Appeals for the District of Columbia Circuit.

Carothers, C., & Crull, P. (1984). Contrasting sexual harassment in female and male dominated occupations. In K. Brodkin-Sachs & D. Remy (Eds.), *My troubles are going to have trouble with me* (pp. 219-228). New Brunswick, NJ: Rutgers University Press.

Coles, F. S. (1986). Forced to quit: Sexual harassment complaints and agency response. *Sex Roles, 14,* 81-95.

Crull, P., & Cohen, M. (1984, March). Expanding the definition of sexual harassment. *Occupational Health Nursing,* pp. 141-145.

Davies, M. W. (1982). *Women's place is at the typewriter.* Philadelphia: Temple University Press.

Dunwoody-Miller, V., & Gutek, B. A. (1985). *S. H. E. Project report: Sexual harassment in the state workforce: Results of a survey.* Sacramento: Sexual Harassment in Employment Project of the California Commission on the Status of Women.

Dworkin, T. M., Ginger, L., & Mallor, J. P. (1988). Theories of recovery for sexual harassment: Going beyond Title VII. *San Diego Law Review, 25,* 125.

Equal Employment Opportunity Commission. (1980). Guidelines on discrimination on the basis of sex (29 CFR Part 1604). *Federal Register, 45*(219).

Estrich, S. (1991). Sex at work. *Stanford Law Review, 43,* 813-861.

Evans, L. (1978). Sexual harassment: Women's hidden occupational hazard. In J. R. Chapman & M. Gates (Eds.), *The victimization of women* (pp. 203-223). Beverly Hills, CA: Sage.

Farley, L. (1978). *Sexual shakedown: The sexual harassment of women on the job.* New York: McGraw-Hill.

Fiske, S. T., Bersoff, D. N., Borgida, E., Deaux, K., & Heilman, M. E. (1991). Social science research on trial: Use of sex stereotyping research in *Price Waterhouse v. Hopkins. American Psychologist, 46*(10), 1049-1060.

Gottfried, H., & Fasenfest, D. (1984). Gender and class formation: Female clerical workers. *Review of Radical Political Economics, 16*(1), 89-104.

Gutek, B. A. (1985). *Sex and the workplace: Impact of sexual behavior and harassment on women, men and organizations.* San Francisco: Jossey-Bass.

Gutek, B. A., Cohen, A. G., & Konrad, A. M. (1990). Predicting social-sexual behavior at work: A contact hypothesis. *Academy of Management Journal, 33,* 560-577.

Gutek, B. A., & Morasch, B. (1982). Sex ratios, sex-role spillover and sexual harassment of women at work. *Journal of Social Issues, 38*(4), 55-74.

Gutek, B. A., Morasch, B., & Cohen, A. G. (1983). Interpreting social sexual behavior in the work setting. *Journal of Vocational Behavior, 22*(1), 30-48.

Gutek, B. A., & Nakamura, C. Y. (1982). Gender roles and sexuality in the world of work. In E. R. Allgeier & N. B. McCormick (Eds.), *Changing boundaries: Gender roles and sexual behavior* (pp. 182-201). San Francisco: Mayfield.

Gutek, B. A., Nakamura, C. Y., Gahart, M., Handschumacher, I., & Russell, D. (1980). Sexuality in the workplace. *Basic and Applied Social Psychology, 1*(3), 255-265.

Hearn, J. (1985, August). Sexism, men's sexuality in management: The seen yet unnoticed case of men's sexuality. In G. Burrell (Chair), *Sexuality, power and organizational theory.* Symposium conducted at the meeting of the Academy of Management, San Diego.

Hemming, H. (1985). Women in a man's world: Sexual harassment. *Human Relations, 38*(1), 67-79.

Jensen, I., & Gutek, B. A. (1982). Attributions and assignment of responsibility in sexual harassment. *Journal of Social Issues, 38*(4), 121-136.

Koss, M. (1990). Changed lives: The psychological impact of sexual harassment. In M. Paludi (Ed.), *Ivory power: Sexual harassment on campus* (pp. 73-92). Albany: SUNY Press.

Lewis, P. (1992, February 8). Savant labels Boeing plant a haven for harassment. *The Seattle Times,* p. A6.

Lindsey, K. (1977, November). Sexual harassment on the job. *Ms.,* pp. 47-51, 74-78.

Lipman-Blumen, J. (1976). Toward a homosocial theory of sex-roles: An explanation of the sex segregation of social interaction. *Journal of Women in Culture and Society, 1* (3, Part 2), 15-31.

Lipman-Blumen, J. (1984). *Gender roles and power.* Englewood Cliffs, NJ: Prentice-Hall.

Littler-Bishop, S., Seidler-Feller, D., & Opaluch, R. E. (1982). Sexual harassment in the workplace as a function of initiator's status: The case of airline personnel. *Journal of Social Issues, 38*(4), 137-148.

Livingston, J. (1982). Responses to sexual harassment on the job: Legal, organizational, and individual actions. *Journal of Social Issues, 38*(4), 5-22.

Loftus, E. F. (1991). Resolving legal questions with psychological data. *American Psychologist, 46*(10), 1046-1048.

MacKinnon, C. (1979). *Sexual harassment of working women: A case of sex discrimination.* New Haven, CT: Yale University Press.

Monahan, J., & Walker, L. (1988). Social science research in law: A new paradigm. *American Psychologist, 43,* 1110-1117.

National Council for Research on Women. (1991). *Sexual harassment: Research and resources.* New York: National Council for Research on Women. (47-49 East 65th Street, New York, NY 10021).

Neugarten, G. A., & Shafritz, J. M. (Eds.). (1981). *Sexuality in organizations: Romantic and coercive behaviors at work.* Oak Park, IL: Moore.

O'Farrell, B., & Harlan, S. L. (1982). Craftworkers and clerks: The effects of male co-worker hostility on women's satisfaction with non-traditional jobs. *Social Problems, 29(3),* 252-264.

Pearman, M. I., & Lebrato, M. T. (1984). *Sexual harassment in employment investigator's guidebook.* Sacramento: State Women's Program of the California State Personnel Board and Sexual Harassment in Employment Project of the California Commission on the Status of Women.

Pogrebin, L. C. (1977, June). Sex harassment: The working woman. *Ladies Home Journal,* p. 24.

Quina, K. (1990). The victimization of women. In M. A. Paludi (Ed.), *Ivory power: Sexual harassment on campus* (pp. 93-102). New York: SUNY Press.

Quinn, R. (1977). Coping with Cupid: The formation, impact, and management of romantic relationships in organizations. *Administrative Science Quarterly, 22*(1), 30-45.

Rivers, C. (1978). Sexual harassment: The executive's alternative to rape. *Mother Jones, 3*(5), 21-22, 24, 28-29.

Safran, C. (1976, November). What men do to women on the job: A shocking look at sexual harassment. *Redbook,* pp. 149, 217-223.

Schneider, B. E. (1982). Consciousness about sexual harassment among heterosexual and lesbian women workers. *Journal of Social Issues 38*(4), 74-98.

Schneider, B. E. (1984). The office affair: Myth and reality for heterosexual and lesbian women workers. *Sociological Perspectives, 27*(4), 443-464.

Sexual tension: Some men find the office is a little too exciting with women as peers. (1981, April 14). *Wall Street Journal,* p. 1f.

Shullman, S., & Watts, B. (1987). Legal issues. In M. A. Paludi (Ed.), *Ivory power: Sexual harassment on campus* (pp. 251-264). Albany: SUNY Press.

Stringer-Moore, D. M. (1982). *Sexual harassment in the Seattle city workforce.* Seattle: Office for Women's Rights.

Tangri, S. S., Burt, M. R., & Johnson, L. B. (1982). Sexual harassment at work: Three explanatory models. *Journal of Social Issues, 38*(4), 33-54.

Terpstra, D. E., & Baker, D. D. (1988). Outcomes of sexual harassment charges. *Academy of Management Journal, 31,* 185-194.

Terpstra, D. E., & Baker, D. D. (1992). Outcomes of federal court decisions on sexual harassment. *Academy of Management Journal, 35*(1), 181-190.

Terpstra, D. E., & Cook, S. (1985). Complainant characteristics and reported behaviors and consequences associated with formal sexual harassment charges. *Personnel Psychology, 38,* 559-574.

The Stapp verdict. (1992, March 5). [Editorial]. *The Seattle Post Intelligencer,* A12.

U.S. Merit Systems Protection Board. (1981). *Sexual harassment in the federal workplace: Is it a problem?* Washington, DC: Government Printing Office.

U.S. Merit Systems Protection Board. (1987). *Sexual harassment in the federal workplace: An update.* Washington, DC: Government Printing Office.

Vermeulen, J. (1982). Preparing sexual harassment litigation under Title VII. *Women's Rights Law Report, 7,* 331-337.

Women's Legal Defense Fund. (1991). *Sexual harassment in the workplace.* Washington, DC: Women's Legal Defense Fund.

Working Women's Institute. (1975). *Sexual harassment on the job: Results of a preliminary survey* (Research Series, Report No. 1). New York: Working Women's Institute.

Author Index

Author Index   *221*

Subject Index

About the Contributors

LAURA A. BAKER received her B.A. (1978) from the University of Kansas and her M.A. (1982) and Ph.D. (1983) from the University of Colorado. She has been on the Psychology faculty at the University of Southern California since 1984, where she is currently Associate Professor. She works on the development, refinement, and application of quantitative genetic models in the study of individual differences in human psychological variables, including both social and intellectual domains. The application of these models to the study of sex differences and in behavioral development throughout the life span is of special interest.

ANDREW CHRISTENSEN received his undergraduate education at the University of California, Santa Barbara. After brief experiences doing social work, teaching college, and traveling, he went to graduate school in clinical psychology at the University of Oregon, where he completed his Ph.D. in 1976 after a year's internship at Rutgers Medical School. He joined the faculty in Clinical Psychology at UCLA in 1976 and is currently a professor there. His research interests are marital and family interaction and therapy.

MARK COSTANZO is Associate Professor of Psychology at Claremont McKenna College and the Claremont Graduate School. He received his Ph.D. in personality and social psychology from the University of California at Santa Cruz in 1986. His research interests include human communication, social cognition, and social influence. He is especially interested in the application of basic theory and research in social psychology to energy conservation, the legal system, and education.

FAYE J. CROSBY received her Ph.D. in social psychology in 1976 and is Professor of Psychology at Smith College. She has taught at Boston University, Rhode Island College, and Yale University. In 1993, she was the Adeline Barry Davee Visiting Professor at the

J. M. Kellogg Graduate School of Management. Her main area of research is gender and work, to which she brings a feminist perspective. Her recent publications include *Juggling: The Unexpected Advantages of Balancing Career and Home for Women and Their Families* (1991) and *Justice, Gender, and Affirmative Action* (1992), coauthored with Susan Clayton. She has served as president of the Society for the Psychological Study of Social Issues (SPSSI) in 1991-1992.

JACQUELYNNE S. ECCLES is currently Professor of Psychology and Research Scientist at the University of Michigan. She wrote this chapter while she was a professor of psychology at the University of Colorado. She has authored or coauthored more than 50 articles and book chapters on topics ranging from gender-role socialization, teacher expectancy effects, and classroom influences on student motivation, to adolescent development in the family and school context. She is also a member of the MacArthur Foundation Network on Successful Adolescent Development in High Risk Settings.

SUSAN T. FISKE is Distinguished University Professor of Psychology at the University of Massachusetts at Amherst. She received her B.A. in 1973 and her Ph.D. in 1978 from Harvard University. Fiske authored *Social Cognition* with Shelley E. Taylor (1984; 2nd ed., 1991) and will edit, with Daniel Gilbert and Gardner Lindzey, the fourth edition of the *Handbook of Social Psychology*. Her federally funded social cognition research focuses on motivation and stereotyping. She won the 1991 American Psychological Association Early Career Award for Distinguished Contributions to Psychology in the Public Interest.

BARBARA A. GUTEK is Professor in the Department of Management and Policy, University of Arizona, and has served on the faculties of UCLA and the Claremont Graduate School. Her Ph.D. is from the University of Michigan in 1975. She is author/editor of nine books and more than 50 articles, is a fellow in the American Psychological Association and the American Psychological Society, and has received grants from the National Science Foundation and the National Institute of Mental Health. She was chair of the Women in Management Division, Academy of Management, in 1990-1991.

RENA D. HAROLD received her Ph.D. in Social Work and Psychology from the University of Michigan. She is currently Associate Professor of Social Work at Michigan State University, and Adjunct Research Scientist at the University of Michigan's Institute for Social Research. Her research interests include social development processes and gender differences, and the impact of macrosocial issues on individuals and families.

CHRISTOPHER L. HEAVEY received his undergraduate education at the University of California, Santa Cruz, and his graduate education at the University of California, Los Angeles. After receiving his Ph.D. in Clinical Psychology in 1991, he spent a year as a visiting Assistant Professor in the Department of Communication at the University of Michigan. Currently, he is Assistant Professor of Psychology at the University of Nevada, Las Vegas. His research interests are marital interaction and therapy.

CAROL NAGY JACKLIN received her B.A. (1960) and M.A. (1961) from the University of Connecticut, and her Ph.D. (1972) in Experimental Child Psychology from Brown University. After working as a research associate at Stanford University from 1972 to 1983, she joined the faculty at the University of Southern California (USC) as a Full Professor of Psychology and Chair of the Program for Study of Women and Men in Society in 1983. She served as Chair of the Psychology Department at USC from 1990-1992 and is currently Dean of Social Sciences at USC. Her research interests include the study of gender socialization in early childhood, the effects of hormones on gender-related behavior, human sexuality, and policy research in feminist issues.

JANIS E. JACOBS received her Ph.D. at the University of Michigan and is Assistant Professor of Psychology at the University of Nebraska. Her research on gender has focused on the relation between parents' gender-typed achievement beliefs and children's achievement beliefs and behaviors. Her other research interests concern the use of base-rates and judgment heuristics in everyday decision making.

KAREN L. JASKAR is a recent graduate of Smith College, with a B.A. in psychology. She plans to pursue a graduate degree in the field of counseling psychology and to open a practice specializing in women's issues.

JANICE R. KELLY is Professor in the Department of Psychological Sciences at Purdue University. She received her Ph.D. in Social Psychology from the University of Illinois in 1987. She is coauthor of two books (with Joseph E. McGrath): *Time and Human Interaction* (1986, Guilford) and *On Time and Method* (1988, Sage). Her research interests include the social psychology of time, temporal patterns in group performance and interaction, and the effects of cognitive and composition (gender) variables on interaction.

LEIGHTON C. KU is Senior Research Associate at the Urban Institute and Associate Professorial Lecturer in Public Policy at George Washington University. Current research interests include teenagers' HIV risk behaviors, Medicaid, and nutrition assistance programs for children.

JOSEPH E. McGRATH is Professor of Psychology at the University of Illinois, Urbana. He received his Ph.D. in Social Psychology from the University of Michigan in 1955. He is author or coauthor of several books on research methodology, group research, and time. His areas of research interest include gender issues, methodology, the social psychology of time, group research, and the use of technology in work groups.

STUART OSKAMP is Professor of Psychology at the Claremont Graduate School. He received his Ph.D. from Stanford University and has had visiting appointments at the University of Michigan, University of Bristol, London School of Economics and Political Science, University of New South Wales, and University of Hawaii. His main research interests are in the areas of attitudes and attitude change, behavioral aspects of energy conservation, and social issues and public policy. His books include *Attitudes and Opinions* and *Applied Social Psychology*. He is a past president of the APA Division of Population and Environmental Psychology and was editor of the *Journal of Social Issues*. He is now President-Elect of the Society for the Psychological Study of Social Issues (SPSSI).

JOSEPH H. PLECK is Senior Research Associate at the Wellesley College Center for Research on Women. His major books are *The Myth of Masculinity* (1981), *The Impact of Work Schedules on the Family*

(1983), and *Working Wives, Working Husbands* (1985). His research currently focuses on adolescent male sexual and contraceptive behavior, and on fathers' use of parental leave (both formal and informal) and other family-supportive employer policies.

JEAN E. RHODES, Ph.D., is Assistant Professor of Psychology and Women's Studies at the University of Illinois, Urbana. She received her Ph.D. in clinical-community psychology from DePaul University in 1988. She has authored a book and several articles on adolescent substance abuse and problem behaviors. Her research interests include adolescent risk and protective factors, and the contribution of mentor relationships to resilience of pregnant African American women.

FREYA LUND SONENSTEIN, a sociologist, is Director of the Population Studies Center at The Urban Institute in Washington, DC. Much of her research has focused on family and children's policy issues. She is the author of several articles about adolescent pregnancy, child care, and child support. Formerly she was the codirector of the Family and Children's Policy Program at the Florence Heller School, Brandeis University.

JANET T. SPENCE, whose Ph.D. is from the University of Iowa, is currently Alma Cowden Madden Professor of Psychology, the University of Texas at Austin. She has served as President of the American Psychological Association and the American Psychological Society. She first became involved in the study of gender during the late 1960s; her current work on gender focuses on a theoretical model of gender identity built on a multifactorial approach to gender-differentiating phenomena.

LAURA E. STEVENS is a doctoral candidate in social and personality psychology at the University of Massachusetts at Amherst. She recently received an M.S. for her work on impression formation in asymmetrical power relationships. Her research interests include impression formation, stereotyping, power, and attribution.

KWANG SUK YOON is an advanced graduate student in Education at the University of Michigan and a Research Assistant at the University of Michigan's Institute for Social Research. He is currently the statistical analyst in Dr. Eccles's research laboratory. He is particularly interested in the impact of parents on children and in the reciprocal influences of parents and children on each other.